SEWING THE UNUSUAL

by
MARY ANNE WOODWARD

Illustrations and Cover Design
by
Delores Eskins Atkins

THE STRODE PUBLISHERS
HUNTSVILLE, ALABAMA

Copyright 1980
By Mary Anne Woodward
All Rights In This Book
Reserved Including The Right
To Reproduce This Book Or Parts
Thereof In Any Form—Printed In U.S.A.
Library Of Congress Catalog Number 79-91426
Standard Book Number 87397-162-0

CONTENTS

PART I.   OUTER GARMENTS

CHAPTER I.	Sweaters	11
CHAPTER II.	Fake Fur	15
CHAPTER III.	Real Fur	21
CHAPTER IV.	Swim Wear	28
CHAPTER V.	Gift Items	59
CHAPTER VI.	Baby Layettes	85

PART II.   UNDER GARMENTS

CHAPTER I.	Simple Sewing Steps	95
CHAPTER II.	Slips	103
CHAPTER III.	Panties	124
CHAPTER IV.	Girdles	138
CHAPTER V.	Garter Belts	149
CHAPTER VI.	Bras	152
CHAPTER VII.	Gowns	158
CHAPTER VIII.	Robes, Negligees, and Scuff Slippers	177
CHAPTER IX.	Male Garments	198

PART III. HOUSEHOLD ITEMS

CHAPTER I.	Sheets and Pillowcases	219
CHAPTER II.	Bedspreads and Coverlets	232
CHAPTER III.	Quilts	243
CHAPTER IV.	Easy Draperies	257
CHAPTER V.	Accessories	265
CHAPTER VI.	Stuffed Toys	280

PREFACE

For years women have been making their family income go farther by sewing. Since World War II, however, there have been certain garments that were thought to be impossible to make at home due to the use of nylon and other "stretchy" and elastic synthetics. Lingerie made of nylon tricot has led the market in sales and popularity, and the "do-it-yourselfer" has had to either do without or buy ready-mades. Special sewing machines are used by the manufacturers of lingerie and elastic garments, and until recently it was thought that standard machines would not sew these fabrics. With the invention of the zigzag machine, however, a new era of fascinating creativity has been introduced. Women, using a standard zigzag sewing machine, can now make the most lavish and luxurious lingerie at home, and even make a swimsuit of elastic fabric or any other popular material.

In this book you will find instructions for making lingerie and swim wear of all kinds, as well as other gift items and notions made of nylon tricot. These are proven methods taught to hundreds of enthusiastic students, who are now making lingerie and swim wear as professional-looking as any bought in stores, but at only a fraction of the price. Nylon tricot and other stretchy synthetics have thousands of uses. Only a few dozen are included here, but the number of designs, products, and possibilities are limited only by the amount of imagination and creativity of the mind.

PART I
OUTER GARMENTS

CHAPTER I
SWEATERS

The development of non-raveling sweater fabrics opened a new dimension to the home seamstress. These fabrics come in all weights and weaves and are usually washable. Ribbed fabric may be purchased for the neck, wrist, and waist pieces; however, strips of the sweater fabric stretched tightly will serve the same purpose. All sweater fabrics should be preshrunk before sewing even though the shrinkage is usually minimal.

SWEATER WITH LONG SLEEVES AND ROUND NECK

Materials Needed:
1½ yards of 60-inch sweater knit fabric or consult the pattern requirements table
12 inches of reinforcement tape or bias tape
12 inches of 60-inch wide ribbed sweater knit, if desired, for wrists, neck, and waist
Sweater pattern or T-shirt pattern
Polyester thread to match fabric

Step-by-Step:
1. Place the front, back, and sleeve pattern pieces on the straight of the fabric and cut with sharp scissors.
2. Baste a strip of bias tape on each shoulder seam.
3. Sew a ¼-inch to 3/8-inch seam using a zigzag or other stretch stitch across one shoulder.
4. Measure the neck edge. Across the width of the binding material, cut a 2-inch wide strip of the binding fabric a ½ inch less than the length of the neck measurement.
5. Fold the 2-inch neck binding in half with wrong sides together and place it on the right side of the fabric on the neck at

the shoulder with the raw edges together and the folded binding edge away from the neck. Stretch the binding slightly.

6. Stitch the binding to the neck with a ¼-inch straight-stitched seam.

7. Sew the remaining shoulder seam and binding ends together in the same manner. The binding seam allowance may be overcast with a zigzag to make it less noticeable.

8. Stretch stitch the sleeve and armhole seams.

9. Measure the wrist of the wearer. Across the width of the binding material, cut two strips 4½ inches wide and the length of the wrist measurement.

10. Fold one wrist binding in half crosswise and stretch stitch a seam across the narrow end.

11. Fold the binding in half lengthwise, and fit the sleeve edge inside the binding so that all raw edges are together. Stitch a ¼-inch seam with a stretch stitch. The binding should be stretched to fit the sleeve, and the sleeve and binding seams should match.

12. Sew the other sleeve and binding in the same manner.

13. Measure the girth of the body where the waist or hip binding should fall. Across the binding fabric, cut a strip 5 inches wide and the width of the waist or hip measurement.

14. Stretch stitch the side seams.

15. With a stretch stitch, sew the binding into place with a ¼-inch seam.

SLEEVELESS SWEATER WITH V-NECK

Materials Needed:
1 yard of 60-inch sweater knit fabric or consult the pattern
12 inches of 60-inch ribbed sweater knit, if desired
12 inches of bias tape or other reinforcement tape
Polyester thread to match fabric

Step-by-Step:

1. Place the front and back pattern pieces on the straight of the fabric and cut with sharp scissors.

2. Baste a strip of tape on each shoulder seam.

3. Straight stitch the shoulder seams with a 3/8-inch seam

allowance.

4. Measure the neck edge. Cut a 2-inch wide strip of neck binding material the required length across the fabric.

5. Fold the 2-inch neck binding in half with wrong sides together and place it on the right side of the garment neck edge. The ends of the binding should be at the point of the V, and the folded edge should be away from the neck edge.

6. With a straight stitch, sew the binding into place with a ¼-inch seam.

7. Turn the binding into position and tuck the two raw ends to the inside so that one side of the binding is on top of the other one at the V. Then straight stitch one binding edge into each side of the V.

8. Cut two 2-inch wide strips of binding fabric across the width of the material so that it will be the proper length to bind the armholes.

9. Fold one armhole strip in half and position it on the right side of the sweater armhole with the sweater and binding raw edges together. The ends of the binding should be placed at the side seam. Stitch the binding into place with a ¼-inch straight-stitched seam. Then sew the other armhole binding.

10. Using a zigzag or other stretch stitch, sew the side seams with a 3/8-inch seam allowance.

11. Measure the girth of the body at the point the sweater binding should fall. Cut a 5-inch wide strip of binding fabric in the proper length.

12. Fold the binding in half crosswise and stretch stitch a seam across the narrow end.

13. Fold the waist binding in half lengthwise, and fit the sweater body inside the binding so that the side seam of the body matches the binding seam, and all raw edges are together. Stretch stitch a ¼-inch seam. The binding should be stretched to fit the body as the seam is stitched.

CARDIGAN SWEATER

Materials Needed:
1½ yards of sweater knit fabric
Polyester thread

12 inches of ribbed or other knit fabric if contrasting binding is desired
Buttons
¾ yard grosgrain ribbon
Sweater or shirt pattern

Step-by-Step:
1. Preshrink the ribbon, as well as the knit fabric.
2. Follow the steps for either long-sleeved or sleeveless sweater. Use the round-neck design.
3. Cut the sweater down the center front.
4. Cut a strip of grosgrain ribbon 2 inches longer than the sweater center opening.
5. Place the grosgrain ribbon so that it overlaps the right side edge of the center front by ¼ inch. The wrong side of the ribbon will be on top of the right side of the sweater. Fold the two ends of the ribbon under with ribbon touching ribbon.
6. Straight stitch the ribbon edge that overlaps the sweater.
7. Fold the ribbon to the wrong side and blindstitch the top and bottom ends of the ribbon to the sweater.
8. Do the other sweater edge in the same manner.
9. Make machine-worked buttonholes on one side of the opening, and sew buttons on the other side.

CHAPTER II
FAKE FUR

Coats and trims of fake fur are among the most exciting and feminine garments. These may be easily sewn with a few special rules and techniques. The first step should be a trip to the local store to try on furs and fakes to determine the style that best suits you. Do not go with predetermined ideas. Sometimes a style that seemed to be off limits will be the most becoming. Check for color, fiber, nap length, and styling.

The next step is to go to a fabric store and find a pattern that most nearly matches the style of the ready-made. Check the fabric suggestions on the pattern to see if fur is recommended, but do not limit yourself to the patterns with this recommendation. Just remember to choose an uncluttered pattern that does not have seams used for visual detail. Seams often do not show at all on a fur garment, so choose a pattern with only necessary seaming.

Choosing And Preparing The Pattern:
   1. Avoid a pattern with intersecting seams. These cause too much bulk and may be too heavy to be sewn on a home sewing machine.
   2. Avoid non-essential seams. Of course, seams are necessary to hold the garment together and give shaping to it, but avoid extra seams that give the garment visual style. These will not show up in fur.
   3. Avoid gathers, pleats, and too much easing. Fur is too thick and heavy to use in this way. Also, gathered or pleated fur would be too fattening to be flattering even if the machine would sew it.

After choosing a pattern, proceed to the fabric section to discover that glamour and luxury come by the yard. There have been tremendous improvements in the quality, appearance, and handling ease of fake furs in the last few years as the textile industry has advanced in textile construction technology. You will be amazed at the variety that is available and the realistic appearance. Some would fool the animals at the zoo. After choosing your fabric, purchase the yardage suggested on the pattern for *napped* fabric. If the fabric is patterned, striped, etc., the recommended amount of extra yardage should be purchased to allow for matching a pattern. Remember that leftover fabric is useful for trims for other garments, purses, hats, collars, etc., but often more fabric will not be available later if needed.

Fake fur is a fabric and will react as one. Fake furs are simply pile fabrics. They come in two types—knitted and woven. The knits will stretch on the crosswise of the fabric as any other knit, and the woven will stretch on the bias. Many fake furs are washable, which can be an advantage if the lining and interlining materials are also washable. Be sure to check the handling instructions.

A contrasting fabric may be combined with the fur to make an attractive and more interesting garment. This helps to vary the garment's visual appearance. It sometimes aids in the construction of the garment, also. A strip of fabric down the center front simplifies the working of buttonholes. Vinyl, suede, contrasting fur, and both woven and knitted fabrics may be used to make the garment more decorative. Imagination is the key to a truly attractive and professional-looking garment. Fabrics may also be used to reduce bulk and simplify sewing. Collars, cuffs, facings, plackets, pockets, and center front strips for the buttonholes are some ideas for using contrasting fabric to simplify sewing. Undercollars and pocket linings may be made from the lining fabric to reduce bulk and make a more professional-looking finished product.

The lining material should be a slippery fabric that is tough enough to withstand the wear both from the body and from the rough surface of the wrong side of the fake fur. A heavy satin or a coated insulated lining works best.

The underlining should be made from a flannel fabric. However, this may be eliminated if the coat is to be worn in a milder climate and if the fake fur fabric has a firm, stable texture that does not need extra body.

The interfacing should be a non-woven interfacing fabric or a hair canvas. It is imperative that an interfacing be used on collars, facings, and any other edge that might stretch.

Although fake fur is bulky, it still requires the use of shoulder pads. A tailor's pad is the best, but homemade pads will do.

FAKE FUR COAT

Materials Needed:
Pellon or muslin for a fitting muslin as per pattern suggestion
Fake fur as per pattern suggestion for napped fabric
Lining fabric as per pattern suggestion
Interlining fabric, if desired
Shoulder pads
Padding for any other area, if desired
Hemming tape
Fasteners, such as buttons, hooks, or snaps, if desired, and fabric, such as grosgrain ribbon or vinyl, to make bound buttonholes, if desired
Pins, transparent tape, scissors, art knife, or single-edge razor blade, tailor's chalk, fabric glue, ½-inch twill tape, wooden block or hammer

Step-by-Step:
1. Fit the pattern and make changes as necessary.
2. Construct a "fitting muslin," a garment made out of pellon or other heavy fabric, to be sure that the pattern is a perfect fit. This garment may be taped together with cellophane tape or masking tape, or it may be sewn with a basting stitch. Upon completion, make any necessary changes or adjustments to this garment. At this time any perfectly straight seams may be eliminated to reduce sewing and bulk. Then take the garment apart so the pieces may be used as a pattern for cutting the fur. The straight seams to be eliminated should remain sewn in the pellon.
3. If the fabric is washable, preshrink the fur by laundering it.

4. Place the fur wrong side up on a table or flat surface. Place the pieces of pellon from the fitting garment on the fabric. Be sure that two pieces are not being cut for the same side. This is an easy mistake since the fabric is not folded. The right side of the pellon may be marked to help insure that this mistake is not made. Also be sure that the fur is lying in the same direction (usually from neck to hem) on all pieces. Sometimes collars and cuffs are cut with the fur going around. Plan your garment before you cut.

5. Short-haired furs may be sewn with a regular 5/8-inch seam allowance and may be cut with regular scissors. The long-haired furs should be cut with an artist mat knife or a single-edged razor blade. This should be done to insure that the fur itself is not cut.

6. Long-haired furs may be sewn in either of two ways. The first way is to allow for an 1/8-inch seam allowance and sew the seam with a wide, overcasting zigzag. The other way to sew the long-haired fur is to use a 5/8-inch seam allowance, cut the fur with the razor blade from the back to insure that the hair is not cut, then trim the hair off the seam allowance as close to the backing as possible. This eliminates the bulk, yet makes a very stable seam. A zipper foot may be used to insure that the seam is as close to the fur as possible. No backing should show from the right side of the garment.

7. After cutting the garment, cut the lining, interfacings, and interlining using standard methods.

8. With a 16 or 18 needle, sew the garment using the seam allowance and method desired. Twill tape reinforcements should be sewn into the shoulder seams and to stabilize the pockets or other pieces needing extra reinforcement. Reduced pressure on the presser foot may be necessary for sewing furs. Long seams may need to be stretched slightly as they are sewn.

9. If a wide seam allowance is being used, glue the open seam allowance flat to the backing with a fabric glue.

10. Seams requiring ease, such as in the sleeve or bustline, pose a slight problem, but this can be eliminated by making very small darts that end just beyond the seam allowance. It may take many darts to remove the excess fabric from the sleeve, but many darts will have a nicer finished appearance

than a couple of very bulky ones. Intersecting seams are also a problem. Simply cut away the excess fur on the seam allowance, trim the seam allowances close to the seam, then sew the intersecting seam. There should have been enough bulk trimmed away to allow the new seam to be sewn without a problem.

11. In making the darts, cut away the dart with a razor blade, but leave an 1/8-inch seam allowance. Fold the right sides together with the raw edges together. Then sew the dart with an overcasting zigzag. Back stitch at the end of the dart and tie the loose thread ends into a knot. Take a straight pin and pull the fur out of the dart seam on the right side. In this way the dart will probably not show. After sewing the darts, press a piece of iron-on mending tape over the dart area to reinforce the fabric.

12. The seams, hem, collar, and darts must be pressed in order to have a neat appearance. Standard pressing methods cannot be used, however. Press by holding a steaming iron two inches above the seam. After the seam has absorbed a little moisture, it should be pounded on the wrong side with a wooden block or a rolling pin.

13. Interfacings should never be caught in the seam because they add extra bulk. Trim away the interfacing seam allowance, and baste or glue the interfacing to the side that will be the top finished layer.

14. Avoid buttonholes if at all possible. Buttons may be added for looks over a snap or a hook and eye closing. However, if a buttonhole is desired, it should be a bound buttonhole using wool, vinyl, suede, or grosgrain ribbon for the binding strips. The hair should be clipped from the area that will be underneath the binding strips to reduce bulk. If a fake fur facing is used, bind a buttonhole on the facing and also one on the outer garment. Then whip the two together into one buttonhole. Experiment before beginning the buttonholes on the finished product.

15. Buttons should be sewn with heavy-duty button and carpet thread that has been waxed. The thread may be waxed by pulling it across parafin if the pre-waxed thread cannot be found. Reinforce the button by sewing through a small button on the underside of the fabric as you sew the front one. A thread shank between the two buttons should be made with an

extra 1/8 inch for movement of the button.

16. Mark the hem by placing strips of transparent tape on the fur where the bottom edge of the hem will be. Then turn the hem up and tape in place. Check the hem to assure that it is even and the right length.

17. Cut a 2-inch piece of pellon or a bias interfacing strip long enough to reach from the front facing all the way around the coat edge to the other front facing. Place the interfacing strip at the bottom edge of the hem and baste into place at the bottom edge. Then catch stitch the top edge to the backing or wrong side of the coat.

18. Stitch hemming tape to the raw bottom edge of the coat. Then turn the hem to the right place and blindstitch the hemming tape into position. The hem should be pressed as in Step 12.

19. Sew the lining using standard seam allowances. If an interlining is desired, cut by using the lining pattern and omitting the back pleat. Then pin the pieces to the corresponding lining pieces and treat as a single piece of material when sewing. Stitch the lining together except for the armholes. Press the seams open.

20. Position the lining against the coat with the wrong side of the lining against the wrong side of the coat. Then baste the lining seam allowances to the garment seam allowances. Sew the armhole seam allowances together.

21. Attach the lining to the facings, which have been blindstitched in place, by whipping with close, tight stitches. Attach the lining to the bottom hem by stitching to the lower edge of the hemming tape. Attach the lining to the bottom edge of the sleeves, which have been hemmed in the same manner as the lower edge hem, with a close, tight blindstitch as in the lower hem. However, a ½-inch slack should be allowed in the lining so the sleeve will not bind. The lining should extend a ½ inch below where it is sewn to the sleeve hem, but it should not extend below the edge of the sleeve.

22. Press the lining into place without getting the iron onto the fur surface.

CHAPTER III
REAL FUR

Real fur is the most luxurious and glamorous of fashions, yet the home seamstress often shies away from making articles from real fur because of a lack of necessary knowledge and skills. Fur can often be purchased from furriers or fur farms in the form of individual pelts or pelts sewn together. Another excellent way to obtain fur for a home sewing project is by checking a used-clothing sale, grandmother's closet, or rummage sales in department stores. Fur rarely wears out, but the length that is fashionable and the style may change drastically. It is also very easy to repair weak and worn spots in an old coat so the fur may be used in a new garment.

After deciding to embark on a fur project, check the local fur department to decide the style and type of fur that is most becoming to you. Do not go with any preconceived ideas; try them all. You may be surprised what suits you best. Then locate your fabric, either new or used. Old and used furs should be tested by pulling on the hair and pulling the skin to test for weakness. If the hair pulls out and the skin tears, beware. An old, worn-out pelt is not worth the time and trouble. If the pelt is still strong in most places, though, a few weak and worn spots may be repaired.

Choosing And Preparing The Pattern:
An old coat will not contain enough fur to make another fur coat of the same size, so you must choose to make it into a smaller garment. With new fur, however, you are limited only by the availability of the pelts.

The seams in fur garments do not show, so avoid patterns with seams used for visual detail. It is best to choose a pattern with very few seams, especially for the first attempt. Gathers, pleats, and lots of ease should be avoided. These will give a fat, unflattering appearance and will be hard to do.

After choosing a pattern, make a fitting garment from pellon to assure proper pattern adjustments for a good fit. Plan for 1/8-inch seams or smaller. Fur edges are whipped edge to edge with no seam allowance. Remember that fur garments, like other outer garments, should be donned over other clothing to allow for a proper fit. Fur garments should not fit too snugly, or there will be wrinkles and puckers.

Preparing The Fur
1. If individual pelts are being used, place them on a wooden cutting board with the fur side down. Using a blade or mat knife, cut the outside edges of the pelts into straight lines so they may be fitted together snugly. Do not cut from the fur side. Then match the pieces together right side up like a jigsaw puzzle. Remember that if curly fur is being used, there is no nap to be considered. However, straight-haired furs have a distinctive nap, and the pelts should be fitted together with the nap going in the same direction on all pieces. In fitting the pieces together, try to match color and texture as much as possible, also.

The pelts should be sewn together edge to edge with a firm whipstitch. Only enough of the hide is caught to make a firm, strong stitch—about 1/8 inch or less. Heavy duty cotton or silk thread should be used. Draw the thread through beeswax to strengthen it. A needle made for leather sewing should also be used. Pull any hair out of the seam if any is caught.

2. If an old garment is being used, carefully remove the lining, interfacing, padding, interlining, etc. Some of these may be in good enough shape to be used again in the finished garment. Next, examine the skin side of the fur. Carefully open any seams, darts, or other stitchings that keep the garment from lying flat. Not all seams will have to be opened.

If there are weak or worn places in the fur, mark the outer perimeter of these from the fur side with straight pins. Turn the garment skin-side up and cut out the worn spot with a razor blade or artist mat knife being drawn in straight lines around the perimeter of the pins. Then, using the removed piece as a pattern, trace a more useable pattern on a piece of paper. Mark the paper as to the fur side and the skin side; it could make a difference. Next, in what will be leftover fur, find a piece of fur that will match the removed piece of fur. Remember to match color, texture, and hair direction or nap. Mark the patch with pins. Then turn the skin side up and, using the paper pattern, remove the patch with a razor blade with the skin side up. Using a needle made for leather and silk or heavy duty cotton thread that has been drawn through beeswax, whipstitch the patch into place by catching only enough of the skin to make a firm stitch. Pull all hair free from the seams. The patch should be undetectable.

Cutting The Garment
   1. Plan the garment; take into consideration the direction of the hair, any stripes, spots, etc. On the skin side mark with pen or magic marker the stripes, spots, hair direction, and any other peculiarities.
   2. Place the pellon pattern pieces on the skin side of the fur. Remember that the hair on a straight-haired fur should point toward the hem of the garment. Special effects may be obtained by special planning for stripes, spots, and hair direction, especially on collars, borders, and cuffs.
   3. Tape the pattern to the skin; then outline the pattern on the skin with magic marker.
   4. Cut the skin along the pattern outline with a single-edged razor blade or an artist mat knife. Only the skin should be cut; the hair will separate by itself. The skin may be lifted from the table while cutting to insure that the hair is not cut.

Preparing The Fur For Sewing
   1. Examine all garment pieces to see if there is any discoloration anywhere on the fur. Hair or fabric dye in the proper color may be brushed on, rinsed in clear water, and allowed to dry to restore the original color or to dye any unwanted light spots. Test on a scrap before applying to the garment.
   2. Imperfections and wrinkles caused by piecing, repair, or age may be eliminated by gently brushing water on the skin side, then gently fastening to a wooden board with pushpins. Be

careful that the hair lies properly. After the skin is dried (takes about twenty-four hours), fluff the hair by holding a steam iron about two inches away from the fur. Check the blocked piece against the original pattern piece. If different, remark and trim the skin by the same method as originally cut.

3. If the skin is fragile, it should be supported by fusing a piece of sheath lining to the skin with a fusible bonding agent. The sheath lining should be cut one inch larger than the pattern piece. The excess sheath lining is pressed back from the seam edge toward the body of the garment. When sewing, catch this fabric along with the skin in the seam.

Sewing The Fur

1. Prepare any darts by cutting the dart area out of the fur. This should be cut with a razor blade or mat knife from the skin side. Then sew ½-inch wide cotton twill tape along the edges of the dart. At the point, reverse the tape by lapping it over itself. A hand zigzag stitch /\/\/\ is the best method to apply the tape. A needle for leather sewing and heavy duty cotton thread rubbed with beeswax are best. Then, with right sides together, sew the dart, with a close, tight overcasting stitch. Push any hair from the seam as you sew. Hair should be pulled from the seam on the right side, also. Be sure to catch just enough skin to allow for stability and also let the needle go through the tape.

2. With a hand zigzag stitch, apply ½-inch wide cotton twill tape along the edge of every seam in the garment except a seam into which fullness must be eased (sleeves, etc.).

3. Stitch all the seams by hand with the special leatherwork needle and heavy cotton or silk thread that has been rubbed with beeswax. The seams should be sewn in an overcasting manner in order to catch the twill tape as well as the skin. Do not stitch deeply into the body of the garment—only 1/8 inch or less.

4. Using paper clips, attach the sleeve in the armhole. Then whipstitch the sleeve into place. Push the sleeve fur between stitches to work the fullness into the seam. Then handstitch twill tape over the top of the seam. The tape can be stitched in the zigzag stitch that straddles the seam or sewn with a large

whipstitch along each edge of the tape. Any other seam that requires easing of fullness should be sewn in this way.

5. At this time sew any shank buttons, hooks and eyes, and snaps, and make any buttonholes by using methods listed later in this chapter.

6. All furs need interfacing—heavier furs need heavier support. Trim interfacings ¼ inch smaller than the piece to be interfaced. Then hand baste the interfacing into place with an uneven running stitch.

7. Measure the hem and mark it with cellophane tape. Cut the fur along the hemline by using a razor blade or mat knife to cut the skin side. The hem should be edged with twill tape as the seams were. Whip a 1¾-inch strip of interfacing to the tape, and then stitch the top edge to the skin. Hand whip 2-inch wide hemming tape to the hem edge. Sew through the tape, interfacing, and skin. To complete the hem, whip the upper edge of the hemming tape to the skin.

Buttons, Buttonholes, Snaps, And Hooks

1. Snaps work nicely in fur and are easy to apply. Simply iron a piece of iron-on tape to the skin side where the snap will be sewn; then sew on the snap in the usual way. Use the heavy-duty thread rubbed with beeswax.

2. Special large hooks and eyes are made for fur garments. See if the hook and eye may be inserted into a seam so only the necessary portion extends beyond the fabric. Then wrap twill tape through the circles to be sewn, cross the tape, and sew the edges of the tape to the skin. This will distribute the pull of the hook and eye. Repeat with the eye in the same manner.

3. Buttonholes are more difficult than other closings, but they are not impossible. Mark the position of the buttonholes on the skin side. Sew twill tape at the outer ends of the buttonhole perpendicular to it. Then sew twill tape along the edges of the buttonhole (top and bottom) along the line to be slashed. The tape may be hand sewn with a zigzag stitch.

Carefully slash the buttonhole with a razor blade on the skin side. Then sew strips of ½-inch wide grosgrain ribbon, leather, vinyl, or suede to the slit edge on the hair side of the garment. Sew these strips carefully with a very close, tight whipstitch. Then pull the binding to the wrong side and whip to the twill tape.

If interfacings are used, construct the buttonhole before inserting the interfacing. The interfacing should be cut 1/8 inch away from the buttonhole edge and then sew to the buttonhole binding with a close whipstitch.

Real fur facings may be slashed and sewn with a tight whipstitch to the binding on the buttonhole edge, or a buttonhole may be worked on the facing and the two buttonholes whipped together.

4. Buttons should be sewn with heavy-duty buttonhole twist that has been coated with beeswax. Sew the button using a smaller button on the back for reinforcement. Leave a wrapped thread shank 1/8 inch above the fur to allow for movement of the button.

Shank buttons may be sewn by making a hole through the outer layer of fur and looping a 3-inch-long piece of cotton twill through the hole, through the button shank, and back into the hole again to the skin side. Then securely attach the tape to the skin with a hand-sewn zigzag stitch down the length of both ends of the tape.

Buttons may be sewn over hooks or snaps to give an attractive look without making buttonholes.

Lining And Interlining

1. An interlining may be inserted to give a warmer, more luxurious feeling. This should be made from flannel or wool and cut from the lining pattern, but the back pleat should be omitted. Baste the interlining pieces to the corresponding lining pieces. Then sew the two as one piece when the lining is stitched.

2. Stitch the lining seams except for the armholes and press the seams open.

3. Position the lining into the garment with wrong side of the lining against the wrong side of the garment.

4. Sew the lining seam allowances to the corresponding garment seam allowances and sew the armhole edges together, also. A hand-basted stitch will do fine.

5. Blindstitch the lining sleeve hem to the sleeve hemming

tape. Allow the lining to be a little loose in the sleeve so it will be comfortable; however, be sure that it does not hang below the sleeve hem.

6. Press under the lining outer edges to make a 5/8-inch hem. Then whip the lining to the facings with a close, tight blindstitch.

7. Press the upper sleeve edge so that it is turned under 5/8 inch. Blindstitch the upper sleeve edge to the armhole. Make sure that the sleeve is comfortable.

Combining Fur With Fabric

Many fur garments are trimmed in leather, suede, wool, or vinyl. Collars, cuffs, pockets, and facings may be too unwieldy if made from fur and also lined with it. Cut the non-fur fabric to allow for a 5/8-inch seam. Press the seam allowance flat against the wrong side of the fabric. Then hand sew to the body of the fur using the same method as sewing two pieces of fur.

SWIM WEAR

CHAPTER VII

SWIM WEAR

Perhaps no other garment costs so much to purchase in comparison with the amount of fabric involved than does the swimsuit. Swimsuits are very inexpensive to make because so little material is required. The methods are similar to making a dress or a girdle. An added feature to making your own is the fact that the swimsuit will be custom fitted. This is a big factor for the person who is not a standard size. Often in the ready-mades, the top fits and the bottom doesn't, or vice versa; and if a swimsuit that fits is found, it may be in an unbecoming color or style.

Most any type of material may be used for swimsuits. Polyester double-knit fabric with a very hard finish is excellent. Do not use the soft, bulky-type double knit, however, because it is too easily picked on the concrete around the swimming pool. Any wrinkle-free fabric, especially perma-pressed materials, are good for swimsuits. Many of the expensive ready-mades are now made from perma-pressed cotton or blends. Some elasticized fabrics, such as Lastex, are available. These are always excellent for swimsuits, and have an added feature of molding the full figure into a more becoming shape. A girdle may be worn under any swimsuit, however, and have the same effect. A girdle made of nylon or specially treated fabric should be used, because rayon fabric deteriorates rapidly in the chlorine water.

If you are using elasticized fabric, be sure that the stretchiest part goes around the body. Otherwise, the swimsuit would tend to slip down. If the fabric is two-way stretch, the straight of the fabric should go around the body. If a one-way stretch fabric is used, the straight of the fabric should go up and down, or top to bottom. One-way stretch fabric and non-stretch fabrics should be used only for two-piece swimsuits, and the two-way stretch fabric may be used for any type suit. A fabric that does not stretch both up and down and across will be terribly uncomfortable when the arms are lifted in a one-piece suit.

All of the pattern books now contain many swimsuit styles. An advantage of buying a pattern is that it will give step-by-step instructions for that particular suit. If you have an old swimsuit that you prefer to copy, however, you may make a pattern for it by using the aluminum foil method explained in the slip instructions in Chapter II. If the swimsuit is worn out, you may consider taking it apart and using the pieces for a pattern. In doing this, consider whether or not the suit has stretched out of shape through the years of wear.

In purchasing fabric for your swimsuit, usually one yard will make any one-piece swimsuit and three-fourths of a yard will make any two-piece one. Consult your pattern for the exact yardage, if you are using one. Usually the fabric is wide enough so that all you need to purchase is enough to reach from the top of the swimsuit to the bottom plus hem allowances—in other words, one length.

Because of the tight fit of the garment and the exercise strain, swimsuit seams must be extremely strong. The best way to insure strong seams is to use nylon thread. The polyester dual duty or regular polyester thread are also very good. These synthetic fibers seem to hold up in the water much better than cotton.

Swim Wear

Elastic used in swim wear should be especially treated to withstand chlorine water. This may be purchased at a fabric store. If the treated elastic is not available, nylon elastic may be used. NEVER use rayon elastic in the swimsuit, because it deteriorates immediately upon contact with chlorine water. Many an embarrassing moment could have been averted by using nylon or treated elastic.

Most swimsuits require a zipper. If the pattern you are using does not have a zipper, you may want to consider using one, anyway, because the suit will be easier to get on and off. An extremely stretchy fabric is required to stretch over 36-inch hips and fit snugly on a 24-inch waist, for example. In this case, the fabric would have to have twelve inches of stretch. Before planning your swimsuit without a zipper, measure your waist and hips, and figure how much stretch is required of your fabric. Then stretch the fabric that many inches and see if it can take that much strain. A zipper may add life to the swimsuit, as well, because the more a fabric stretches, the sooner it will stop retaining its shape. In inserting a zipper in the back of the swimsuit, be sure to insert a facing underneath the zipper to assure maximum comfort. When inserting a decorative zipper in the front of a swimsuit, however, do not have the facing extend to the top of the zipper, especially if the suit is designed to leave the zipper unzipped slightly for a more exposed look.

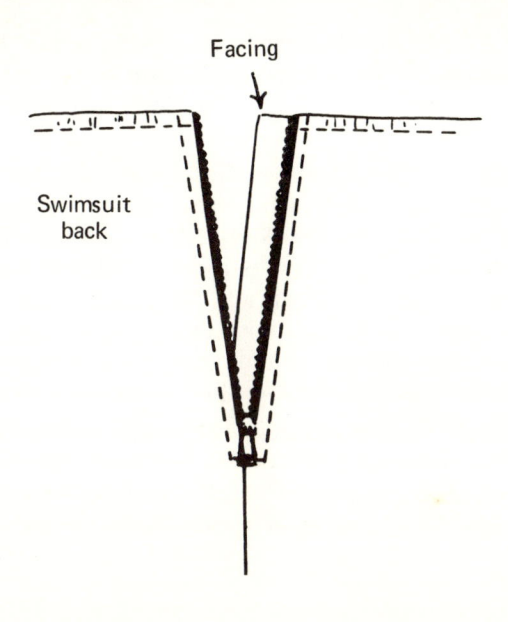

When elastic fabric is being used, all seams must be zigzagged. After stitching a ½-inch zigzagged seam, push the seam allowance to one side, open both sides of the fabric flat on the machine, and overcast the seam with a zigzag on the right side of the fabric. If your machine does a variable stitch, sometimes called a three-step zigzag, like this ᴠᴠᴠᴠ , overcast the seam with it rather than the standard zigzag. This stitch is stronger and helps prevent skipping of stitches, which is a plague sometimes when sewing elastic fabrics. Increasing the pressure on the presser foot and using a ballpoint needle also help prevent stitch skipping. In sewing both tricot and elastic or stretchy fabrics, the new roller-type presser foot helps eliminate the top layer of fabric from stretching as you sew. This stretching can cause puckering of the seams and uneven fabric lengths at the bottom of the seam. Before you make your swimsuit of elastic fabric, refer to Chapter IV on girdles for extra pointers, because the two garments are very similar in construction methods.

Swim Wear

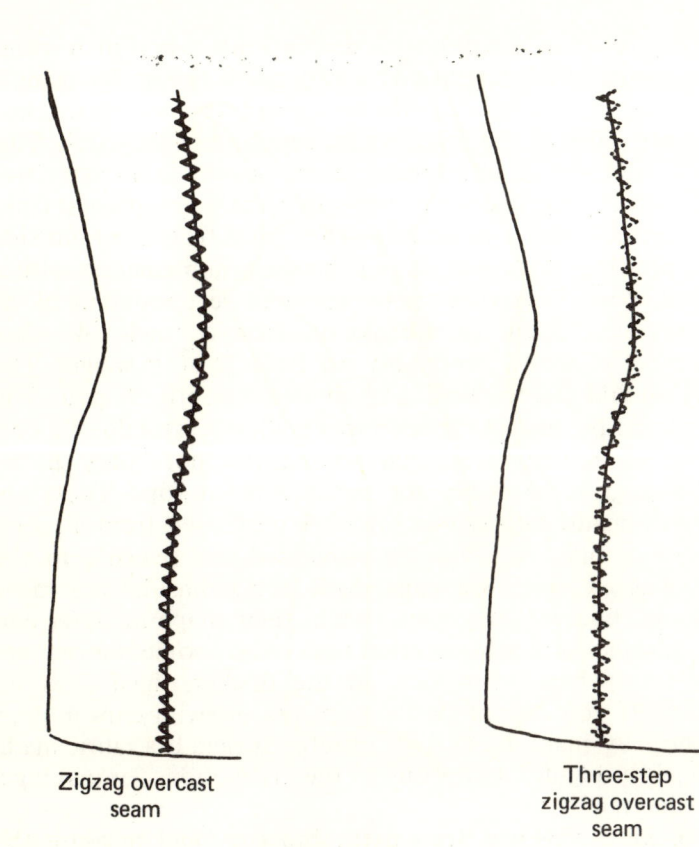

Zigzag overcast
seam

Three-step
zigzag overcast
seam

Roller-type presser foot

If you are using the polyester double knits, use ¼-inch seams with a regular stitch length and a very small zigzag. By using a small zigzag, the seam can still be opened up and top-stitched down both sides of the seam with a regular straight stitch. This makes a very strong, reinforced seam, as well as an attractive one. If you do not choose to top-stitch the seam, press it from the wrong side with a steam iron. Then press from the right side with a pressing cloth and pound the seam immediately with a pounding block. If you are unable to purchase a pounding block from your local fabric store, make one from a 2-inch x 4-inch x 8-inch piece of wood, preferably oak because of its weight. The corners should be rounded and sanded smooth. A pounding block should be used in this manner on all polyester double knit garments to insure professional-looking, flat, non-bulky seams.

A bra-liner is necessary for most swimsuit tops. These are very easily made with sew-in bra cups purchased from a fabric store. Swim bras may also be purchased and sewed into the lining of your suit. Bra cups made for swimsuits are more serviceable, because they must retain their shape in water and resist chlorine and salt deterioration. Also, some fabrics are almost transparent when wet, so the thicker, lined cups are necessary. If you cannot find a swim bra or swim cups in your size, you may make them from fibrefill or rigid bra fabric made for a slightly padded bra. Consult the instructions for making a bra in Chapter VI.

To make a bra-liner, try on the bra cups and measure the correct distance between them. Then position the inside of the bra cups on the wrong side of the lining fabric the correct distance apart. Pin them securely in the correct position on the straight of the fabric and mark around the cups. Next, remove the cups and cut the fabric one-fourth of an inch inside the cup marks.

After cutting the holes for the cups in the lining material, position the cup holes against the wrong side of the swimsuit top and pin the fabric in place. Next, cut out the lining fabric to match the swimsuit top so that it can be sewed into the swimsuit. With right sides together, sew the cups into the liner holes. Then stay stitch the lining into the swimsuit top. This method of inserting a bra-liner into a swimsuit may also be used for ready-mades with ill-fitting tops. A large piece of elastic may also be zigzagged across the bottom of the swimsuit liner to help it stay in position and fit better.

Swim Wear

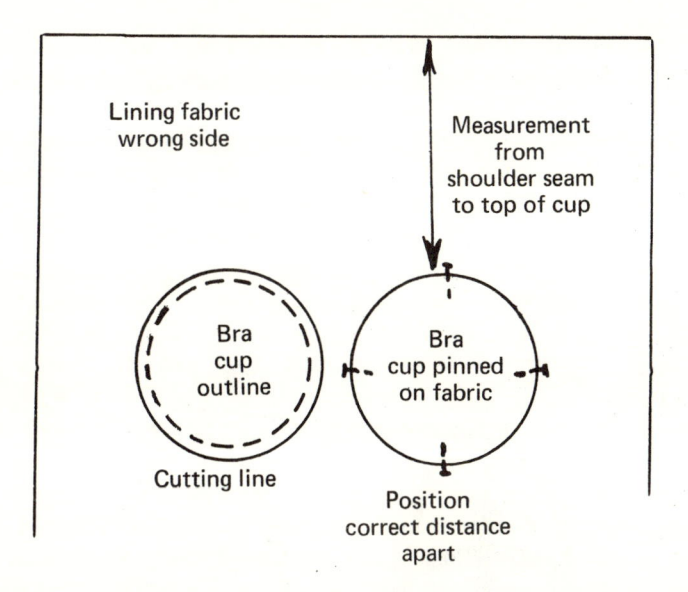

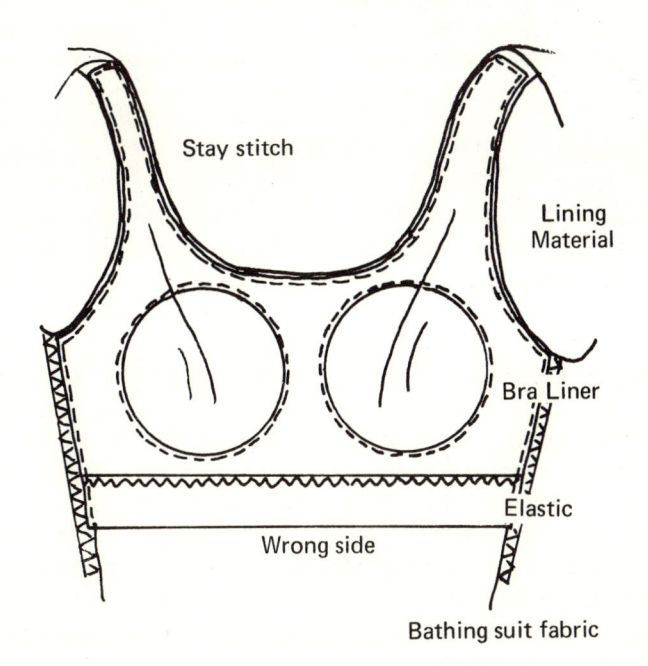

(Diagram: Lining fabric wrong side — Bra cup outline / Cutting line; Bra cup pinned on fabric; Measurement from shoulder seam to top of cup; Position correct distance apart)

(Diagram: Stay stitch, Lining Material, Bra Liner, Elastic, Wrong side, Bathing suit fabric)

To insert bra cups in an unlined swimsuit, either purchase or make the bra cups that fit you perfectly. Then cut a piece of 1-inch or wider elastic to extend between the two side seams.

Pin the bottom of the cups in the correct position on the top edge of the elastic. After fitting the cups to you to make sure they are correctly positioned, zigzag them onto the elastic. The elastic ends may then be sewed onto the side seams. To stabilize the top of the cups, sew one end of a narrow piece of elastic to the top of the cup and the other end onto the shoulder seam.

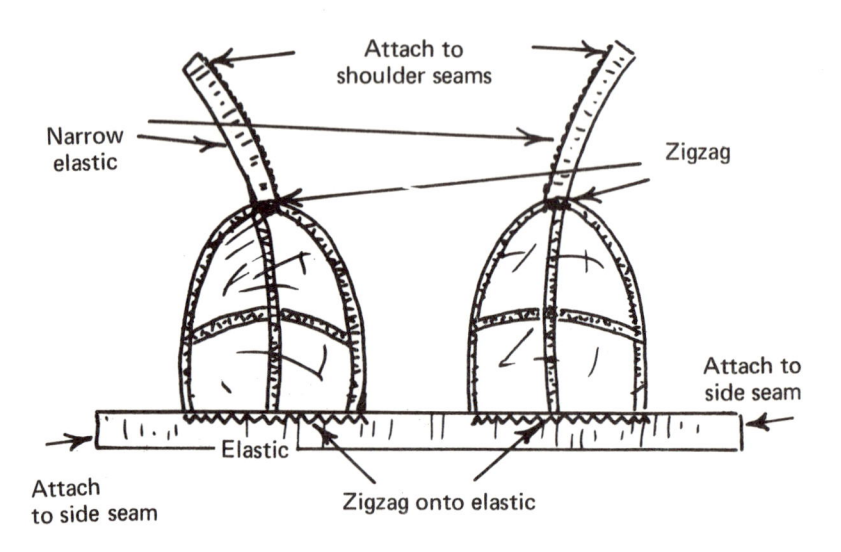

Attach to shoulder seams

Narrow elastic

Zigzag

Attach to side seam

Elastic

Attach to side seam

Zigzag onto elastic

The bra portion of the swimsuit should be inserted after the swimsuit is completely finished. This is the only way to assure that the cups are correctly positioned.

It is not necessary to completely line most swimsuits. If your fabric lacks body or is transparent when wet, then a lining becomes necessary. The crotch of a swimsuit is always lined with tricot, and this may be sewed in the same manner as the panty or girdle crotch pieces, as discussed in previous Chapters III and IV. Tricot or any other two-way stretch fabric may be used for lining elastic fabric swimsuits. Sometimes nylon elastic fabric or elastic fabric treated to withstand chlorine water is used to line the swimsuit from the waist down or across the abdomen to lend support to the fuller figure. The elastic fabric lining should be cut slightly smaller than the outer fabric in order to be effective.

Any type lining fabric may be sewed into the seams with the swimsuit fabric and treated as one piece of material. This will prevent the lining seams from showing through the outer fabric,

Swim Wear 37

especially when wet. To hide some of the raw seam allowances, place the right sides of the lining fabric together and the right sides of the swimsuit fabric together. Then place the wrong side of the linings on top of the wrong side of the swimsuit fabrics. Next zigzag the center seam. When the fabrics are opened up, the raw edges will be hidden. The raw edges of the side seams will show, however, unless you turn the fabrics inside out similar to the way the crotch of panties is applied. This is a little complicated, but possible. Consult Chapter III if you decide to use this method. Often it is only necessary to line the front abdomen and crotch sections, and you can use the unbound leg sections for turning the raw seams into a covered position.

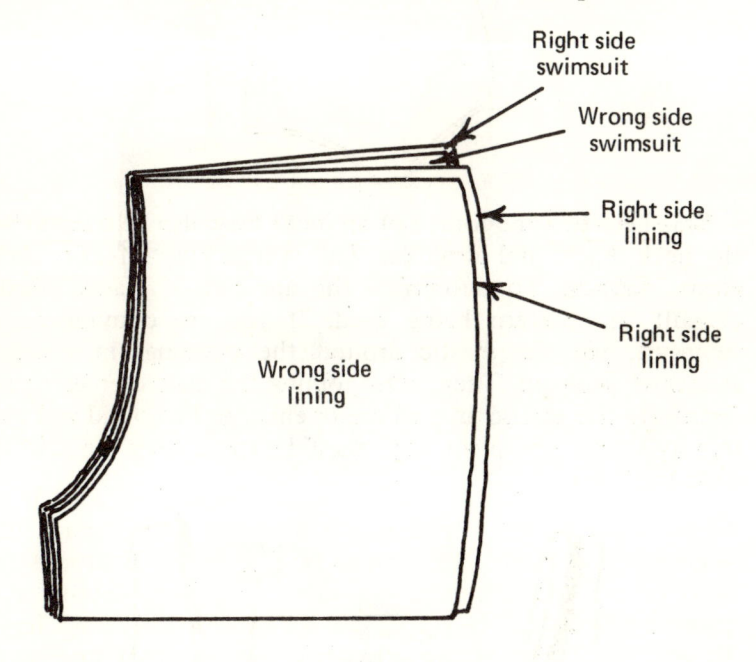

The raw edges of the swimsuit must be bound in some way. Unless the suit is completely lined, there will be raw edges around the legs, neck, arms, and back. Three-inch wide sheer or tricot bindings are available at lingerie fabric shops and are excellent for an attractive, non-bulky binding. This binding should be applied in the same manner as the double-fold binding discussed in Chapter VIII, Gowns. A ½-inch seam should be used on the bindings so that it will make a prettier edge.

Small elastic (one-fourth of an inch) may also be used to bind the neck, back, and armholes. This is especially effective on the elastic fabrics. To determine the amount of elastic needed, consult the pattern being used. If you are copying an old swimsuit, pin the elastic around the openings in a slightly stretched position. Then, after joining the elastic ends, equally distribute the elastic around the opening to be bound and pin it into position. The picot edge should extend over the raw edge onto the fabric.

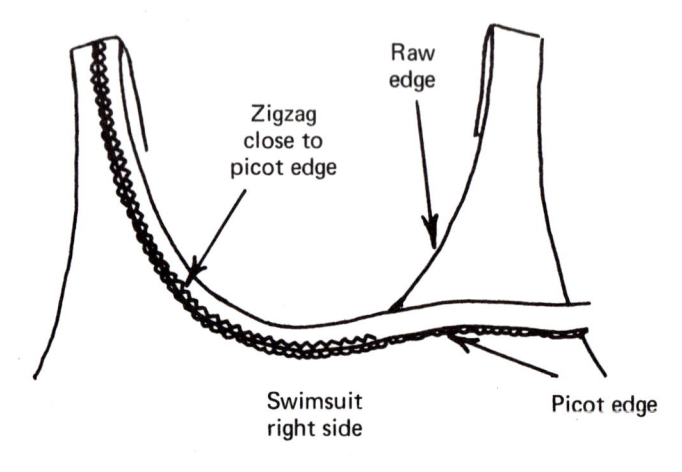

Swim Wear 39

Zigzag close to the picot edge, but do not let the needle overcast the elastic into the fabric. Then turn the elastic to the wrong side and zigzag it into place by allowing the needle to overcast the elastic edge into the fabric, then swing back into the elastic. In binding the armholes with elastic, you should not stretch the elastic under the arm, but only on the shoulder section. This gives greater comfort.

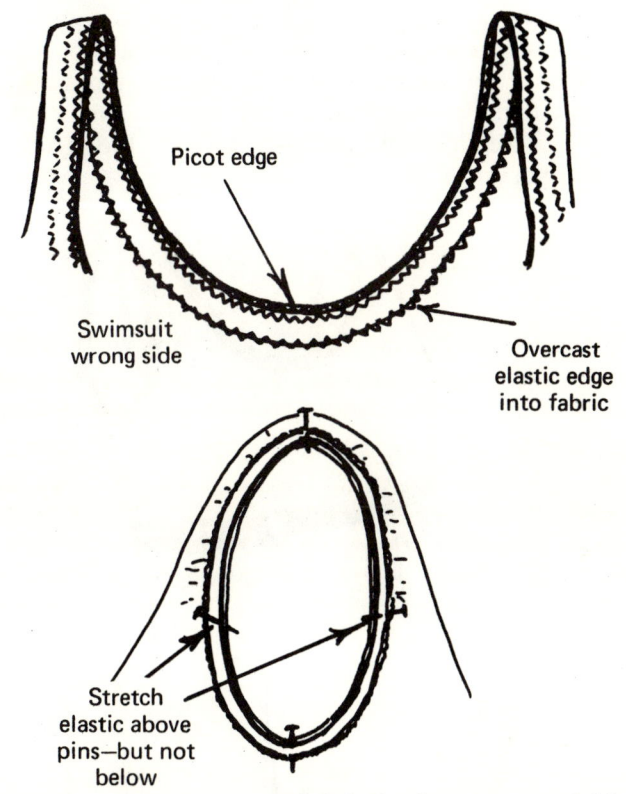

Picot edge

Swimsuit wrong side

Overcast elastic edge into fabric

Stretch elastic above pins—but not below

A bias strip of the swimsuit fabric is always a good binding for the raw edges. This method will be more expensive, however, than using elastic or sheer tricot.

The swimsuit legs should be bound with ½-inch elastic similar to that used in a panty waist. See Chapter III for instructions on applying elastic in the panty waist, and apply the leg elastic in the same manner. The elastic should be turned to the wrong side, instead of showing on the right side of the suit. If the boy panty-leg type swimsuit is desired, make a pair of tricot panties for the lining, and join the lining and the swimsuit at the waist.

For the larger woman or the older woman who does not wish to have the exposure of the standard one or two-piece swimsuit, a very becoming suit may be made by making a sleeveless shell and a pair of short shorts or hot pants with a tricot panty lining. Standard sewing methods may be used in making this swimsuit, except for the panty lining. A pattern may be found in all of the standard pattern books. If large hips are a problem, try binding the neck with a contrasting color of braid or other fabric. This will draw attention away from the hips to the face. If a small bust and large hips are a problem, add a tie belt or a strip of braid under the bustline. A bow in the center of the braid or to one side will also help to give the figure a more balanced appearance.

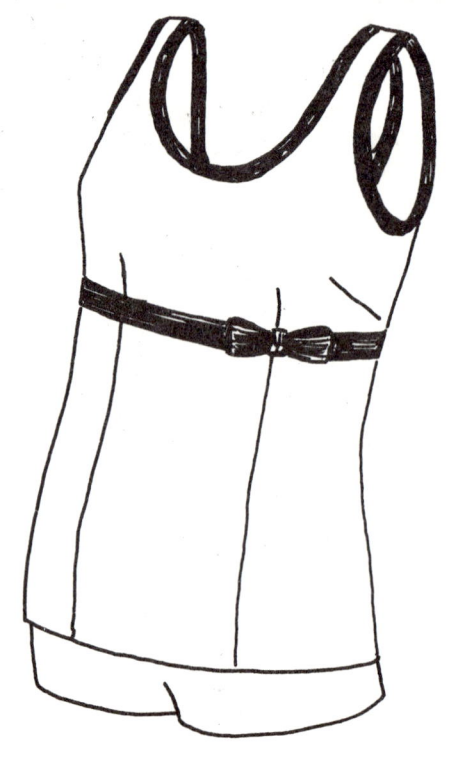

Swimsuits for males are also very easy to make. A standard shorts pattern may be used, or a pattern may be taken from an old swimsuit. Some patterns are available in the pattern books, also. Usually, the legs of the shorts pattern should be shortened for the swimsuit. A tricot lining may be easily made by following the instructions for making panties in Chapter III. This lining may be sewed in the top of the swimsuit before applying the top elastic. Men's swimsuits do not usually have a fly, so they are really very simple to make. A fly does appear in the new, long-leg type swimsuit, but it is applied in the standard method used for other men's apparel. The methods of sewing the seams in men's elastic fabric swimsuits are the same as those used in women's. The men's cotton swimsuits are straight-stitched in the standard methods.

Swimsuit sets are extremely attractive, but are usually found only in a very expensive store. You may make one at a fraction of the cost by making a jacket, slacks, shorts, skirt, scarf, and swimsuit from matching fabric. This will give you a wonderful vacation or weekend outfit that will go anywhere, do anything, yet not take up as much suitcase room as separate outfits would. You may also want to consider making His or Hers, Mother-Daughter, or Father-Son swimsuits. At a crowded beach it is easy to spot your family if you all have on swimsuits in a wild, matching fabric.

BEACH SLIPPERS

To make beach slippers, follow the instructions for making scuff slippers in Chapter IX, except that for a covering you should use terrycloth or fabric to match your swimsuit.

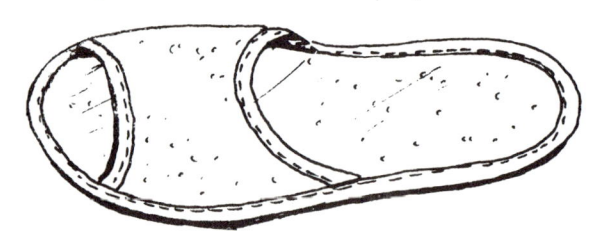

Swim Wear 43

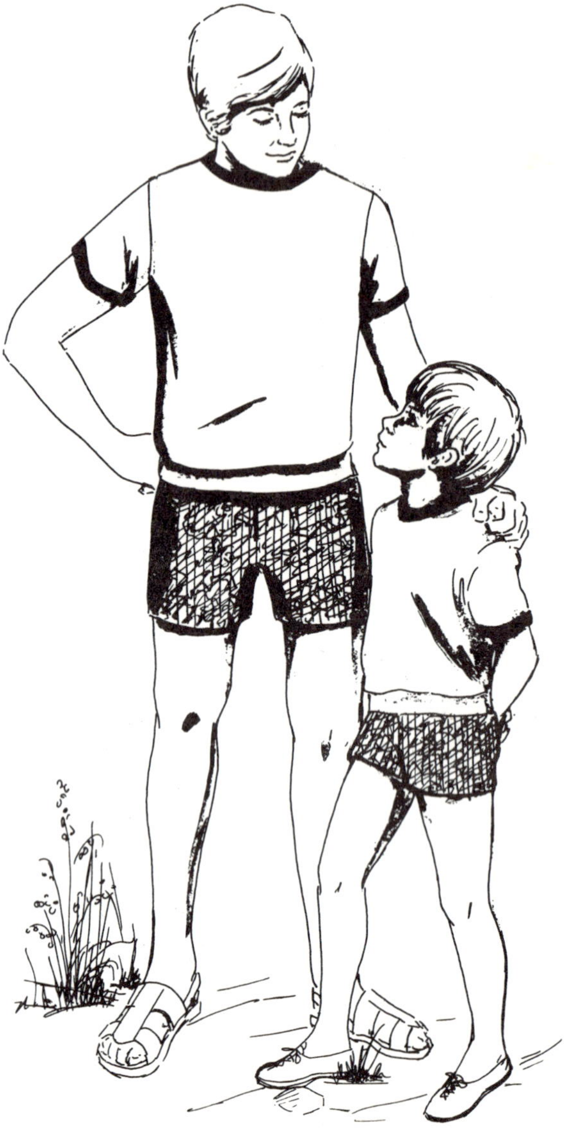

Swim Wear 45

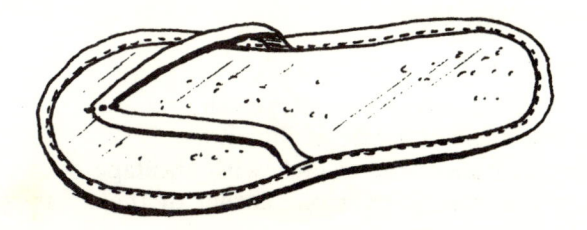

THONG SANDALS

These very popular sandals may be constructed of a variety of fabrics. Construct the sole portion by using the methods in steps 1, 2, and 3 of the scuff slipper instructions in Chapter IX. Terrycloth, swimsuit fabric, or denim, duck, etc., may be used for the top covering. Instead of making the instep piece, use 14 inches (for each sandal) of spaghetti strap string made according to the instructions in Chapter VIII or a soft cord or rope. Place your foot on the sole piece, and mark the exact spot to sew the thong. Divide the strap in half and stitch it into position by sewing front to back. Do not sew sideways or the toe will be uncomfortable. Then place the foot in the thong and position the ends of the straps on the sides of the sole and straight stitch into position. Then bind the sole as in Chapter VIII, step 10, of the scuff slipper instructions. Complete the other sandal in the same manner as the first.

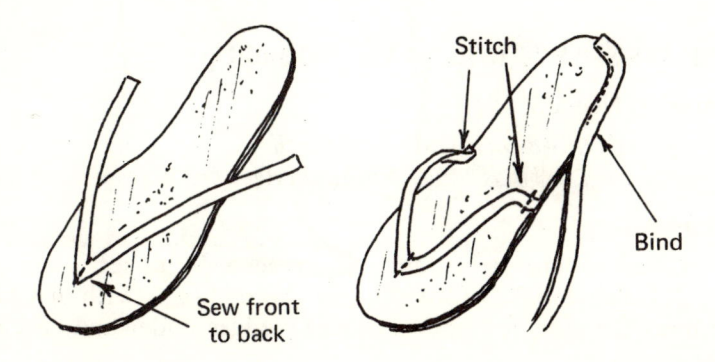

Sew front to back

Stitch

Bind

CHILD'S SWIM TOWEL (Up to 3 yrs. old)

Materials Needed:

1 yard of 48-inch wide terrycloth
4½ yards of bias tape

Step-by-Step:

1. Cut a 36-inch square of terrycloth.
2. Cut a triangle of fabric as illustrated.
3. Bind the base of the triangle with bias tape.
4. Place the triangle over one corner of the square piece of cloth, and pin it into place.
5. Bind all raw edges with bias tape.

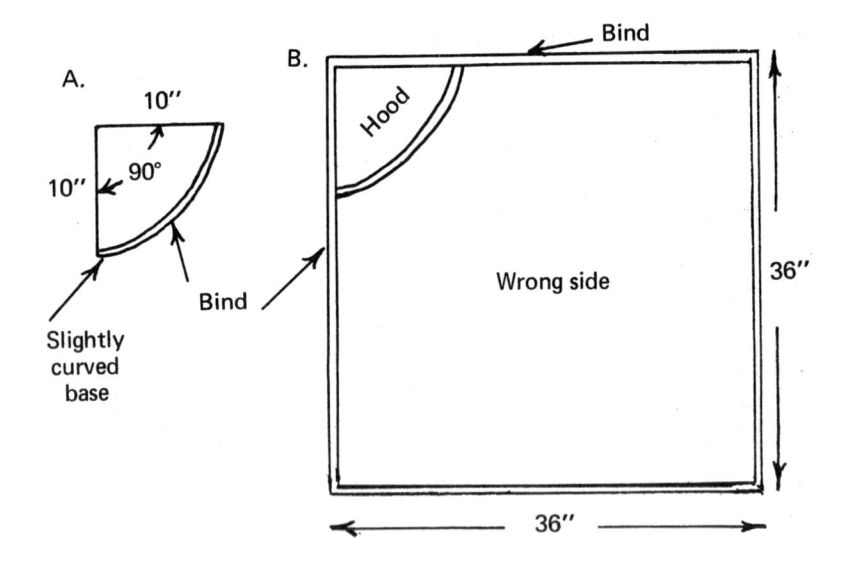

CHILD'S SWIM TOWEL (4 Yrs. Old and Up)

Materials Needed:

1½ yards of 48-inch wide terrycloth
8-1/3 yards of bias tape, if bound edges are desired

Step-by-Step:

1. Cut a rectangle of fabric 36 inches x 48 inches.
2. Either bind all four sides of the rectangle with bias tape, or hem the sides by rolling the raw edges under and stitching into place.

Child's swim towel

Note: Line with terry, and make outside to match swimsuit

Older Child's Swim Towel

Swim Wear

3. Cut a rectangle of fabric 10 inches x 20 inches.
4. Bind or hem all edges of the 10-inch x 20-inch rectangle.
5. Placing right sides together, fold the 10-inch x 20-inch fabric in half crosswise so that it is 10 inches x 10 inches.
6. Stitch a side seam perpendicular to the fold.
7. Open up the hood section opposite the fold, and center it on the edge of the 36-inch side of the towel. Then stitch it into place.

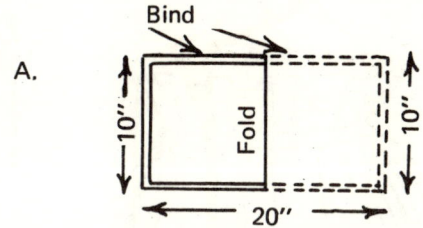

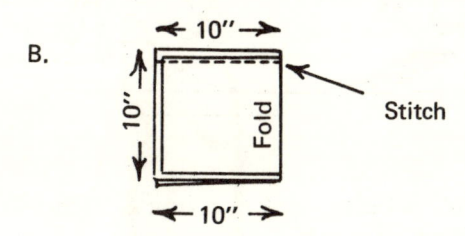

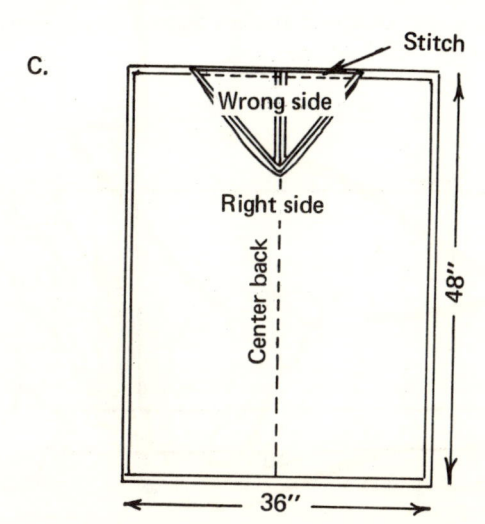

A.

B.

C.

BEACH BAG

Materials Needed:

16-inch x 36-inch piece of vinyl fabric

16-inch x 36-inch piece of cloth fabric, if you desire to cover the vinyl. Fabric matching your bathing suit is attractive.

2½ yards of rope, decorative cord, or grosgrain ribbon

Step-by-Step:

1. If the vinyl is being used as a lining, it should be sewed with the outer fabric as one piece of material.

2. Fold each end down 3 inches across the 16-inch sides so that the right sides will be together.

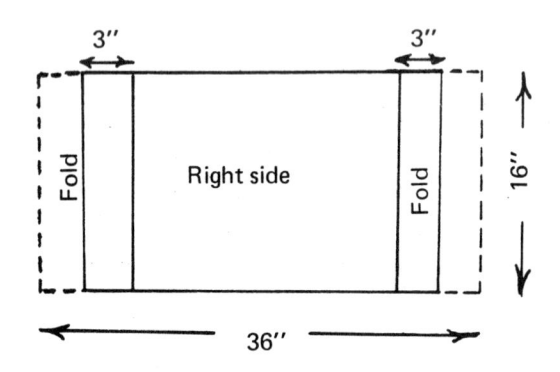

Swim Wear

3. Using a long stitch length, straight stitch from the folded edges down to three-fourths of an inch from the raw edge on all four corners.

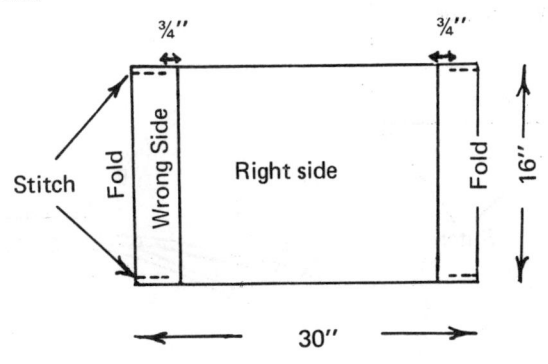

4. Turn the folded ends right side out, and straight stitch the raw edge ends in place. Then sew another seam parallel to this one. Begin this seam where the side stitching was completed.

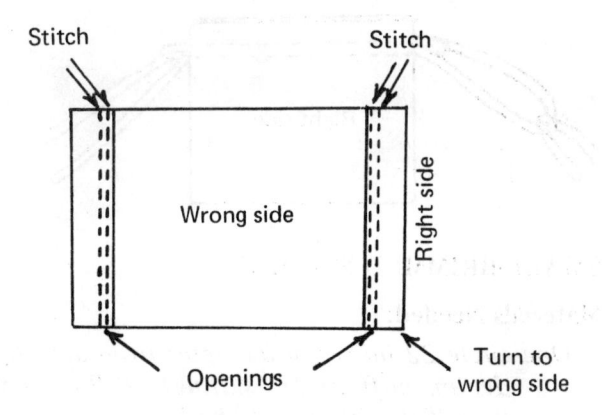

5. Fold the fabric in half with right sides together, and stitch from the folded bottom edge to the first parallel seam. Then repeat this seam on the other side of the bag.

6. Cut the rope in half. Then attach a safety pin on one end of one piece, and thread it through one side of the bag between the parallel stitching and back through the other. Then tie the two ends in a knot. Next, take the other piece of rope, and repeat this process by starting on the opposite side of the bag from the knotted rope.

A.

Wrong side

Fold

Stitch

B.

Right side

C.

Right side

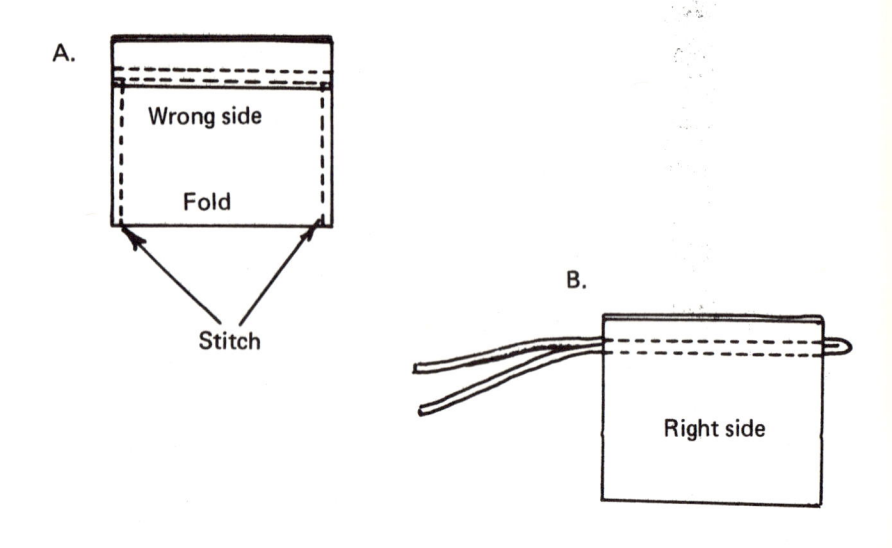

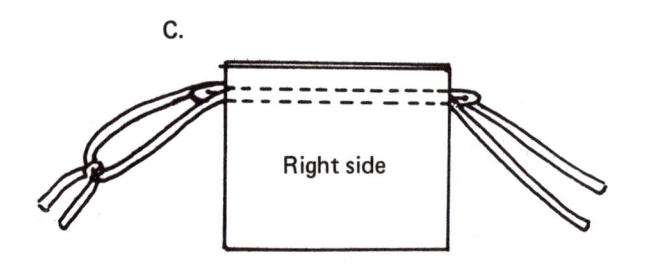

SMALL-BRIMMED SUN HAT

Materials Needed:
One circle 22 inches in diameter from any stiff fabric (duck, denim, stiff nylon, suiting) Pellon may be used as a liner if the fabric lacks body.
2 yards of lace edging, rickrack, etc.
Bows, flowers, or other trim, as desired

Step-by-Step:
   1. Fold the circle in half with right sides together.
   2. Stitch a half-inch seam from the folded edge around the brim to a point one inch from the center; then stitch the other side in the same manner.
   3. Turn the right side out through the one-inch opening.

Swim Wear 53

4. Stitch the trim along the edge of the brim. Be sure to tuck in the raw edges on the center of the brim.

5. Placing right sides together, fold the hat in half and sew folded edges together.

6. Decorate as desired.

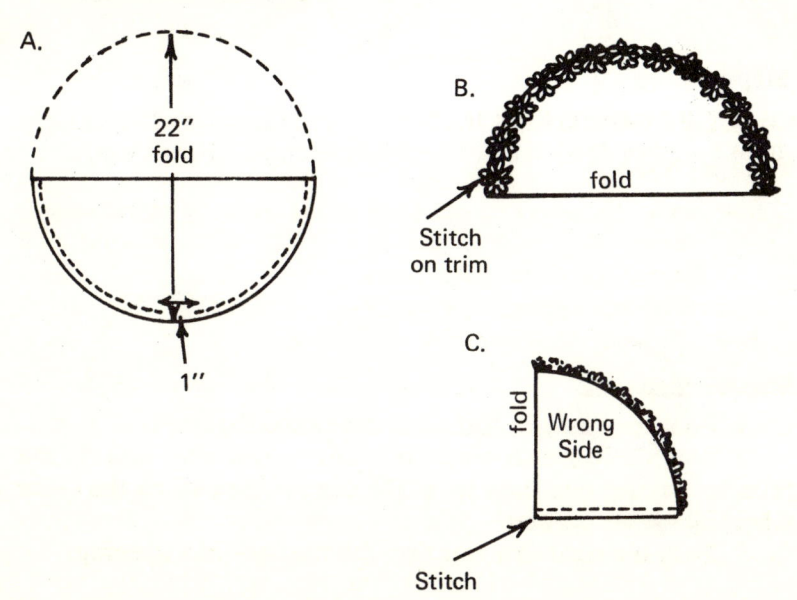

A.
22" fold
1"

B.
fold
Stitch on trim

C.
fold
Wrong Side
Stitch

LARGE-BRIMMED SUN HAT

Materials Needed:

1 yard of 48-inch fabric, such as denim, duck, suiting, or bonded
24-inch grosgrain ribbon
Decorative scarf or flowers

Step-by-Step:

1. Cut a 6½-inch circle, two 20-inch circles, and a parallelogram 5 inches deep with a 22-inch base and a 21-inch top.

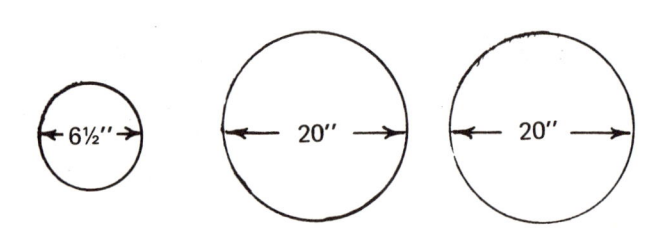

```
         ←——— 21" ———→
        ┌─────────────────┐  ↑
        │                  │  5"
        └─────────────────┘  ↓
       ←———— 22" ————→
```

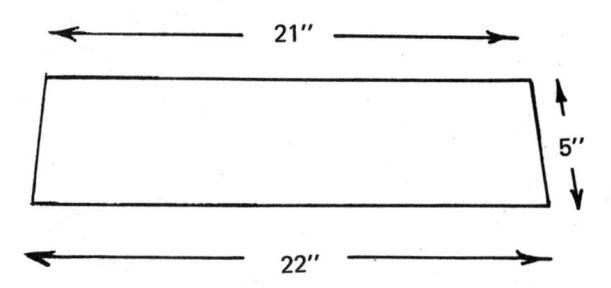

2. Join the ends of the parallelogram by placing the right sides together and straight stitching a ½-inch seam.

3. Place the right side of the 21-inch edge against the right side of the 6½-inch circle and join by straight stitching a ½-inch seam.

4. Pull the side fabric down so that the raw edges are inside the hat. Then place the 22-inch edge of the crown in the center of the two 20-inch circles, and mark around the crown with a piece of chalk.

5. Cut out the circle a half-inch inside the markings drawn for the crown. This forms the brim pieces.

6. Place the right sides of the brim pieces together and stitch the outer edges all the way around the brim. Then turn the right sides out.

7. Place the brim around the bottom of the crown section with the raw edges together. Then pin the grosgrain ribbon around the brim so that it will be caught in the seam and cover the raw edges.

8. Stitch the crown, brim, and ribbon together in this position.

9. Turn the grosgrain ribbon and the raw seam to the inside, and either tack the ribbon up by hand or sew by machine.

10. Trim with a scarf, a garland of flowers, or a ribbon.

Sewing The Unusual

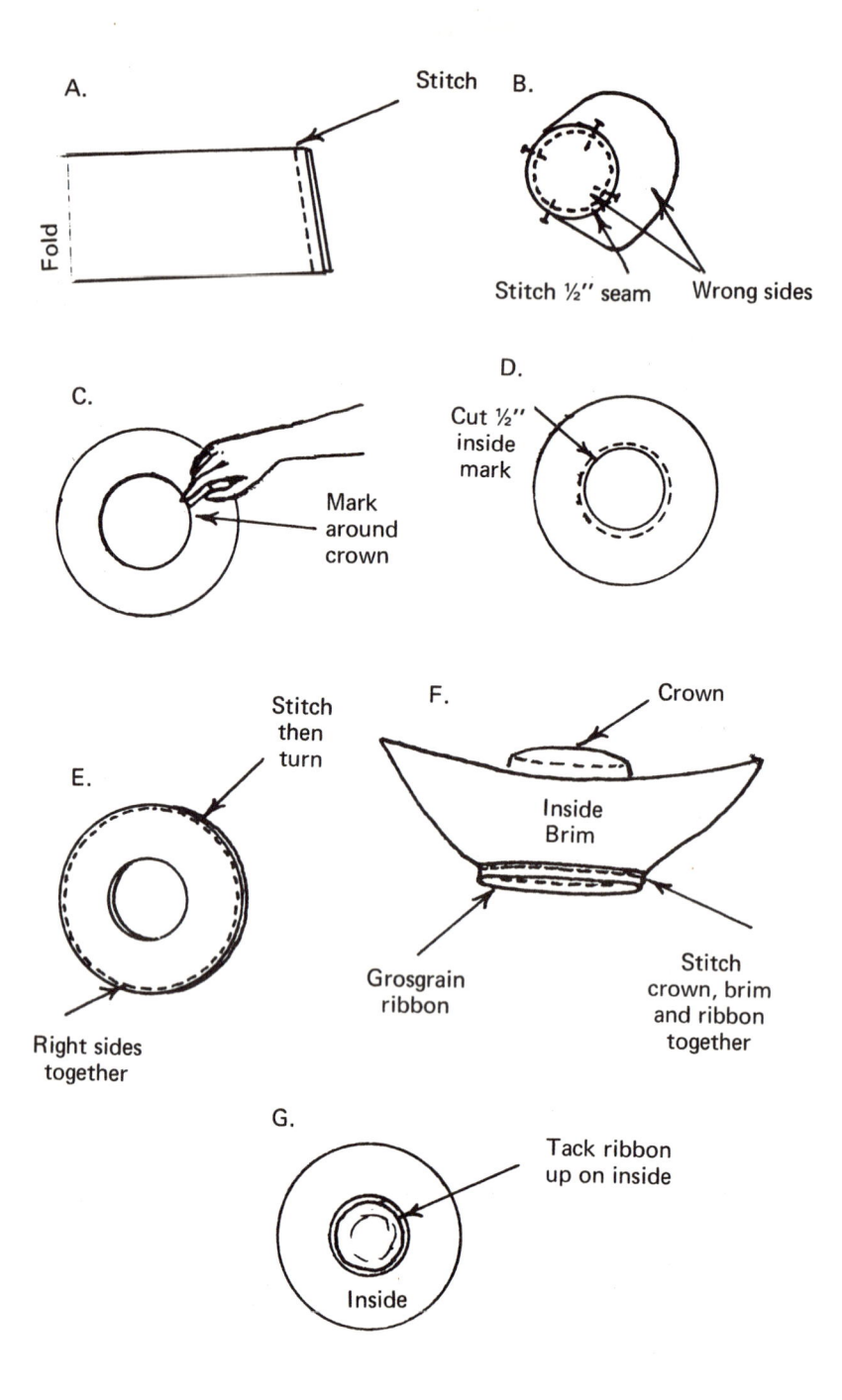

A. Fold / Stitch

B. Stitch ½" seam / Wrong sides

C. Mark around crown

D. Cut ½" inside mark

E. Stitch then turn / Right sides together

F. Crown / Inside Brim / Grosgrain ribbon / Stitch crown, brim and ribbon together

G. Inside / Tack ribbon up on inside

Swim Wear

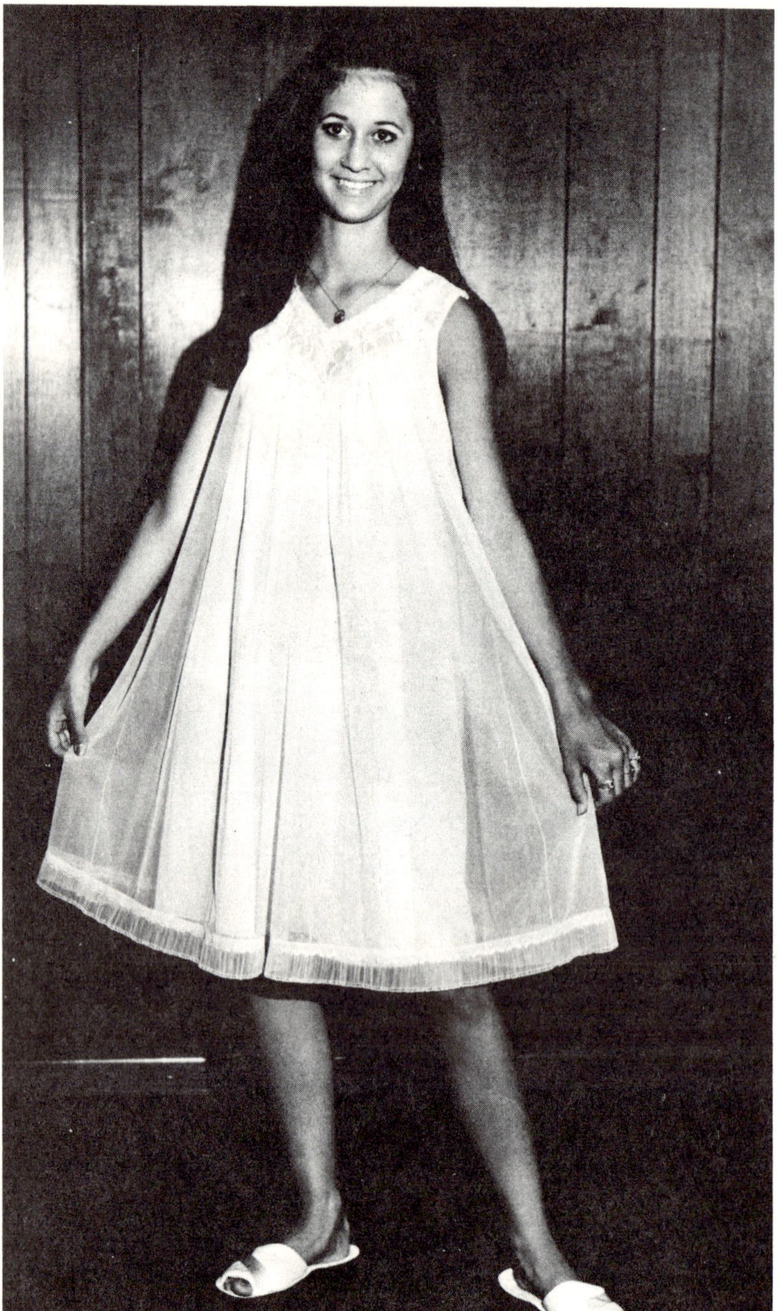

Gift Items

CHAPTER V

GIFT ITEMS

SMOKE RING SCARF

Materials Needed:

24-inch x 14-inch piece of fabric, either nylon, chiffon, tricot, whipped cream, jersey, etc.

Step-by-Step:

1. Cut a 27-inch x 14-inch pattern from a piece of paper, and place it on the fabric. If a woven fabric is being used, cut the fabric so that the length is on a true bias. If a stretchy fabric is used, such as tricot, cut the fabric on the stretch so that the stretch goes lengthwise. Since the stretch is across the width of tricot, cut the scarf so that the straight of the fabric is 14 inches

Gift Items

long and the stretch or width is 27 inches.

2. Fold the scarf lengthwise with right sides together, and stitch the long side of the scarf. Use a straight stitch; then overcast the stitch and the fabric edge with a zigzag.

3. Stitch the ends together in the same manner, but leave a 2-inch gap.

4. Turn the scarf right side out, and close the 2-inch gap by hand.

RING SCARF

Materials Needed:

18-inch x 42-inch piece of sheer nylon
3¼ yards of narrow edging nylon lace
¾-inch bone ring (purchase this at a knit shop or drapery store)

Step-by-Step:

1. Cut one end of the fabric in an oval shape, and leave the other end straight.

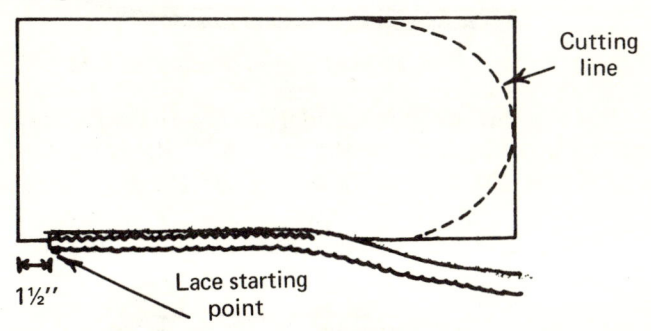

2. Place the edging lace on top of the sheer fabric just beyond the edge. Zigzag the lace onto the edge of the fabric all the way around the scarf. Start the lace at a point 1½ inches from the square end on the long side of the scarf.

3. Zigzag the lace ends together. Then, without breaking the thread, run a gathering stitch straight across the end of the scarf 1½ inches from the end.

4. Overlap the two lace edge sides of the scarf by folding it in half lengthwise. Place the lace joint on top of the non-joint edge.

5. Pull the gathering threads so that the fabric is gathered as tightly as possible.

Gathering stitch

Lace joint

1½"

Fold scarf with lace sides together

Lace joint on top of solid lace side

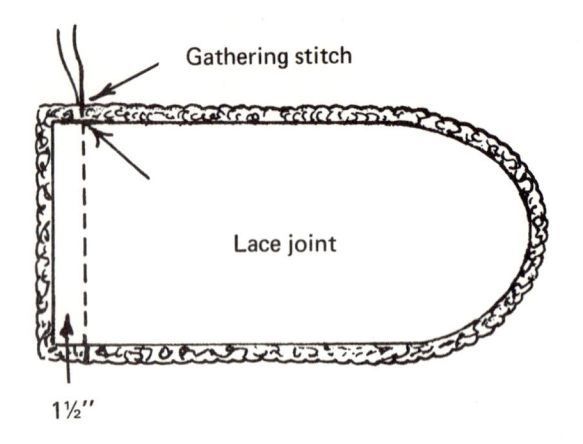

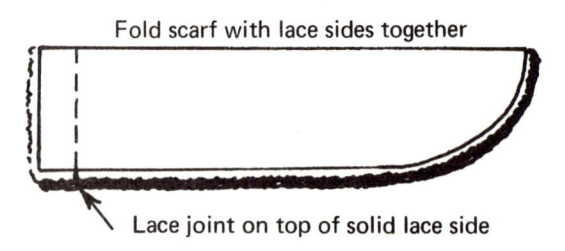

6. Push the gathered end through the bone ring. Then the lace joint will be underneath the other side of the lace piece.

7. Place the lace joint on top of the solid lace as it feeds through the ring. Then flatten the lace and sheer over the ring so that the gathering stitch is on the inside of the ring.

Ring with fabric and lace pulled through it

8. Arrange the gathers evenly inside the ring. Then flare the lace and fabric over the ring edge with the gathering stitch against the inside of the ring.

Gift Items

9. Position the four lace pieces on top of one another. Then straight stitch the fabric in this position as close to the ring as possible. A zipper or cording foot is very useful for this seam.

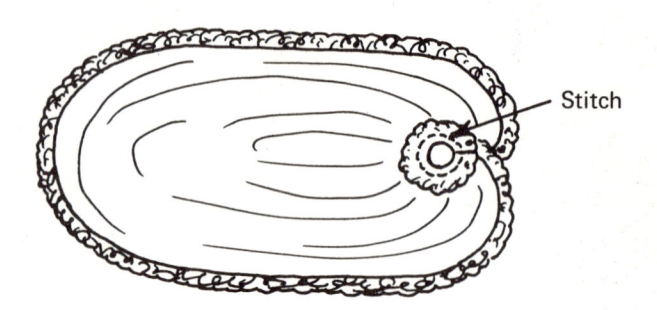

10. To wear this scarf, simply place the fabric either over the head or around the neck; then tuck the oval end through the ring, and draw the scarf up to the desired length.

DRESS-UP EVENING SCARF

Materials Needed:

18-inch x 72-inch piece of sheer fabric
4¾ yards of edging lace
½ yard of 3-inch to 4-inch wide lace with one scalloped edge, plus enough extra lace to cut two appliqués

Step-by-Step:

1. Cut both ends of the fabric into an oval shape by rounding the corners.
2. Fold the scarf in half and mark the halfway point.
3. Then, fold the 18-inch wide piece of wide lace in half, and mark the halfway point in it.
4. Place the wide lace on top of the scarf with halfway marks together and the scalloped edge extending slightly over the edge of the fabric.
5. Stitch the lace to the fabric by zigzagging down the fabric edge and then along the edge of the lace on all sides.
6. Place the edging lace on top of the sheer along the fabric edge; begin the edging lace at the end of the wide lace. Then zigzag the edging lace into place. Edge the sheer scarf completely with the narrow lace, except where it is already edged with the wide lace.

Gift Items

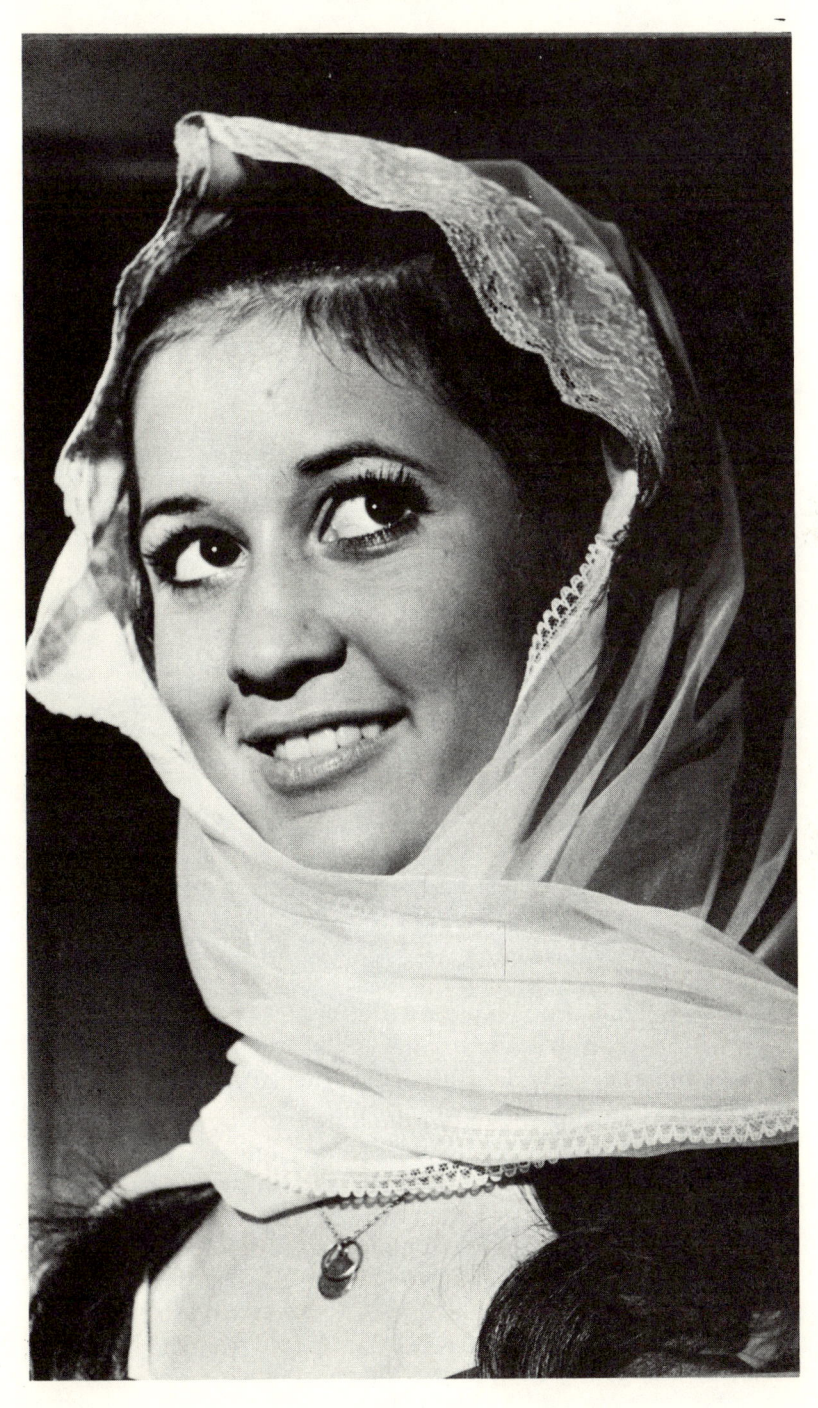

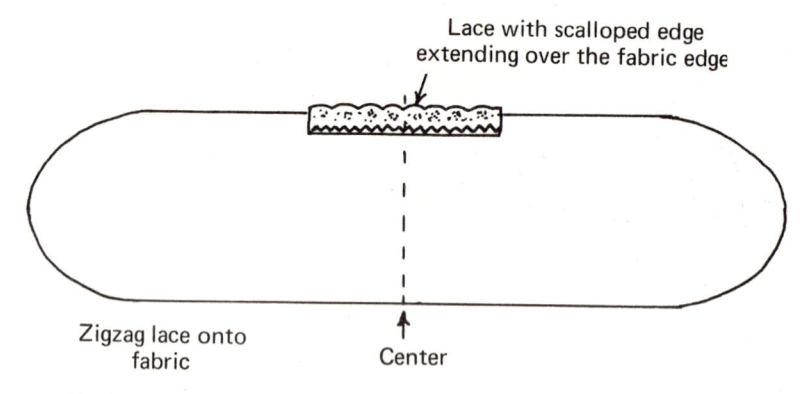

66   Sewing The Unusual

Lace with scalloped edge extending over the fabric edge

Zigzag lace onto fabric

Center

7. At the point where the narrow lace joins the wide lace, put three rows of gathering stitches from the edge of the scarf to a point 6 inches from the edge.

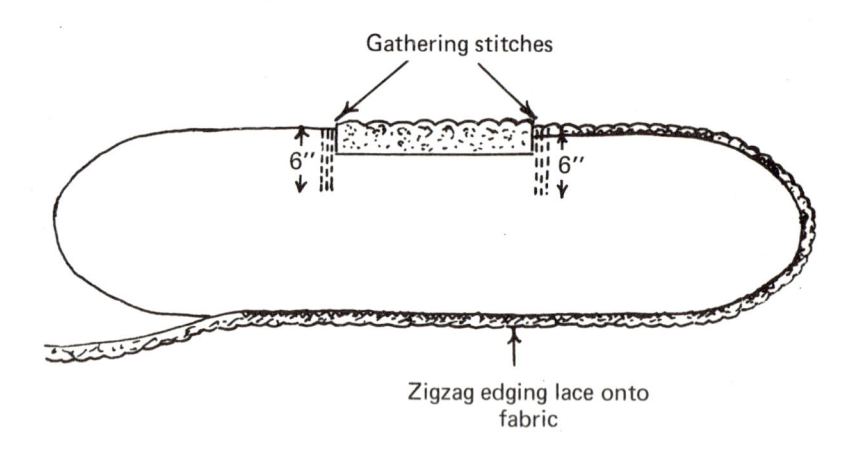

Gathering stitches

6" *6"*

Zigzag edging lace onto fabric

8. Pull the gathering stitches tight.

9. Cut two appliqués from the leftover wide lace, and zigzag them over the gathered stitches. To make an appliqué, cut out a flower decoration from the lace. Be careful not to cut into the heavy outline threads. Then place the flower on the fabric in the proper place, and overcast the edges with a zigzag. Be sure to completely outline the flower with stitches so it will be secure.

10. To wear this scarf, place the wide lace over the hair at the forehead and gently tie it under the chin.

Gift Items

WINDY DAY SCARF

Materials Needed:

36-inch x 27-inch piece of sheer tricot or net
1 yard of 1-inch wide ribbon

Step-by-Step:

1. Fold the fabric in half lengthwise.
2. Then fold the fabric in half crosswise. This will make two folded sides and two raw-edge sides.
3. Starting one inch from the folded edge, cut in a semicircle from the short side to the other folded edge.

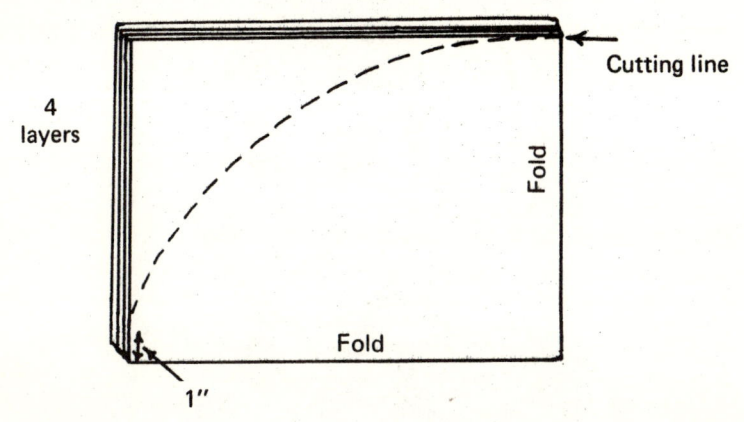

4. Unfold the fabric, and trim the cut edges if they appear to be uneven.
5. Fold the fabric in half lengthwise with the wrong sides together.
6. Beginning 1 inch from the folded edge, run a gathering stitch one-eighth of an inch from the fabric edge along the semicircle to a point 1 inch from the folded edge on the other side.

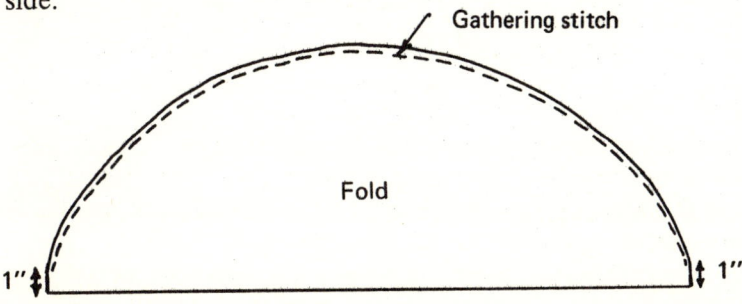

7. Draw the gathers evenly until they measure 14 inches across.

8. Center the ribbon along the gathering stitches. Then sew the gathered raw edge to the wrong side of the ribbon with a 1/8-inch, straightstitched seam.

9. Fold the ribbon in half lengthwise so that it will cover the raw tricot edge, and top stitch along the unfolded edge the entire length of the ribbon.

DICKIE-TYPE SCARF

Materials Needed:

21-inch square of sheer nylon tricot
Two-thirds of a yard of edging lace
6-inch piece of ribbon or other material for a tie

Step-by-Step:

1. Fold the square of material diagonally with the right sides together so that it is triangular in shape. To determine which side is the right side, stretch the fabric crosswise until it rolls up on the edge. It will roll toward the right side.

2. Straight stitch along the one raw edge of the triangle about one-fourth of an inch from the edge. Turn the corner at

the apex of the triangle and stitch about an inch up the other side. Then lock the stitch and break the threads.

3. Stitch up the other side from a point about an inch from where the stitches were discontinued.

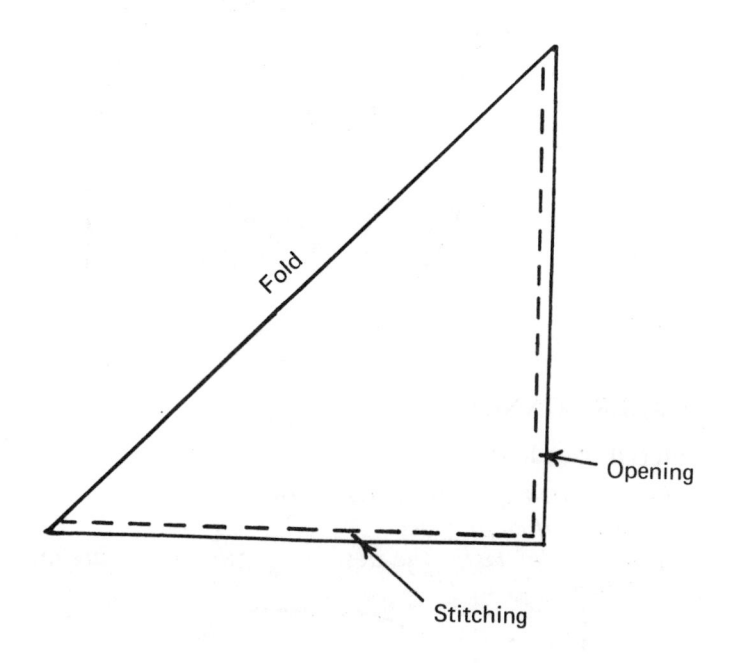

Fold

Opening

Stitching

4. Turn the scarf right side out by pulling it through the opening.

5. Hand stitch the opening so that it will be neatly closed.

6. Zigzag lace across the folded edge of the scarf.

7. Evenly pleat the lace edge of the scarf so that it is 11 inches to 12 inches long. Then zigzag along the bottom edge of the lace again to secure the pleats.

8. Straight stitch the tie on the corner of the triangle at the end of the lace. Then sew a hook and eye on the tie end and on the other side of the scarf top.

9. To wear this scarf, simply hook it around the neck. It is excellent to fill up any V-neck dress, sweater, or suit neck opening. These little scarves cost $4.00 to $5.00 ready-made, but may be made at home from scraps or leftover fabric. Although dickies are usually used for suits, they can work wonders for a plain, V-neck dress.

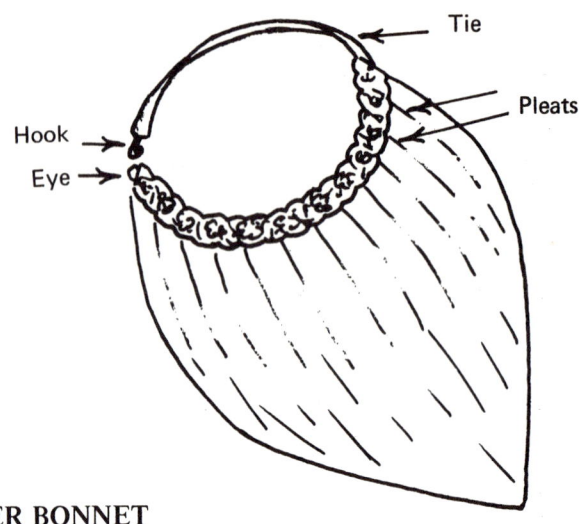

CURLER BONNET

Materials Needed:

Two 24-inch squares of nylon tricot sheer
2¼ yards of edging lace
¼-inch wide elastic the desired length to be snug around the head

Gift Items

Step-by-Step:

1. Place the two squares of sheer on top of one another with the wrong sides together.

2. Cut the two squares into 24-inch circles. The best way to cut the squares into circles is by making a newspaper pattern and placing it on top of the fabric layers to be used as a guide. To make a pattern, spread the paper on a table. Tie a string around a pencil. Hold the string against the newspaper 12 inches from the pencil. Draw a circle by moving the pencil completely around the point where the string is being held.

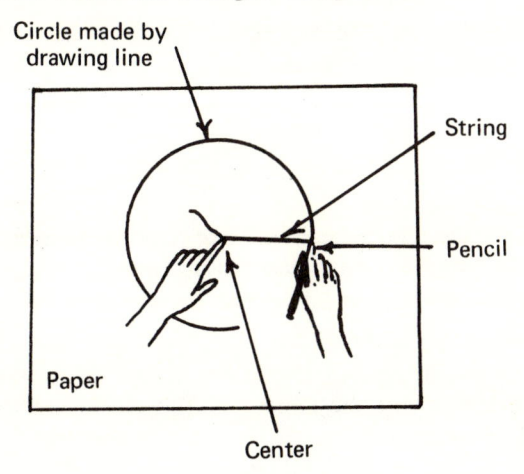

3. Pin the edges of the circle together.

4. Zigzag the lace on the top of the fabric along the edge.

5. Run a gathering stitch all around the bonnet about one-half inch from the stitched edge of the lace.

6. Gather the gathering stitch enough so that the bonnet is *almost* the head size.

7. Overlap the elastic ends, and join them by straight stitching the length of the overlap.

8. Quarter the elastic and the bonnet, and mark with pins at the quarter marks.

9. Pin the quarter marks of elastic onto the inside of the bonnet at the quarter marks along the gathering stitch.

10. Stretching the elastic so that the quarter marks match, zigzag the elastic along the gathering stitch. Use a regular length zigzag stitch; let the needle overcast the elastic edge and go into the fabric, then swing back into the middle of the elastic. It is necessary to stitch only the edge of the elastic.

LONG, DECORATIVE SCARF

Materials Needed:

12-inch x 72-inch long piece of any type knit fabric (tricot, jersey, double-knit, etc.). Whipped cream or crepe may also be used.
13 inches of fringe in the desired length

Step-by-Step:

1. Fold the fabric in half lengthwise with the right sides together.
2. Place the fringe between the fabric pieces with the fringe solid end even with the fabric edge.

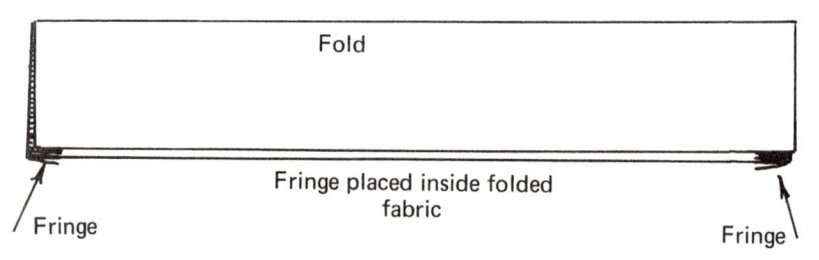

Fold

Fringe placed inside folded fabric

Fringe   Fringe

3. Straight stitch ½-inch seams from the folded edge to a point one inch from the center of the scarf. Sew a similar seam on the other end.

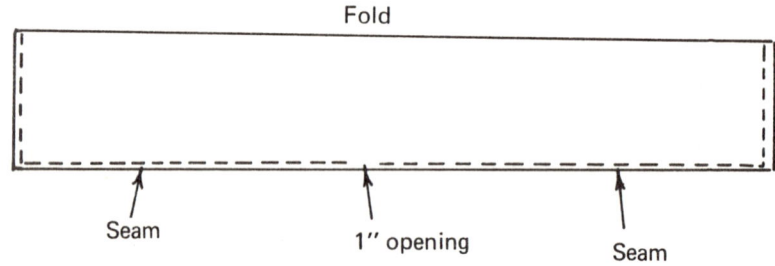

Fold

Seam   1" opening   Seam

4. Turn the scarf right side out and press. Often it is not necessary to hand stitch the turn opening, because it will not show.

TIE SCARF

Various designs of scarves may be made from leftover fabric or fabric purchased especially for a decorator scarf. Design your own scarf by making a paper pattern in the desired shape. Fold the paper in half, and use the fold as the scarf center; then cut the paper into the desired shape. In this way, both sides of the scarf will be the same. When designing your scarf end, perhaps you would like to consider a triangular-shaped end, instead of the regular square type. If both ends of the scarf are to be alike, use the same pattern for both ends so that they will be identical. Beautiful scarves and gloves may be made from leftover fabrics to make a truly attractive, custom-made outfit. Often a pretty scarf will be made of leftover dress fabric to be worn as a hair band with the dress. These little extras are what make a garment into an ensemble. They tie the whole person together in a totally groomed look.

LARGE TRIANGULAR SHAWL

Materials Needed:

53-inch square of velvet, brushed-type nylon fleece, or other fabric (Nylon is more practical.)
30 yards of yarn

Step-by-Step:

1. Fold the fabric in half diagonally with the right sides together.
2. Straight stitch a seam one-half inch from the edge on all the raw edges. Leave a 2-inch opening for turning.
3. Turn the fabric right side out through the opening.
4. Thread a large needle with a long piece of yarn. Push the needle through the fabric one-fourth of an inch from the edge. Then push the needle back through the fabric about one-eighth of an inch from where it came through. Pull the thread through until the yarn left before entering the fabric is the desired fringe length. Cut the yarn on the needle side of the fabric to match the length of the other end. Then pull the string ends through the loop. Continue making the yarn fringe down both sides of the scarf.

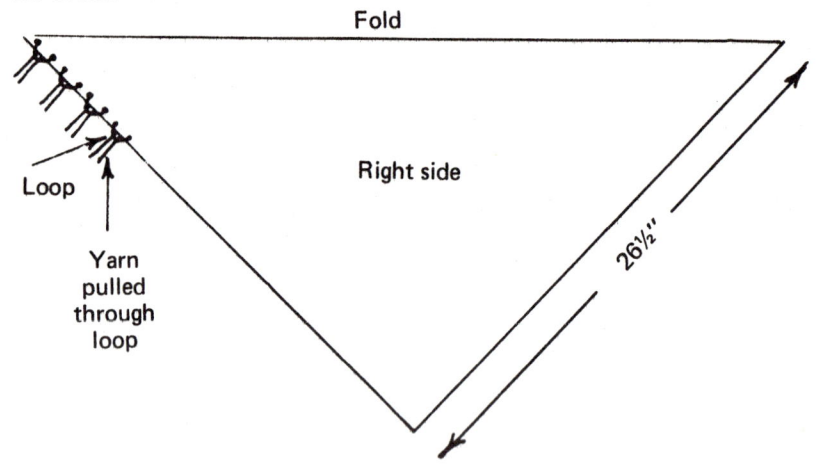

5. This scarf is excellent for warmth as well as beauty. Ponchos may also be made in this manner. Hand-fringed scarves sell for $35.00 to $40.00 but are very inexpensive to make. They are time-consuming but make excellent handwork projects for television viewing, waiting rooms, etc.

TRAVEL SHOE BAGS

Materials Needed:
Two 9½-inch x 15-inch pieces of tricot (stretch in the 9½-inch direction)
24 inches of cord

Gift Items

Step-by-Step:

1. Fold the fabric in half lengthwise, and sew a ½-inch seam down the side and across the end. This end may be ovalled slightly. Then overcast the seam with a zigzag.
2. Fold a 1-inch hem to the wrong side across the top and stitch. Leave an opening at the seam side for the cord.
3. Run a cord through the hem; then tie the two cord ends together.
4. Make another bag for the other shoe.

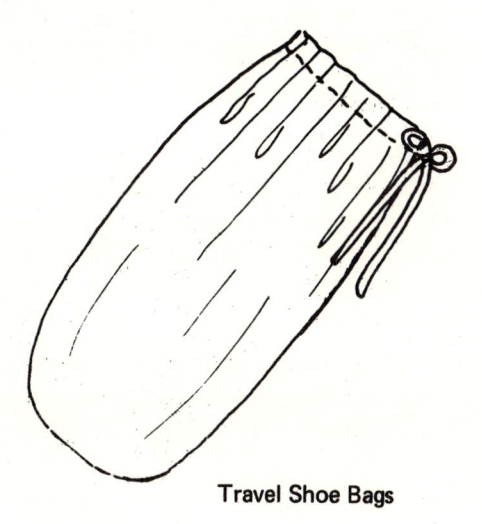

Travel Shoe Bags

GLOVES

Materials Needed:

12-inch length of tricot (other type fabrics may be used, especially leftovers from dresses.)

GLOVE PATTERN

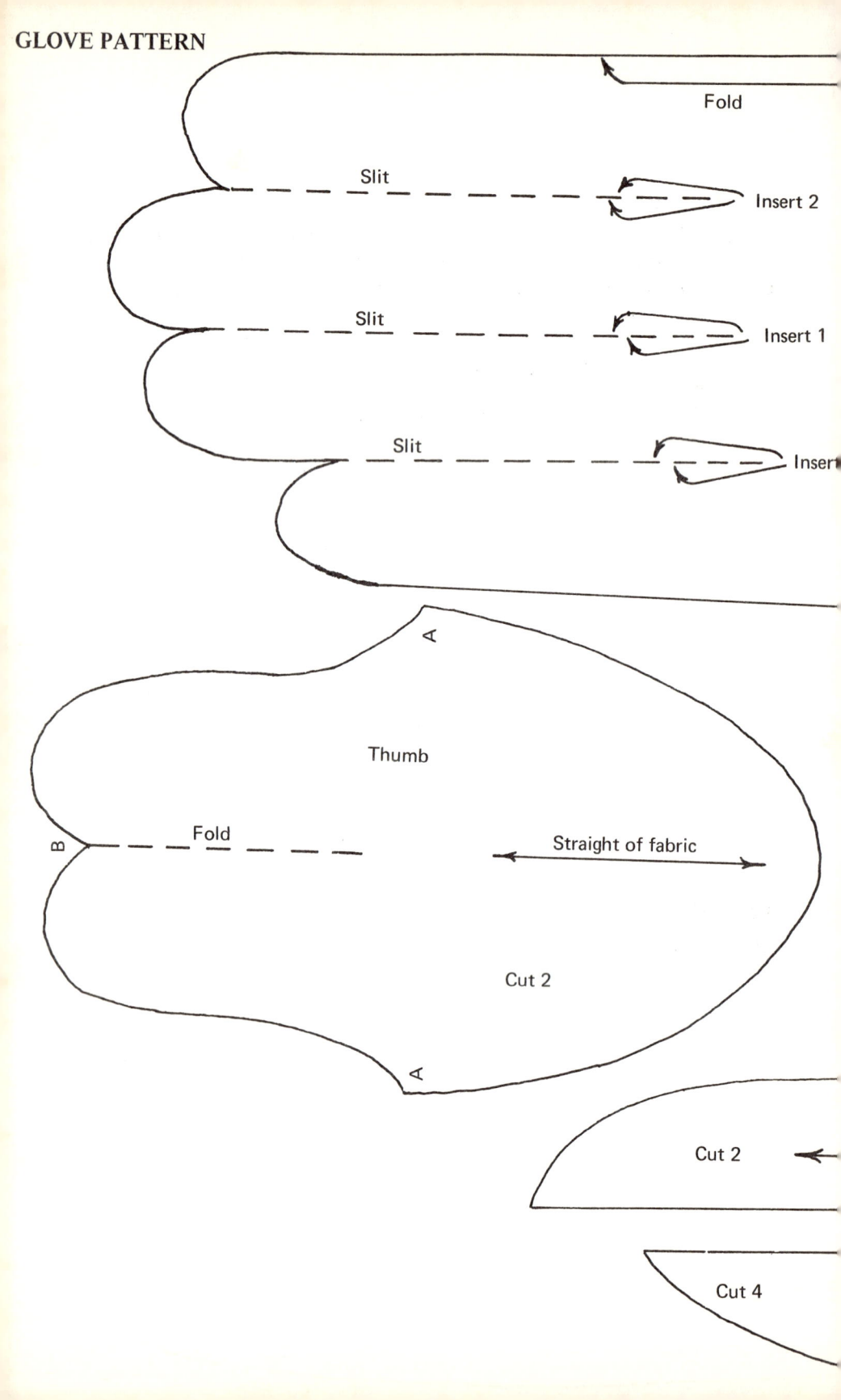

Fold

Slit — Insert 2

Slit — Insert 1

Slit — Insert

Thumb

A

B — Fold — — — — — Straight of fabric

Cut 2

A

Cut 2

Cut 4

Fold

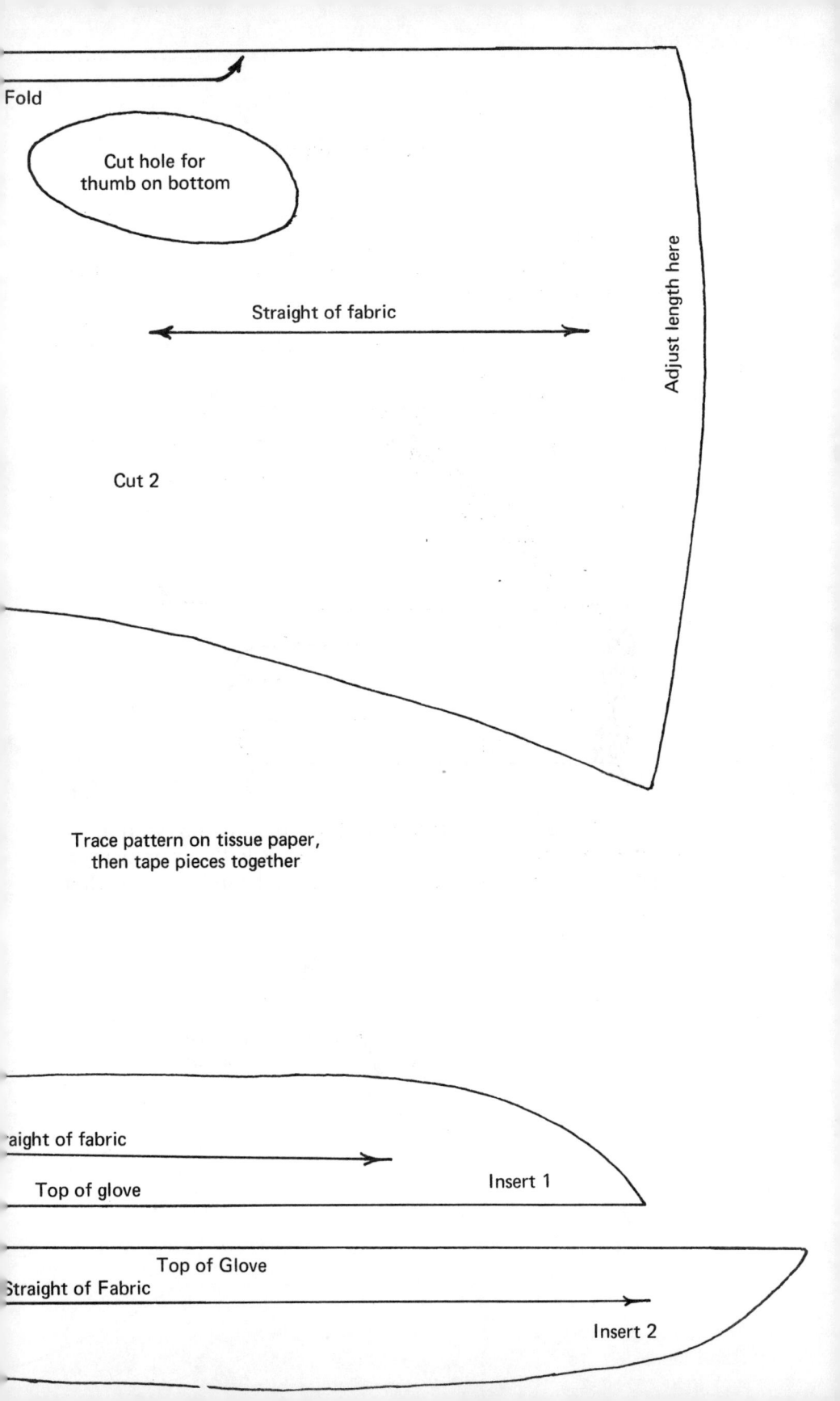

Cut hole for
thumb on bottom

←——— Straight of fabric ———→

Adjust length here

Cut 2

Trace pattern on tissue paper,
then tape pieces together

Straight of fabric

Top of glove

Insert 1

Top of Glove

Straight of Fabric

Insert 2

78 *Sewing The Unusual*

Step-by-Step:

1. Place the pattern on the straight of the fabric and cut as indicated on the pattern.

2. Zigzag any lace or other decoration on the top edge of the glove, or hem with a decorative stitch. If an edging lace is not desired, use a rolled hem.

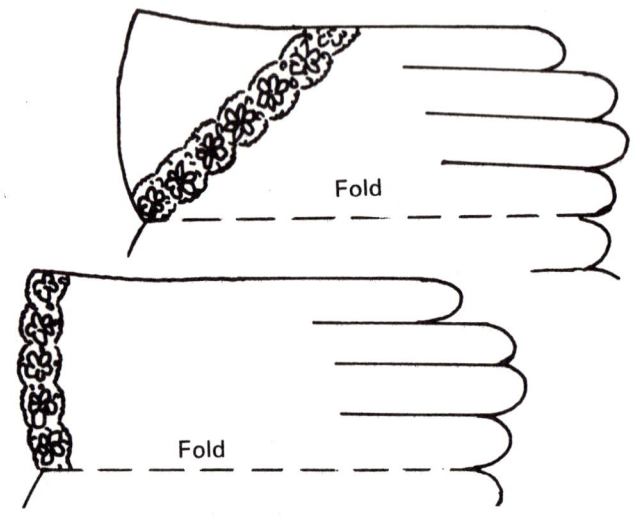

3. With right sides together, fold the thumb section as indicated on the pattern. Sew from A to B with a very narrow straight stitch; then overcast the seam and fabric edge with a zigzag.

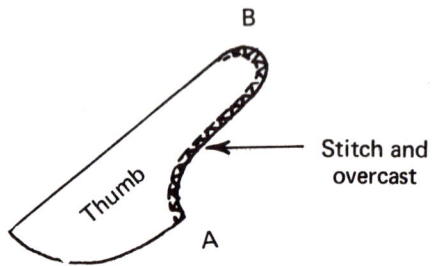

4. Cut out the thumb hole on the underneath side of each glove.

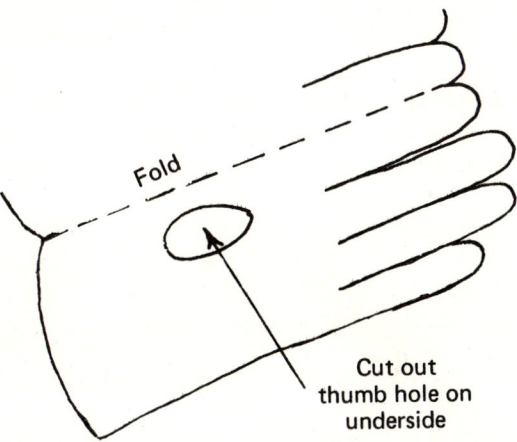

Fold

Cut out thumb hole on underside

5. Place the thumb section in the thumb hole. Place the right sides of the two pieces together, and straight stitch the thumb in place. Then overcast this seam with a zigzag. Use VERY narrow seams throughout the glove.

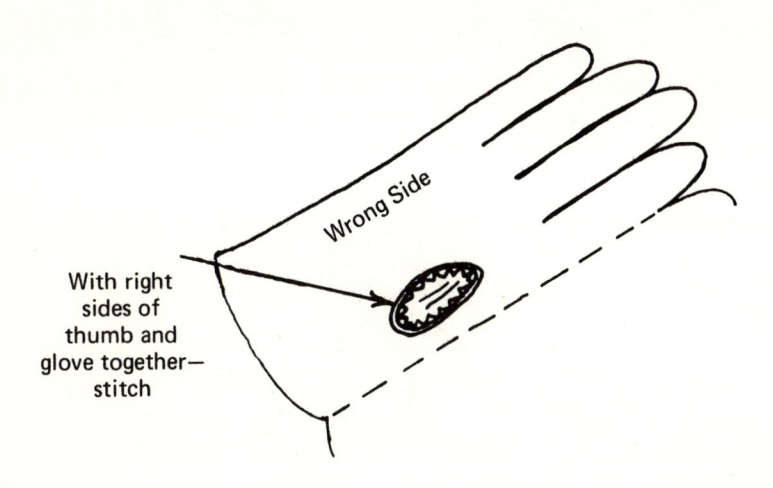

Wrong Side

With right sides of thumb and glove together— stitch

6. Place one "Insert 2" on the top of the glove at the inside of the index finger with the flat side of the Insert at the seam edge. At the base of the finger, extend the Insert up the side of the middle finger.

7. With right sides together, straight stitch this Insert into position. Then overcast the seam with a zigzag. Be sure to lock each zigzagged seam before and after sewing by stitching two stitches with the stitch length at "0."

8. Place an "Insert 1" on the top of the middle finger with right sides together. The Insert should extend to the base of the finger and up to the top of the third finger.

9. Stitch this Insert into place as before.

10. Place the flat side of an "Insert 2" on top of the third finger against the outside seam so that it extends to the base of the finger and up the inside edge of the little finger.

11. Straight stitch into position as before, and overcast with a zigzag.

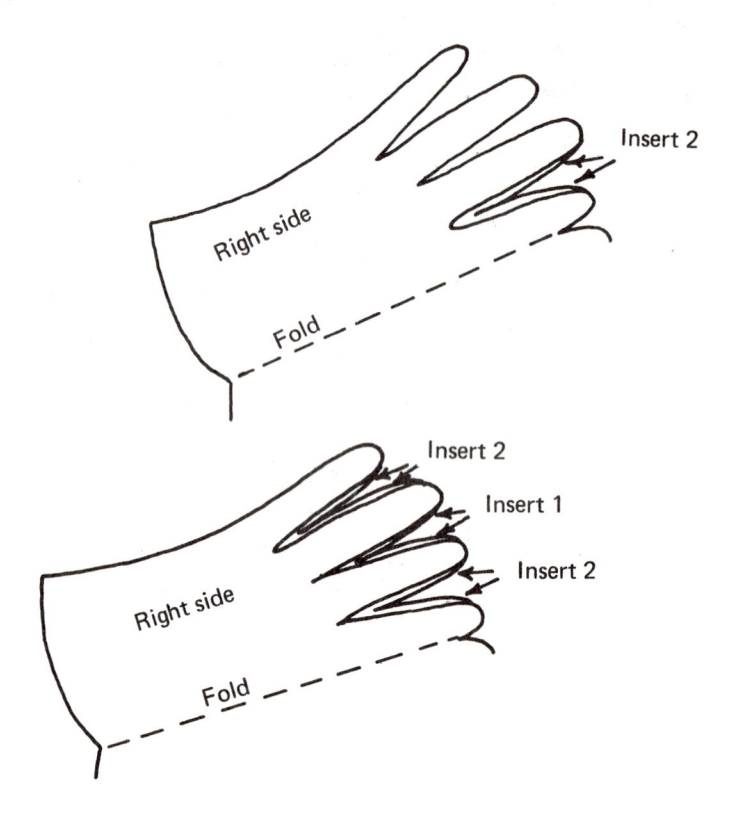

12. Turn the glove inside out; straight stitch across the top of the index finger, down the bottom of the insert at the side of the finger, up the side of the middle finger, etc., until all of the bottom seams are completed. Then stitch from the top of the little finger back to the glove hem. After stitching these seams, overcast them with a zigzag.

13. Make the other glove in the same manner as the first.

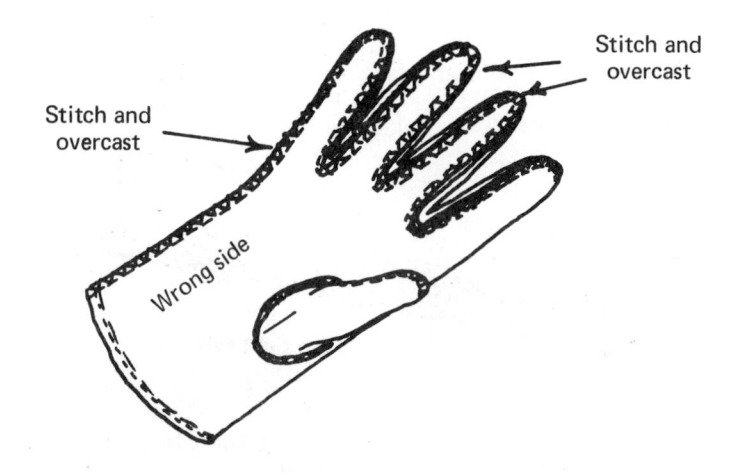

BRIDAL GARTER

Materials Needed:

22-inch length of 1½-inch wide satin ribbon
22-inch length of ½-inch wide lace
11-inch long piece of 1-inch wide elastic

Step-by-Step:

1. Zigzag the lace to the right side of the ribbon edge the entire length of the ribbon.

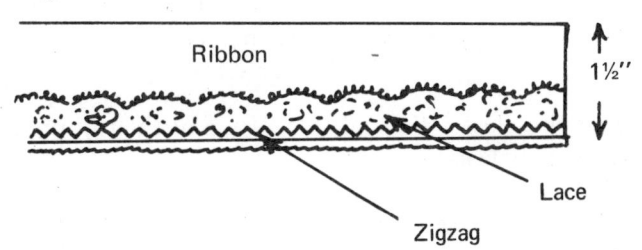

2. With right sides together, stitch the ribbon raw ends together with a straight stitch.

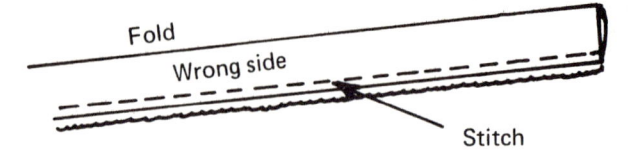

Fold
Wrong side
Stitch

3. Turn the ribbon right side out, and fold in half lengthwise.

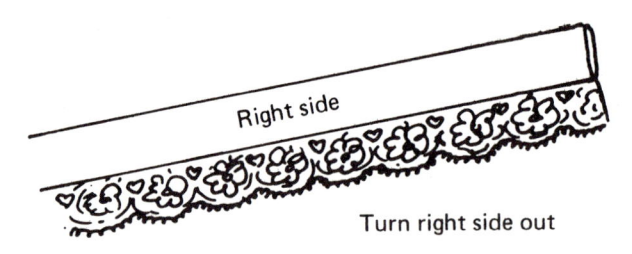

Right side
Turn right side out

4. Straight stitch the ribbon edges together, but leave a tiny opening through which to insert the elastic.

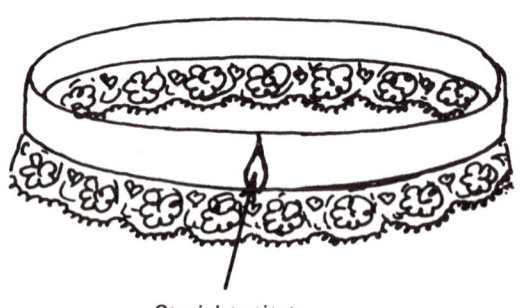

Straight stitch but leave tiny opening inside

5. Pull the elastic through the inside of the ribbon, and join the ends of the elastic.
6. Close the tiny opening.
7. The garter may be trimmed with a small flower appliqué or a bow.

Gift Items 83

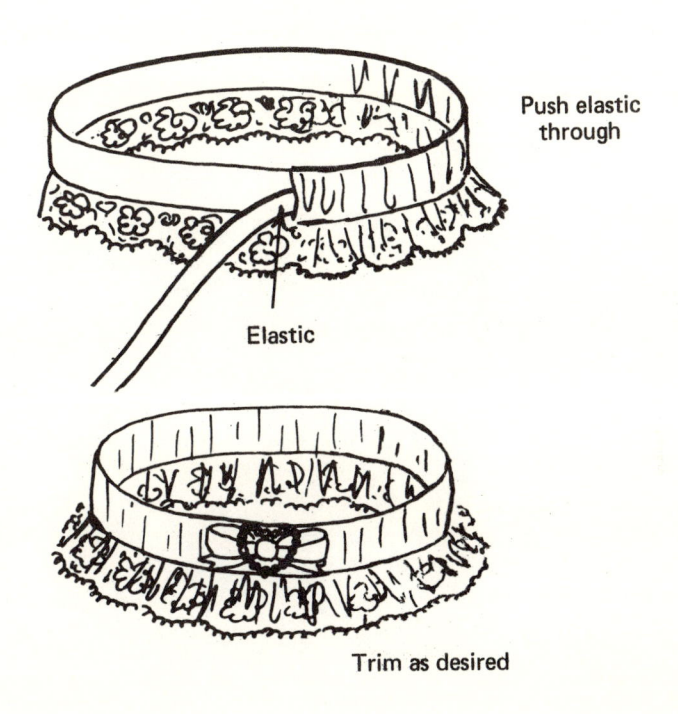

Push elastic through

Elastic

Trim as desired

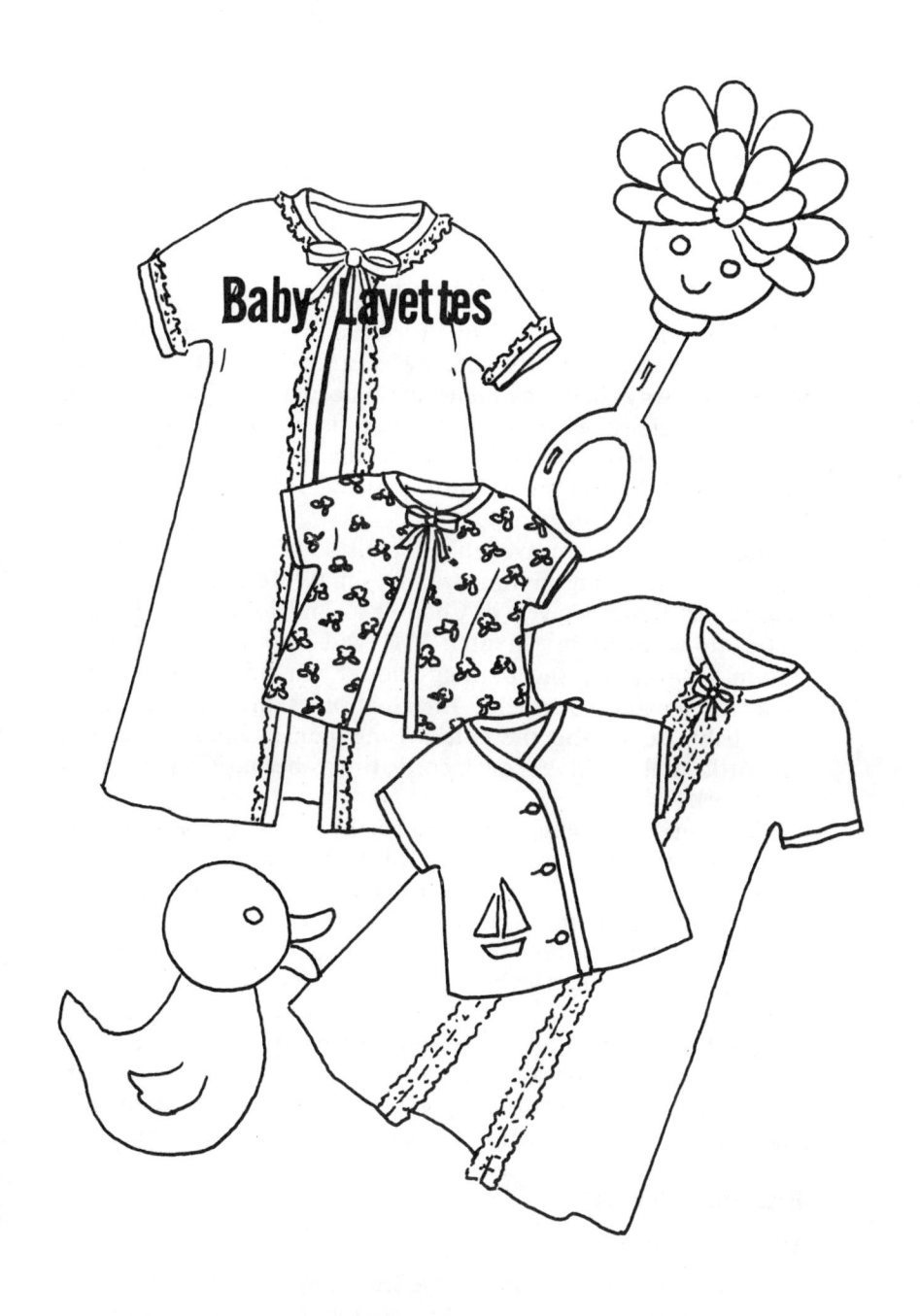

Baby Layettes

CHAPTER VI

BABY LAYETTES

Nylon tricot is especially versatile and useful for baby garments, because of its softness, laundering ease, and stain resistance. Any baby garment may be made from the nylon tricot, especially when you consider its many forms, such as antron, satinnette, quilted, and the many weights of brushed nylon tricot. Nylon should not be used for diapers, however, because it lacks absorbency.

Many patterns are available for all sorts of baby items. In making these using nylon tricot, simply follow the general sewing instructions given in Chapter I. The double-fold binding instructions given in Chapter VIII will also prove useful for bindings, although the binding should not be as wide as one used for an adult garment. Imagination is the key to darling little baby items, and the enterprising woman can make beautiful little baby things in record time, because there is no handwork.

When making baby items, especially those for a baby girl, you immediately think of lots of lace, and lace is certainly necessary. Be very careful to choose a very soft lace, however, and do not place the lace in such a position that it will rub against the baby's tender skin. Many a fussy baby becomes suddenly quiet when the beautiful lacey dress is removed.

In this chapter you will find many ideas for baby apparel that are probably not in a pattern book or printed elsewhere. With the tips and instructions given in previous chapters, plus the items given in this chapter, you will be able to come up with many other baby garments of your own design and ingenuity.

BABY BLANKET

Materials Needed:

1 yard of 54-inch wide brushed nylon in the weight that meets the need of the season (This will make one blanket and one sacque.)

Baby Layettes

4¼ yards of edging lace

Step-by-Step:

1. Cut a 1-yard square of fabric.
2. Zigzag a 6-inch to 8-inch strip of lace across one corner for decoration, if desired. A tiny bow is very pretty attached to the middle of this strip of lace, also.

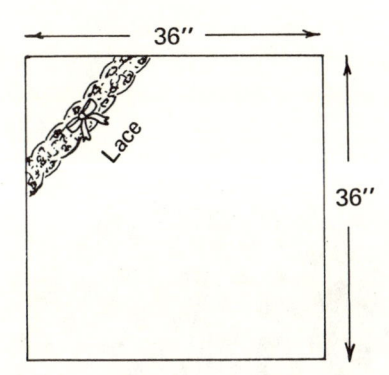

3. Place the rest of the lace on the right side of the fabric edge about the middle of one side. Allow only the scallop to extend over the edge of the fabric. Zigzag around the edge of the fabric near the scallop.
4. Miter the corners by folding the lace into a right angle so that the inner edge is in line with the corner and makes a pretty, squared angle.

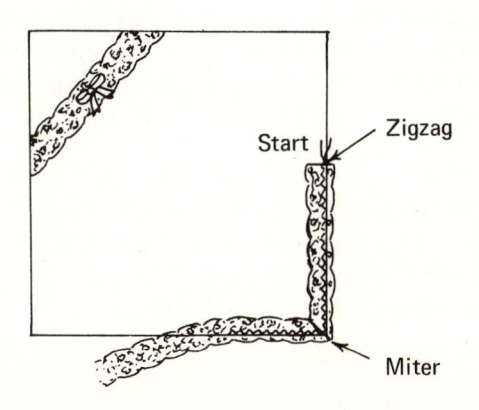

5. Zigzag around the inside or straight edge of the lace so that both sides of the lace will be secured to the tricot.

SACQUE OR GOWN

Materials Needed:
*Use leftover fabric from blanket, or
One-fourth of a yard of tricot, brushed nylon, etc., for sacque
One-half yard of tricot, etc., for gown
Patterns are available in pattern books.
Lace*

Step-by-Step:
1. Place the pattern on the straight of the fabric and cut.
2. Straight stitch the seams, and overcast the seam and the fabric edge with a wide zigzag and short stitch length.
3. Zigzag lace on the sleeves and all other edges in the same manner as the blanket.
4. If lace is not desired, edge the sleeves, etc., with a doublefold binding as described in Chapter VIII, or apply a satin ribbon or a nylon sheer strip binding. These bindings may be purchased at a lingerie fabric store.
5. For closings, loops and buttons (see Robe and Gown Instructions) or gripper snaps are excellent. Ties are pretty but impractical because babies untie them. For decoration, satin bows or appliqués are very pretty sewed over the gripper snaps.

CRIB QUILT

Materials Needed:

1 yard of 54-inch wide quilted nylon tricot fabric
5¼ yards of washable satin binding
Decorations as desired

Step-by-Step:

1. Apply any decorations.
2. Seal the raw edges with a zigzag so that the fiber-fill will remain between the tricot.
3. Place the fabric edge inside the folded satin binding about the middle of one side of the quilt. Lock the stitch by sewing a couple of stitches with the stitch length at "0." Then, using the widest zigzag, stitch along the inside edge of the binding.
4. Fold the binding into a miter at the corners. Then tuck the raw edge under at the finish of the binding, and lock the stitch again. This quilt will cost $2.00 to $2.50 to make, but costs about $8.00 to $10.00 in the stores ready-made.

BUNTING

Materials Needed:

1 yard of heavy brushed nylon fleece
4¼ yards of tricot binding, lace, or sheer binding
12 inches - 14 inches of beading lace, a self-fabric casing, or a satin ribbon casing
1 yard of very narrow ribbon or spaghetti strap string

Step-by-Step:

1. Cut a 1-yard square of the nylon fleece.
2. Fold the fabric into a triangle by placing the opposite corners together.
3. Measure 4 inches down from the corner, and cut straight across from this point to the edge of the fabric. Measure on the straight edge of the triangle, and cut from the straight edge straight across to the diagonal edge.
4. Turn the fabric so that the right sides are together, and straight stitch these cut edges together; then overcast the stitch and the fabric edge with a zigzag.

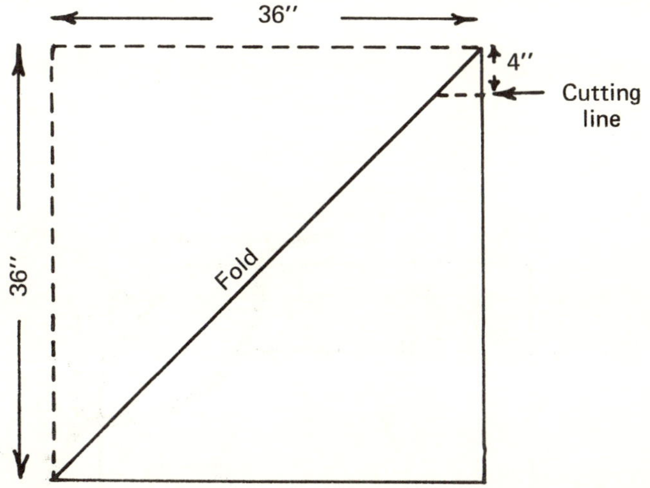
36″
4″
Cutting line
36″
Fold

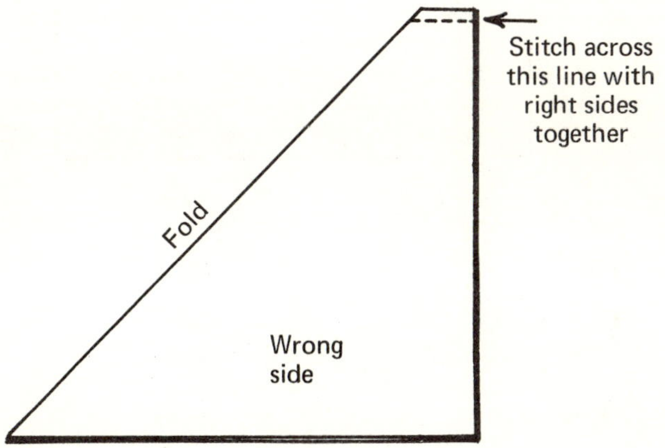
Stitch across this line with right sides together
Fold
Wrong side

5. Measure 9 inches from the seam down on the raw edge. Zigzag the beading lace or other casing from this 9-inch point to the 9-inch point on the other raw edge in a semi-circle.

6. Run a draw string–either a narrow piece of ribbon, a spaghetti-type string as illustrated in Chapter VIII, or other decorative string–through this beading lace or casing.

7. Finish the edge with lace or a binding in the same manner as quilts or blankets discussed previously in this chapter.

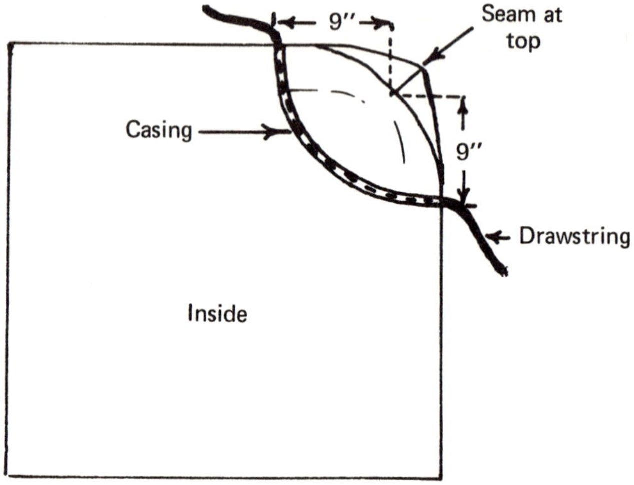
9″
Seam at
top
Casing
9″
Drawstring
Inside

PART II
UNDER GARMENTS

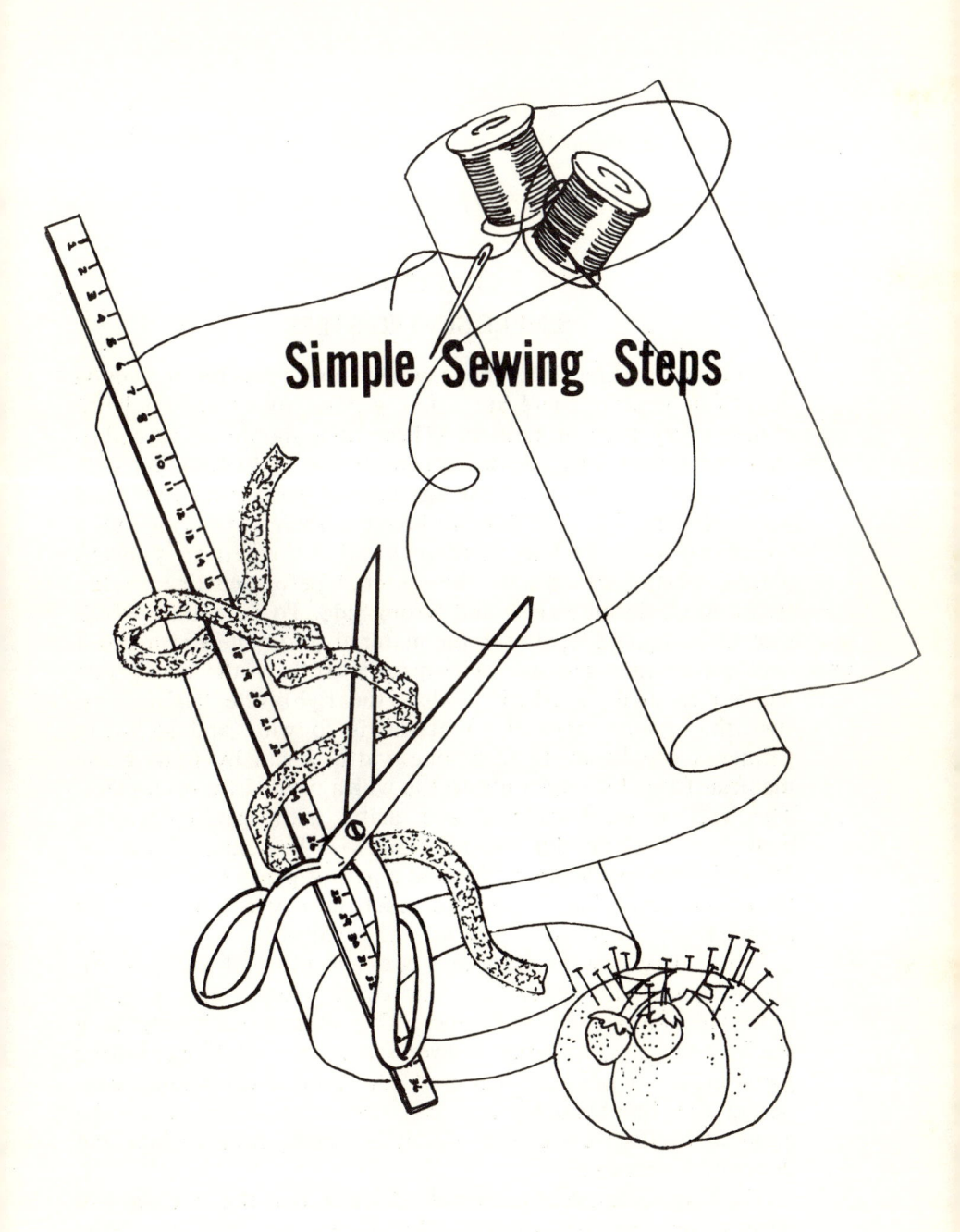

Simple Sewing Steps

CHAPTER I
SIMPLE SEWING STEPS

When embarking into the new skill and pleasure of making beautiful lingerie, there are a few general rules that apply to almost every type of garment. These rules should be learned so that the industrious person can improvise and create her own designs and be able to fashion any type of garment as styles and needs change. The first thing to be remembered in sewing nylon tricot and other stretchy synthetics is that the pattern is always placed on the straight of the material before cutting. Nylon tricot has a definite right and wrong side. To determine which side is the right side, stretch the material across the width and it will roll to the right side. The material rolls to the wrong side when stretched lengthwise. Also, the right side has a finer, smoother grain. Since the material is so wide and so many garments can be made from one width, begin by folding the material from the edge only to the width needed for each piece. This will conserve material and enable many garments to be made from fabric that would otherwise be scraps. Since the fabric is 108" wide, two slips and a pair of panties can be made from one yard. This is why so much money can be saved by sewing lingerie instead of buying ready-mades.

In deciding how to place and cut each piece of the garment, always ignore all center back and center front seams possible, especially on gowns and robes. This eliminates sewing long seams and saves material. Fewer seams mean a longer-lasting garment, a quicker-made garment, and a more economical one. Seams are line-breakers and can destroy the beauty of the garment by distracting from the eye-catching trims of lace and decorative stitching.

The scissors must be extremely sharp so that the material will have a smooth, non-gapped edge when cut. Pinking shears should never be used on tricot because the material never ravels. Nylon dulls scissors rapidly, and sharpening will be needed more often for smooth cutting. To sharpen scissors, hold them in the left hand with the point toward you. With an ordinary, general-use file, rub down the slant of the scissors' blade with long, hard strokes beginning at the point and continuing to the center. Then turn the other point toward you and repeat the process. Be sure to follow the slant of the blade and not file directly down on the sharp edge, as this will dull the scissors.

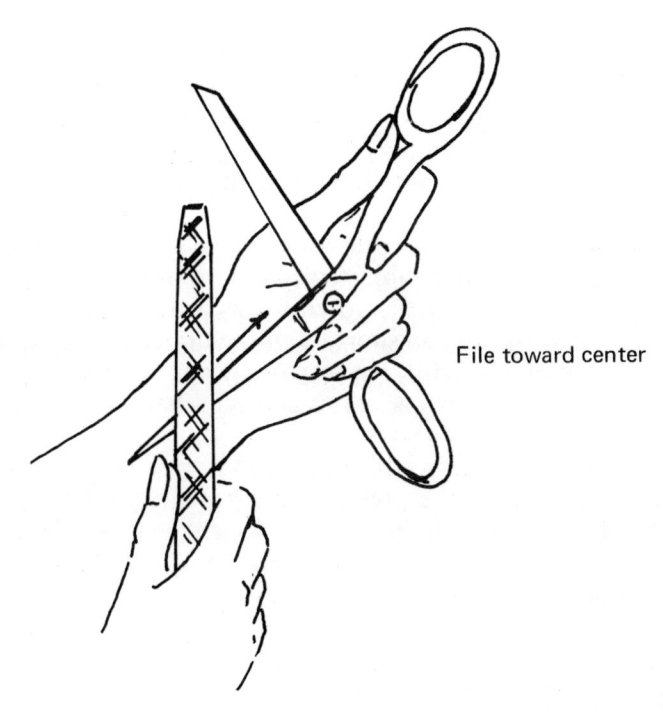

File toward center

The sharpening process is the act of thinning the cutting edge.

In placing the material for cutting, use as few pins as possible. In place of pins, use weights like heavy books, pot lids, or table knives to hold the material in place.

In sewing nylon and other stretchy synthetics, a zigzag sewing machine is imperative. If straight stitching alone is used, the thread will break when the material stretches. The zigzag attachment, which can be purchased for most machines, will do the job, but is not quite as handy to use. A very small needle—a size 9 or 11—must also be used. A larger needle will not pierce the tough fabric and will pull the material down into the bobbin cavity with it. More stores are now stocking small needles because of the new demand caused by the nylon lingerie sewing.

Nylon thread is also a necessity, because nylon material will cut the cotton thread. Also, in a nylon garment made with cotton thread, the material will outlast the thread threefold. The large, tube-type spools of thread are the most economical and work better. Sometimes smaller spools can cause backlashing of the thread, although they may be used. If the small spool is used, it should be placed on the floor in a cup or can and then threaded through the machine in the usual way. The large spool should also be placed on the floor instead of on the spool spindle up on top of the machine. This insures the best stitch possible. In buying thread, the finer thread should be used. The coarse nylon thread will cause stitch-skipping. A number 15 nylon thread weight in the large spool is by far the best thread for nylon sewing.

In preparing the machine for nylon sewing, the regular upper thread tension and bobbin tension as set for regular sewing will usually be correct. If the stitch seems a little too tight and the stitch length is not too short, then the upper and lower tensions can be loosened slightly to match one another and sew smoothly. Refer to the sewing manufacturer's handbook for instructions on adjusting tensions.

If you have a sharp edge or burr that snags the material in the sewing area or on the presser foot, smooth it out by coating it with clear nail polish. Nylon snags easily, and an entire garment may be ruined by an ugly snag from a minute rough spot that would not bother most other materials.

When sewing most seams, especially the long side seams where there is no pressure from tight fit, the 1/8-inch seam using the medium zigzag width and a very fine stitch-length is used. Do not overcast the edge of the seam, but be careful to let the needle stop close to the edge of the material and not beyond it. If the seam is overcast it causes stretching, puckering, and unsmooth seams. When starting seams, be sure to hold the thread in the back of the needle to help prevent clogging of the thread in the bobbin. It will be a pleasant surprise to find the ease with which the seams can be sewed in spite of the slippery material and the fine thread.

All seams are sewed one-eighth of an inch from the edge of the material. Some seams, which need extra strength because of tight fit, are first sewed with a straight, regular-length stitch and then overcast with a zigzag. Places where this seam is used will be brought out in later chapters as applied to specific garments.

Simple Sewing Steps 99

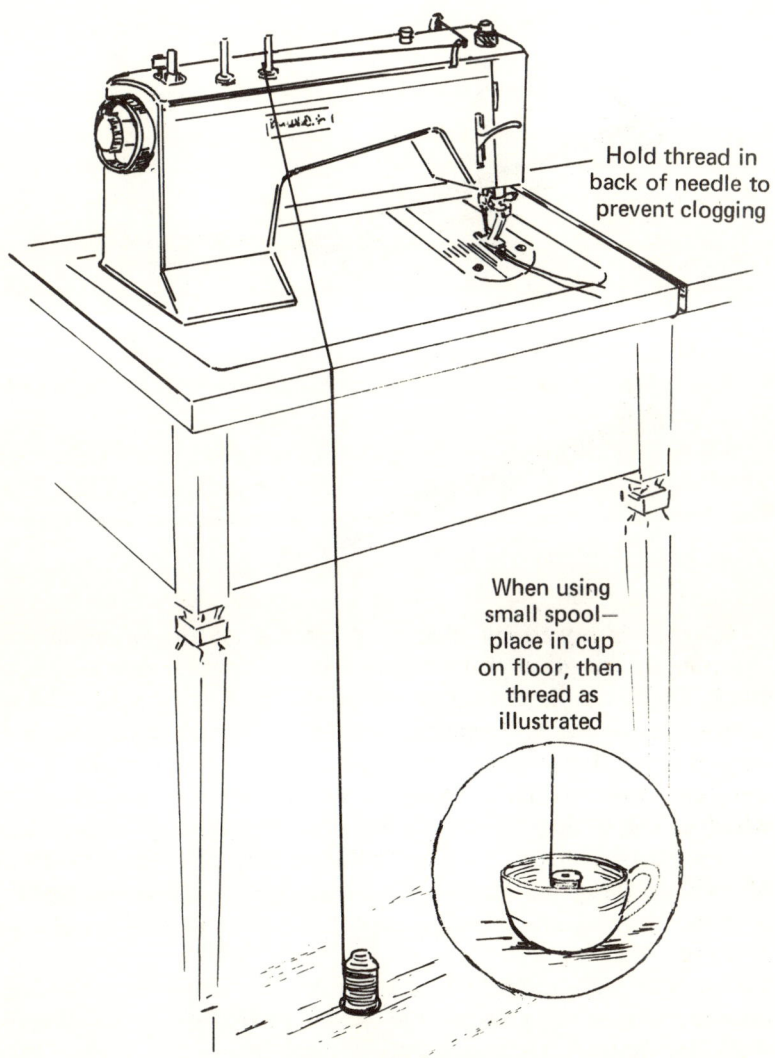

Hold thread in back of needle to prevent clogging

When using small spool—place in cup on floor, then thread as illustrated

Tube spool on floor and threaded through machine
No. 15 nylon thread weight in large spool

Zigzagged seam, trimmed

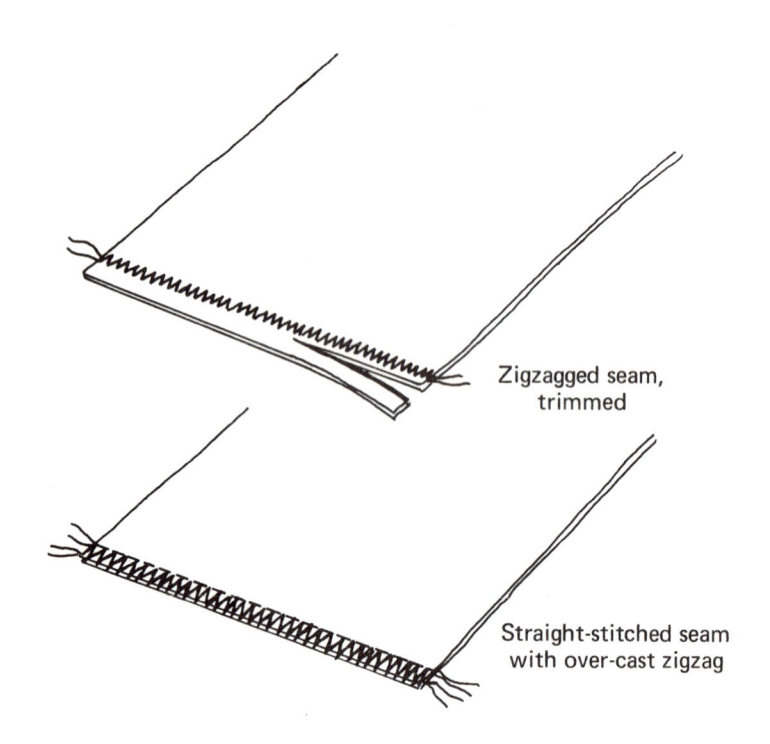

Straight-stitched seam with over-cast zigzag

All lace is sewed by placing it on top of the material and stitching it in place with a small-width zigzag and a regular stitch length. All lace used on nylon should be nylon, also. Most cotton lace requires ironing and must be ironed with a warmer temperature than nylon can withstand. Cotton lace also wears out three times faster than nylon lace or the nylon material on which it is sewed.

The busy woman of today will welcome the ease and speed of nylon sewing. All of the work except sewing on the buttons is done by machine. There is no hand work, no basting, and no pinning. A complete slip can be made in one hour. A very fancy, lacy nightgown can be made in 2½ hours. The practical, conservative woman may find more difficulty in learning to wear the lingerie of a millionaire than in making it. Practical gowns and slips may be made, but the creative woman is usually drawn toward the more beautiful because it lifts the spirits and satisfies the need to create an artistic thing of beauty. The lingerie novice may find her artistic ability lies in the sewing of lavish trouseaus. Anything manufactured by lingerie companies can be made by the novice at home at a fraction of the cost and a small amount of time, with the joy and satisfaction of having created a thing of beauty as a bonus.

Nylon tricot is truly an easy-care fabric. It resists dirt, soil, and stains, and can be laundered in cold or warm water with any mild soap or detergent. Separate light and dark colors to avoid any bleeding of the dyes, even though nylon dyes rarely bleed. If white nylons turn gray or yellow, simply bleach with an all-fabric bleach. A chlorine bleach, however, should never be used. Body stains can be removed with rubbing alcohol. Blood stains should be soaked in cold water, and ball-point pen stains may be removed by applying hairspray. Nylon may be machine dried. For best results, place a damp bath towel in the clothes dryer with the lingerie to absorb the moisture and insure wrinkle-free results. If a clothes dryer is not available, garments may be rolled in a towel to remove excess moisture, then hung to dry. Foundation garments will retain their life longer if allowed to dry naturally away from heat. Hot water should never be used on garments containing elastic, as heat deteriorates it. A hot iron should not be used on nylon garments, either, since excessive heat will dissolve both the fabric and the thread.

Although nylon tricot does not usually shrink when laundered, it is always advisable to pre-shrink the fabric by laundering and drying before making the garment. Gowns with sheer overskirts seem to shrink most, with the sheer overskirt sometimes shrinking several inches shorter than the underskirt.

The entire family can enjoy the garments made by the enterprising mother at home. A great part of being intelligent is the ability to make much out of little. Nylon tricot and its many forms, such as jersey, sheers, velvety brushed jersey, quilted, florals, abstracts, stripes, and solids, are so versatile that garments may be made from them for every member of the family. The husband will enjoy the underwear, T-shirts, sport shirts, dress shirts, pajamas, and robes made of nylon tricot. The family will sleep more comfortably between smooth, soft tricot sheets with lacy tricot pillowcases. The baby enjoys having all of his apparel made from soft, non-allergic nylon in its many forms. Little boys and girls enjoy having their underwear, robes, gowns, pajamas, shirts, blouses, dresses, and little suits made from nylon tricot. This unique material may be used for carefree draperies, bedspreads, tableclothes, and shower curtains. The industrious woman will find herself caught up in a world of lavish, beautiful lingerie. A noted designer once said that whether or not a woman's undergarments are of expensive materials shows on her face and the way she carries herself. Certainly beautiful grooming from the skin out does pay off in self-assurance.

Slips

CHAPTER II

SLIPS

Beautiful nylon slips come in a wide variety of styles—all of which may be made at home with a zigzag sewing machine. A few patterns are now available in the pattern books, and many more will be available in the future as more people become acquainted with nylon lingerie sewing. Slips with darts on the bodice are usually more satisfactory than those with the gathers, since the gathers often show through the dress in bulky, wrinkled lines. Until you are able to purchase the pattern of your choice, however, you may make a pattern from your favorite slip by using aluminum foil. Simply place the garment flat down on the foil, tracing over each seam and dart with the index finger. This running your fingers over the foil along the seams and darts will make a clear outline of each piece of the garment from which to cut a pattern. Next, cut the foil pieces along the seam indentations. Then place these foil pieces on paper to be used for a pattern and cut around each piece one-fourth of an inch from the edge of the foil. This will allow for seam allowances and any necessary trimming. In making the pattern for the bodice, simply flare the lower, underarm seam to the side 1½ to 2 inches to allow for any darts or gathers.

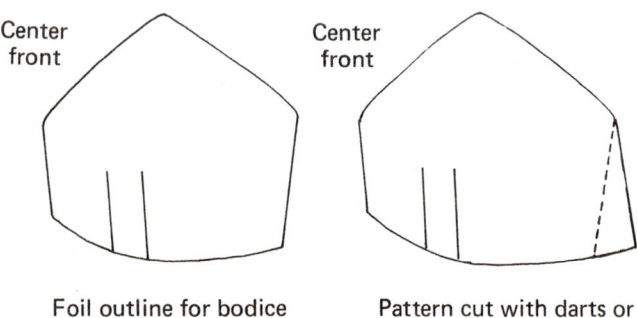

Foil outline for bodice

Pattern cut with darts or gathers allowances

Slips

The bodice of the slip may be made in a variety of decorative styles. A very beautiful and practical slip bodice is one made with a single layer of tricot and a layer of over-all lace. If a less fancy slip is desired, use a single layer of tricot edged with lace. A tailored slip bodice may be made with a double layer of tricot.

INSTRUCTIONS FOR SLIP WITH OVER-ALL LACE BODICE

Materials Needed:

> 1 yard of 108-inch wide nylon tricot (This will make two slips up to size 38 plus one pair of panties, but a yard must be purchased to get the length.)
> 1½ yards of nylon lace for edging the slip top (This is sufficient for all sizes up to size 36. Increase the amount two inches per size above size 36.)
> 1½ yards of nylon lace to edge slip bottom (Increase two inches per size for sizes above size 36.)
> 1/3 yard of over-all lace for slip top
> Two slip straps

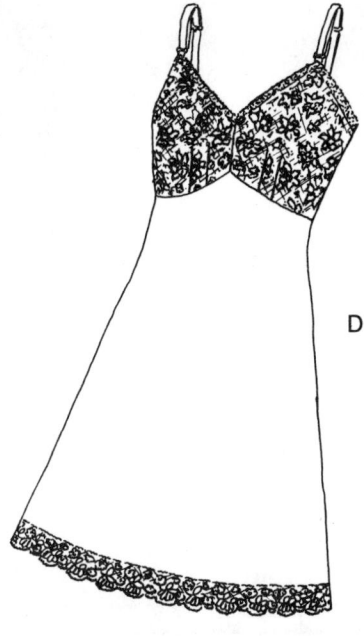

Drawing of over-all lace bodice slip

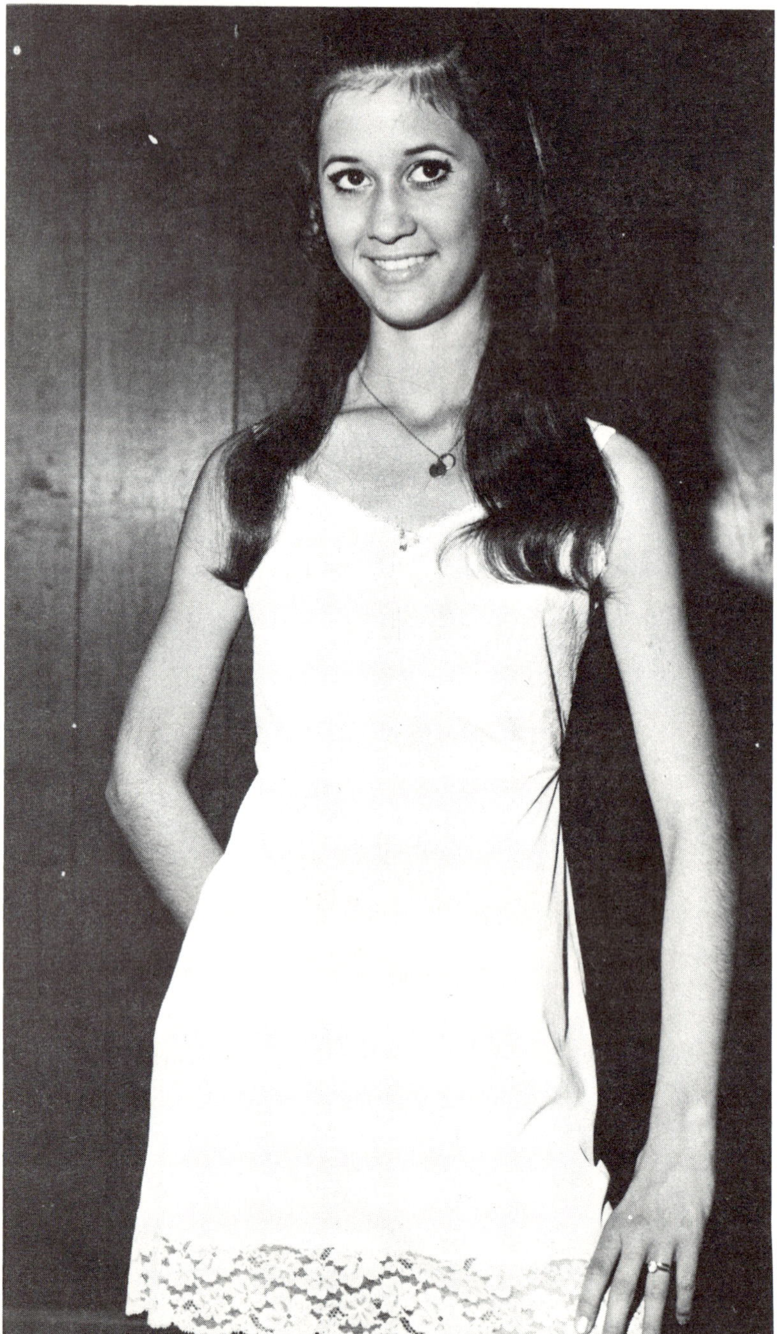

Step-by-Step:

1. Place the pattern pieces on the straight of the tricot material and cut around each piece with sharp scissors.
2. Using the slip top pattern, cut the over-all lace bodice.
3. Mark the dart points with pins, and mark the large ends of the darts with a pencil dot or very small cuts.
4. Lay the over-all lace over the tricot, and treat the lace and tricot material as one piece of fabric. Starting at the points, sew the darts. Setting the stitch length at "0", sew a couple of stitches to secure the thread. Then, with a regular stitch length and straight stitch, sew to the edge of the dart. Lock the stitch at the bottom end by turning the stitch length to "0" and sewing a couple of stitches. This prevents tying thread ends. All seams should be locked at the ends by this method so that they will not ravel loose.

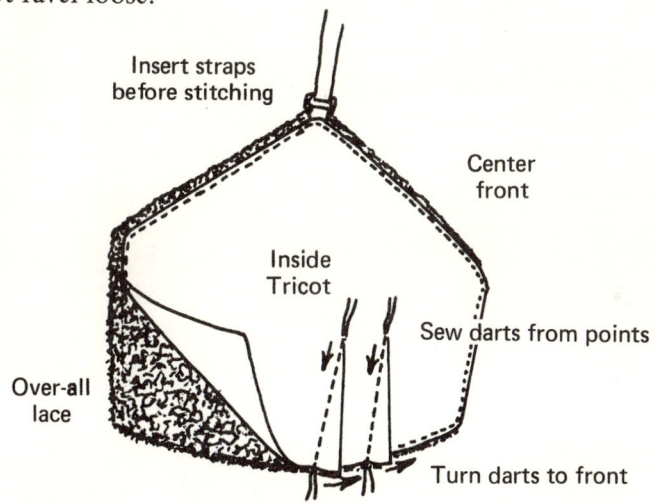

5. Turn the darts toward the center front and stay stitch all around each section of the slip top with a straight stitch to hold the lace and tricot in place. Insert the slip straps in position between the over-all lace and the tricot, and stay stitch them in as you sew.
6. Sew the center front seam by stitching the two pieces together with a 1/8-inch seam and a straight, regular length stitch. Then overcast the seam with a wide zigzag and a short distance between stitches.
7. Using the same method as the center front seam, sew one bodice side seam.

8. Edge the top of the slip with narrow lace by sewing the lace on with a narrow zigzag and a regular stitch length. The lace must be mitered in the front at the straps and the center front. To miter lace, begin sewing along the inner edge of the lace. Stop sewing a short distance from the corner to be mitered. At the corner, fold the lace back over itself. Hold the lower edge of the fold with the index finger. Realign the lace with the vertical edge of the fabric. When the inner edges of the lace meet perfectly, the mitered corner is correct. Then continue sewing along the inner edge of the lace. At the mitered corner, zigzag along the fold to the top of the lace to secure it in the mitered position. Then continue sewing along the inner edge of the lace.

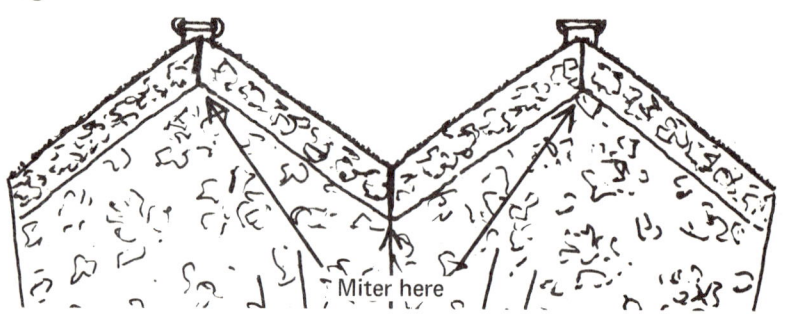

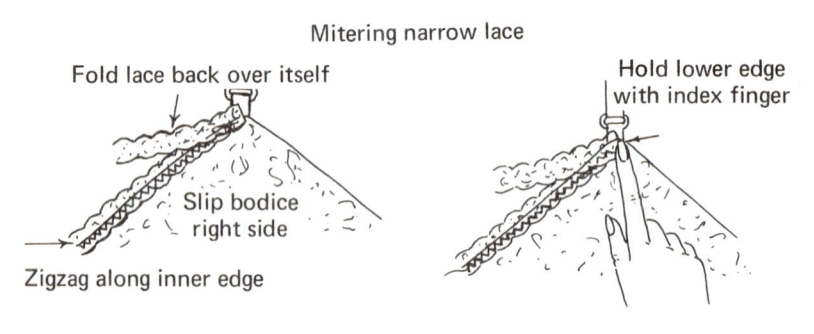

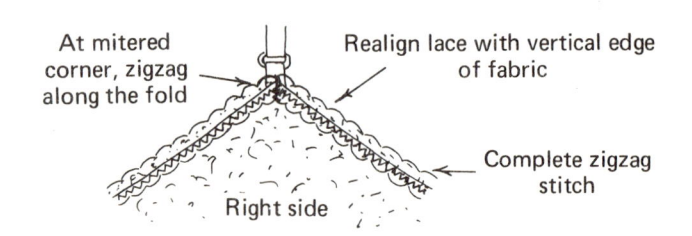

Miter here

Mitering narrow lace

Fold lace back over itself

Slip bodice right side

Zigzag along inner edge

Hold lower edge with index finger

At mitered corner, zigzag along the fold

Realign lace with vertical edge of fabric

Complete zigzag stitch

Right side

Slips

Mitering wide lace

Fold lace back over itself

Slip bodice right side

Hold lower edge with index finger

Zigzag along outer edge

At mitered corner, zigzag along the fold

Zigzag stitch along inner edge

Realign lace with edge of fabric complete zigzag stitch

Right side

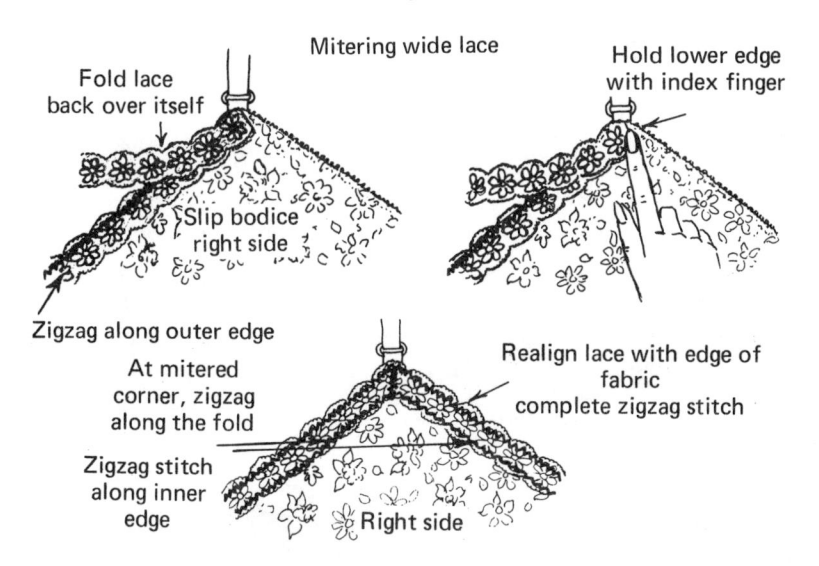

9. Sew the second side seam of the bodice with a 1/8-inch seam by straight stitching, then overcasting the seam with a wide zigzag and a short stitch length.

10. Sew one side seam of the slip skirt by using a medium width zigzag and a short stitch length. Be careful not to overcast this seam, or it may pucker. The seam may need to be trimmed slightly if the rough, cut edge is unsightly or too wide. The seam should be trimmed as close to the stitches as possible.

11. The slip length should be adjusted before sewing on the lace at the hem.

12. Zigzag the lace on the bottom of the slip either by attaching it to the bottom edge of the tricot or placing the lace as an overlay. The lace should be laid on top of the right side of the tricot and zigzagged. If the lace is used as an overlay, it should be zigzagged at the top edge of the lace and again along the bottom edge of the tricot with the lace extending slightly below the tricot.

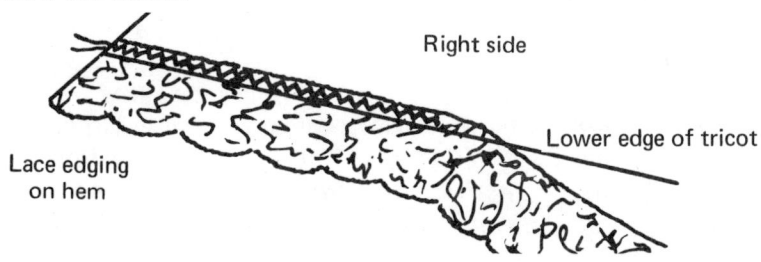

Right side

Lower edge of tricot

Lace edging on hem

Lace overlay hem

Right side

Lower edge of tricot

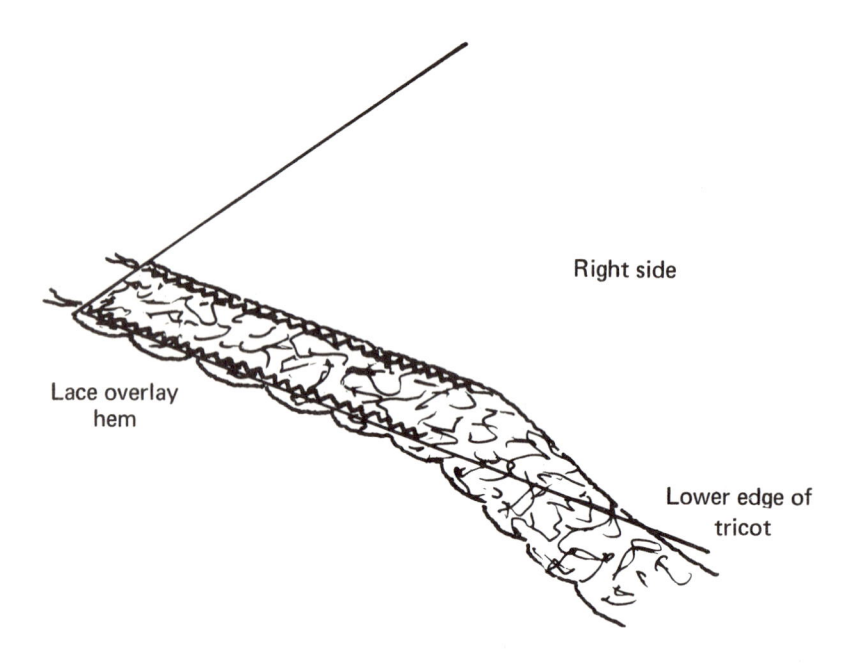

13. Sew the second side seam of the skirt in the same manner as the first side seam.

14. Starting at the point of the skirt in the center front, join the skirt and the top by using the straight stitch and then overcasting the seam with a wide zigzag and a short stitch length. When joining lace over-lay top and tricot skirt; let the skirt material be relaxed and the lace overlay top be stretched or held firm to make the side seams and center front match.

15. Press the slip with a steam iron at a low temperature. If there are any puckered seams, they should press out.

INSTRUCTIONS FOR HALF SLIP

Materials Needed:

Nylon tricot sufficient for the desired length (approximately ½ yard)

1½ yards of lace for edging the hem if lace is desired

¾-inch elastic for the waist. Measure the waistline and subtract 2 inches to calculate the necessary amount.

Pattern, which can be obtained from any pattern book

Small piece of ½-inch wide satin ribbon (about 1½ inches long)

Slips

Half Slip Illustration

Half Slip
Illustration
with appliqué

Step-by-Step:

1. Zigzag any appliqués before sewing any seams. Appliqués may be purchased at many stores, but you may cut your own from suitable lace. In making your own appliqué, cut around the flowers or designs in the lace. Be sure to clip the lace design just outside the heavy or raised thread (cordonnet) outlining the design of the flower. Stitch around each appliqué edge with a zigzag.
2. Sew the side seam along the seam allowance with a medium zigzag and a regular stitch length. Be sure to lock the thread at each end of the seam by doing a couple of stitches with the stitch length at "0".
3. Zigzag the lace around the hem as in Step 12 of the over-all lace bodice slip instructions.
4. Sew the second side seam by the same method as the first one in Step 2.
5. Join the ends of the elastic by machine or otherwise. Quarter the elastic and mark each quarter by using pins. These pins will mark where the elastic should meet the center front and back and the side seams.

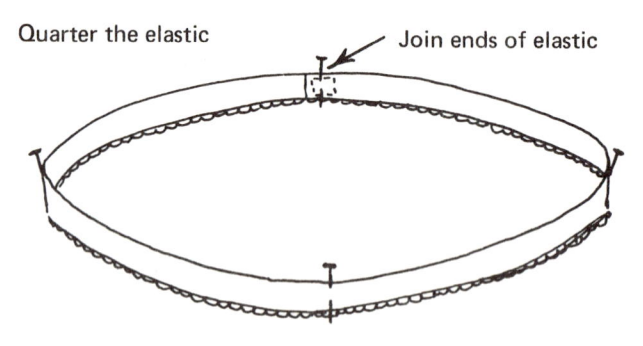

Quarter the elastic   Join ends of elastic

6. Notch the slip slightly at center back and center front. Use the side seams as the other quarter marks.
7. With the slip right side out, lay the joint of the elastic on the wrong side of the fabric at the center back notch with the top scalloped edge or picot edge of the elastic facing down on the wrong side of the fabric. Place a small piece of satin ribbon between the elastic joint and the tricot. Keep the elastic positioned so that the raw tricot edge does not extend above it. Zigzag close to the picot edge with a regular length stitch and a small width zigzag. Use the pin quarter marks on the elastic to

match the elastic to the side seams and the center front notch. Keep the fabric well under the elastic in order to have a good seam. Do not let the needle extend beyond the edge of the elastic onto the fabric.

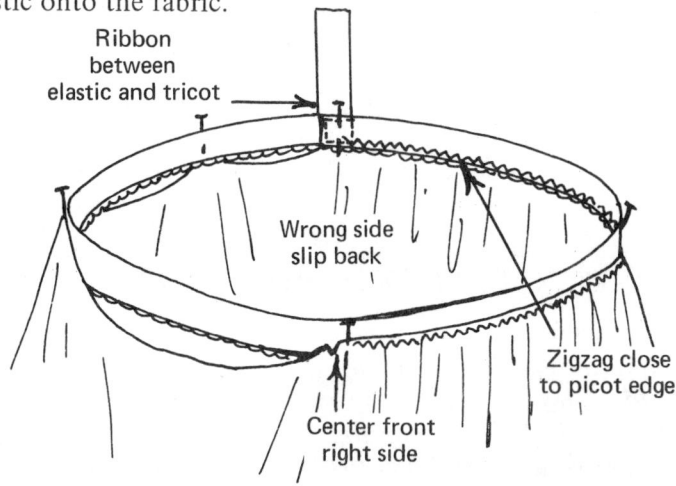

Ribbon between elastic and tricot

Wrong side slip back

Zigzag close to picot edge

Center front right side

8. Turn the garment wrong side out and turn the elastic to the right side. Cut the joint cover ribbon to the necessary length and tuck the bottom edge under. Using the widest zigzag, stitch around the bottom edge of the elastic; let the needle go into the elastic, then over the elastic edge into the tricot. Be sure that the needle is overcasting the elastic onto the tricot. This will prevent the elastic from stretching out of shape. Try to keep the needle from cutting the large elastic threads that run through the elastic, as this weakens it.

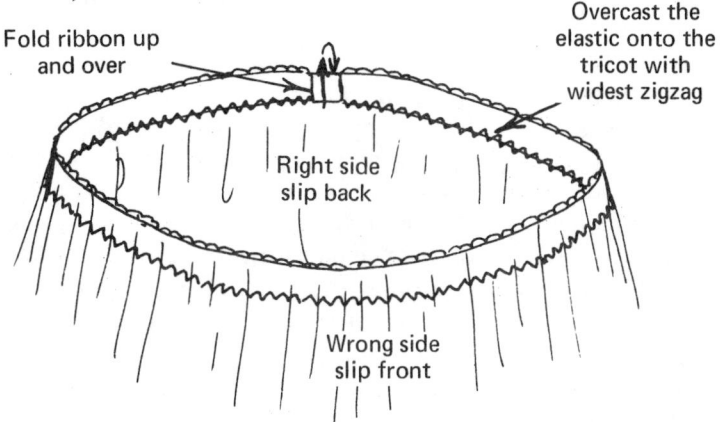

Fold ribbon up and over

Overcast the elastic onto the tricot with widest zigzag

Right side slip back

Wrong side slip front

9. Straight stitch around all four sides of the ribbon as it is tucked over the elastic joint. Be sure to lock these threads well by stitching a couple of stitches with the stitch length set at "0."

Turn ribbon under and straight stitch

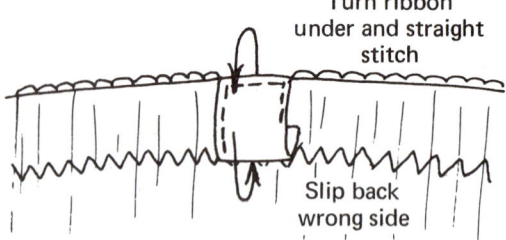

Slip back wrong side

INSTRUCTIONS FOR LADIES CHEMISE SLIP

Materials Needed:

¾ yard of nylon tricot or enough to get the desired length
Two slip straps
1 3/8 yards of lace for slip top
1½ yards of lace for slip bottom

Step-by-Step:

1. Place pattern pieces on the straight of the tricot material and cut around each piece using sharp scissors.

2. Mark any darts in your favorite method as you would any other fabric.

3. Stitch the darts by locking the thread by sewing two stitches with the stitch length at "0"; then adjust the stitch length for regular stitching. Straight stitch to the end of the dart and again lock the thread by setting the stitch length at "0" for a couple of stitches. This prevents tying threads, and all seams should be secured by this method. If wider lace than 2½ inches is to be used around the slip top, zigzag the lace on the front as in Step 6 before stitching the darts.

4. Zigzag one side seam by using a medium width zigzag and a short stitch length going down the seam line. Be sure to lock the stitches at the top and bottom of the seam. Do not let the needle go beyond the material edge or it will cause puckering. Then trim the seam allowance close to the zigzag stitch.

5. Zigzag the lace around the slip bottom either by placing it on top of the fabric as an overlay or on the edge as a lace edging.

The lace overlay hem requires zigzagging at the top edge of the lace and again at the edge of the tricot.

6. Zigzag the lace around the top as in the lace overlay hem. Place the slip straps in position between the tricot and the lace at the top edge of the tricot as you zigzag. Matching colors of satin ribbon may be used if slip straps are not available in the desired color.

This method of finishing the top by overlaying the lace is far easier and more serviceable than merely edging the top with lace, especially since the pattern would have to be adjusted to make room for the lace edging by cutting off the top edge.

7. Sew the second side seam by using the method explained in Step 4.

8. Press the slip with a steam iron set at a warm temperature.

Ladies Chemise Slip

Child's Chemise Slip

INSTRUCTIONS FOR CHILD'S CHEMISE SLIP

A pattern for the child's chemise may be made by measuring the child's body at the underarm chest section. Take a large piece of paper and fold it in half lengthwise. Measure the paper from the fold crosswise to one-fourth the child's body measurement. Angling down slightly (about 1 inch) from the center to the underarm seam mark, cut from the fold to the one-fourth body measurement mark (the underarm seam). Then measure the desired length of the chemise, and cut down the side from the top to the bottom. Angle in slightly at the waistline and then flare out to the hemline. A pattern back may be made by using the same piece of paper, except the back should be straight across.

Slips

Pattern front (Fold)

Pattern back (Fold)

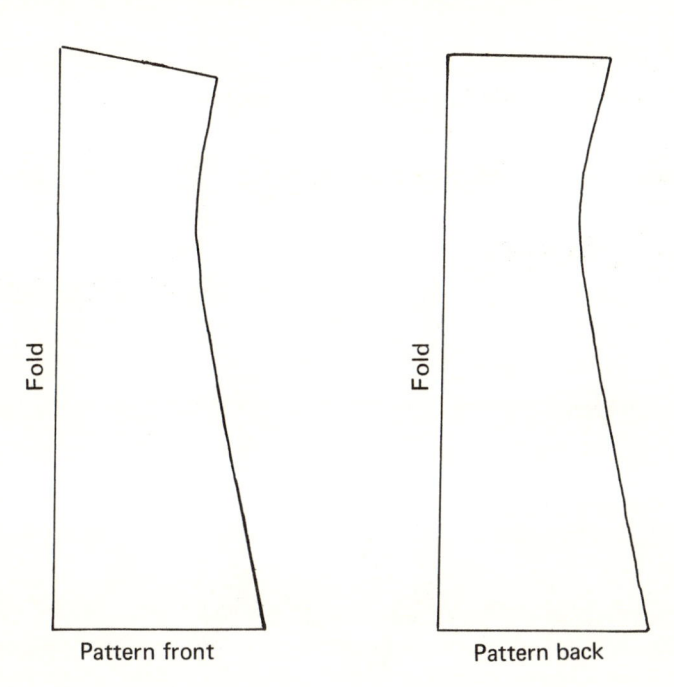

To make a chemise slip, purchase enough material to get the slip length. The amount of lace needed can be determined by measuring the top and bottom edges of the chemise pattern and adding enough to make the shoulder straps.

Shoulder straps should be made from the same lace used at the top and bottom of the slip. Simply center under the lace a piece of narrow satin ribbon the same length as the lace, which has been cut the correct length needed for shoulder straps. Zigzag along both sides of the ribbon edges the entire length of the straps. Be sure that the ribbon is centered under the lace pieces. The satin ribbon under the lace makes a more rigid and more comfortable strap than one made of lace alone. Set the straps a little closer to center front on the child's chemise.

Zigzag ribbon on under side of lace for shoulder strap

Finish the chemise by using the same methods used in making the ladies' chemise.

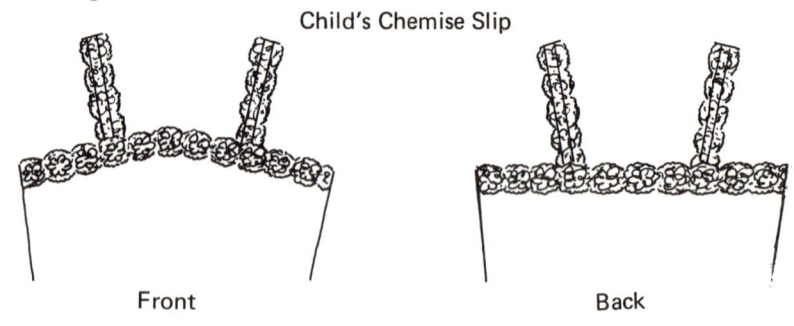

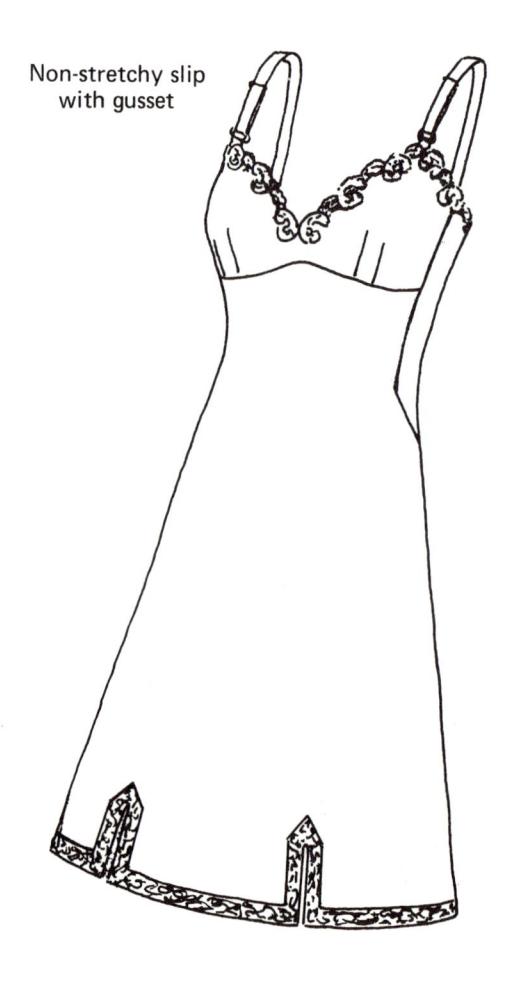

Child's Chemise Slip

Front

Back

Non-stretchy slip with gusset

NON-STRETCHY SLIP

Slips made of non-stretchy fabrics, such as stabilized nylon or taffeta, plain cotton or dacron, are very desirable for wear under knit garments and garments with a great amount of static electricity. Nylon tricot is not a very thick material, nor does it have a great deal of body; therefore, thicker, heavier, more rigid materials without any static electricity may be more serviceable under sheers and knits. Slips made of these non-stretchy fabrics must either have a zipper or a gusset made of stretchy tricot. The gusset seems to be the more desirable, since it is just as simple to insert as a zipper and makes dressing so much easier. The zipper may also cause discomfort or show through the dress. The slip with the gusset may be made in any style—whole slip or half slip—and will be an extremely comfortable garment.

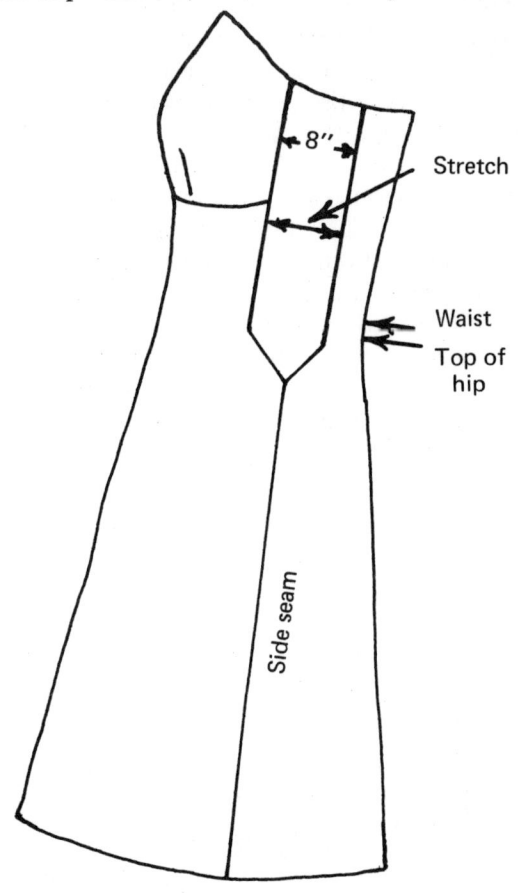

In making a whole slip with a gusset, use your slip pattern, which may be purchased from any fabric store. Using ½-inch seams, sew the slip in the same manner as a dress. Complete the entire slip except finishing the top with the lace and straps. For gussets, cut two pieces of nylon tricot 8 inches wide and long enough to reach from the top of the slip under the arm down to an inch below the top of the hip. The bottom edge may be pointed. These pieces should be cut on the straight of the material so that the stretchy part of the tricot will be crosswise of the gussets. Center a gusset over each side seam at the top edge of the slip. Cut out the non-stretchy fabric behind each gusset, but leave a ½-inch seam allowance to be sewed to the tricot. Sew in the gusset by using a medium zigzag and a short stitch length. This seam may be trimmed if desired. The gusset should be applied in the same manner on both sides.

After completing the gusset, apply the lace at the top and bottom of the slip in the same manner as any other slip. Refer to the overall lace bodice slip instructions given previously.

In making a half-slip of a non-stretchy material, complete the half slip except for the elastic and the hem. Cut two triangular pieces of nylon tricot on the straight of the fabric so that the stretch of the tricot will be across the base of the triangles. The triangles should be 8 inches across the base and 8 inches from the base to the apex or point. Apply these triangular pieces centered over the side seams of the half slip in the same manner as the gussets were sewed in the full slip. After sewing in the gussets, finish the bottom edge of the slip in any desired method. Refer to previous instructions in this chapter.

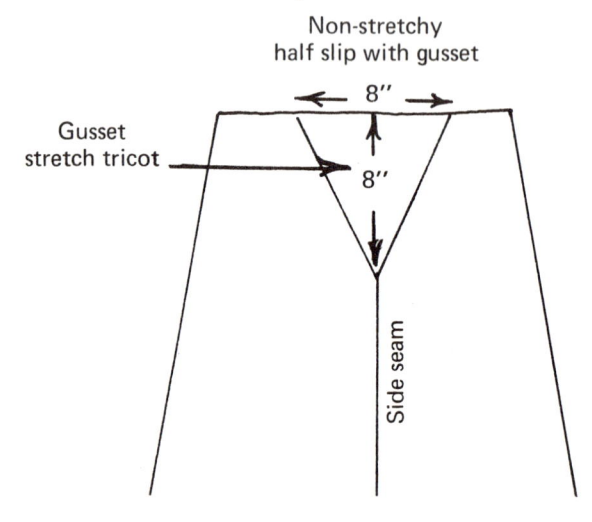

Non-stretchy half slip with gusset

Gusset stretch tricot

8"

8"

Side seam

Slips

In applying the elastic to the top of the half-slip made of non-stretchy material, use a piece of elastic 2 inches less than the waistline measurement. The elastic should be placed on the right side of the slip; allow the material to come almost to the top of the elastic. Then, stretching the elastic only at the gusset area, zigzag around the top edge of the fabric. Next, zigzag around the bottom edge of the elastic; use a wide zigzag and a regular stitch length. Let the needle go off the elastic onto the fabric; then swing back into the elastic. Try to keep the needle from cutting through the large elastic threads by overcasting the large threads and hitting only the small woven fabric in the elastic. This will make stronger, more durable elastic.

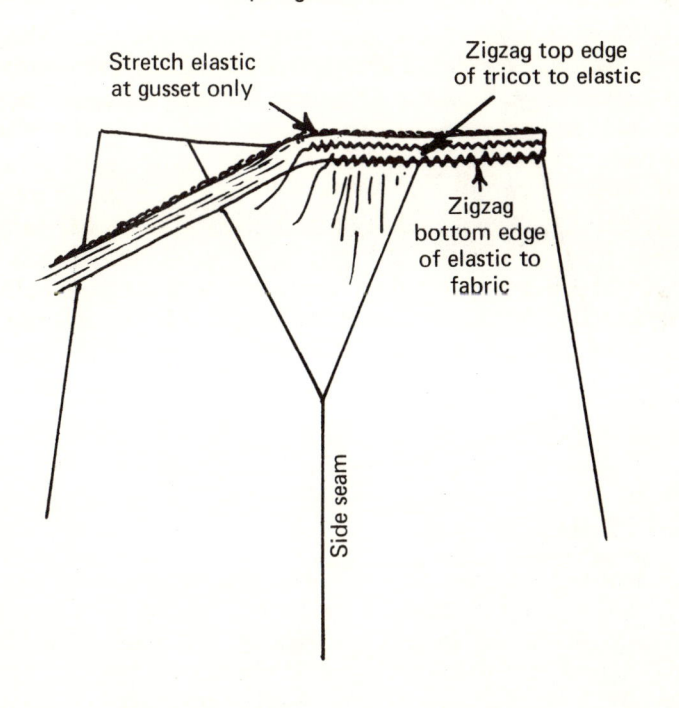

TAILORED SLIP

A tailored slip may be made by using the regular slip pattern, except the bodice should be a double thickness of tricot. Sew the side seams of each layer (lining and top) of the bodice separately in the manner discussed previously. (Refer to Steps 1 through 7 of the overall lace bodice slip instructions). Then place the right sides of the bodice together (lining and top) and straight stitch around the top edge. The straps may be inserted between the two layers as the top is sewed. Then turn the bodice right side out. The lining works as a facing to the top edge. A decorative stitch may be used around the top edge about one-half inch from the edge if desired. Treat the two layers of fabric as one, and sew the bodice darts through both layers at the same time. This helps to stabilize the two pieces and also makes less bulk.

Finish the slip skirt in the same manner as other slips, except that the hem should be turned up like a dress or any other garment. A 1-inch hem is sufficient, and a decorative stitch may be used to secure the hem or two rows of straight stitching about an eighth of an inch apart.

Panties

CHAPTER III
PANTIES

In making panties of all designs and varieties, the same general rules for nylon sewing apply. The size 9 or 11 needle, nylon thread, and a zigzag sewing machine are necessary as in the sewing of other tricot garments. Any style panty may easily be made by the beginner. Patterns are available in some pattern books, or may be made by using a pair of ready-made panties in your size. Refer to the instructions for making patterns with aluminum foil discussed at the beginning of the Slip Chapter (II).

INSTRUCTIONS FOR LADIES BRIEFS
Materials Needed:

½ yard nylon tricot for sizes 4 through 9. Three pairs of sizes 4 or 5 may be made from this amount of material because of the fabric width.

½-inch wide waist elastic 2 inches shorter than waist measurement

1 yard of ¼-inch wide leg elastic for sizes up to 6. Increase the amount by 2 inches per size above size 6.

1½ inches of ½-inch wide satin ribbon

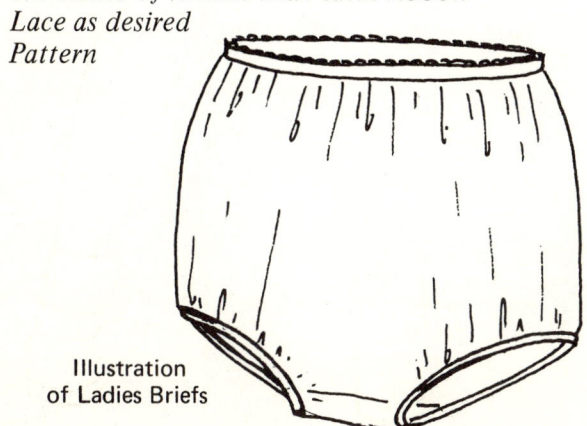

Lace as desired

Pattern

Illustration of Ladies Briefs

To determine the correct panty size, refer to the following table:

BODY MEASUREMENTS

SIZE	4	5	6	7	8	9
HIP	34-37	37-39	39-41	41-44	44-47	47-50

Panties

Step-by-Step:

1. Lay the pattern pieces on the straight of the fabric so that the stretchiest part of the material will be going around the body. This is very important for proper fit and wearing ease.

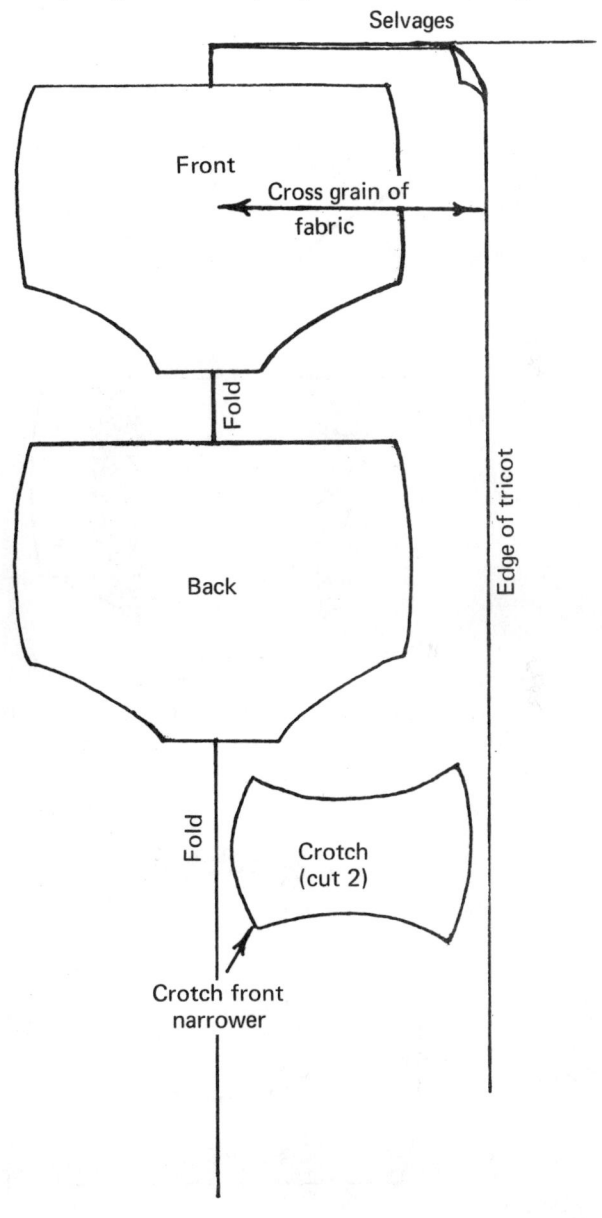

2. Using a small zigzag stitch, trim the panty with lace or appliqués as desired. Refer to the instructions for making a half-slip to obtain more details on appliquéing.

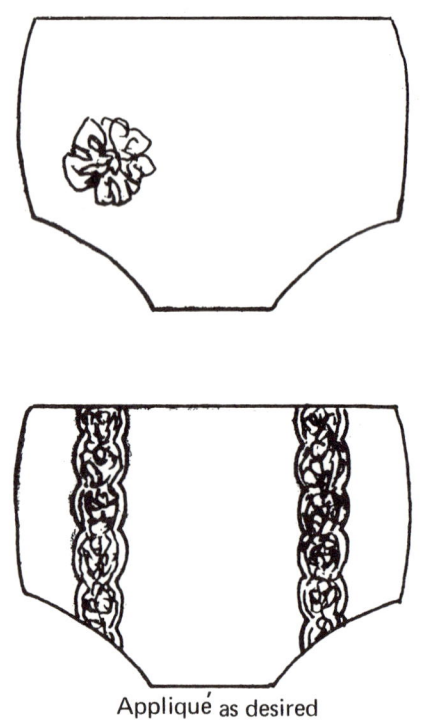

Appliqué as desired

3. Place the panty front between the two crotch pieces with the right sides of the crotch against the panty front. The crotch front will be narrower than the crotch back.

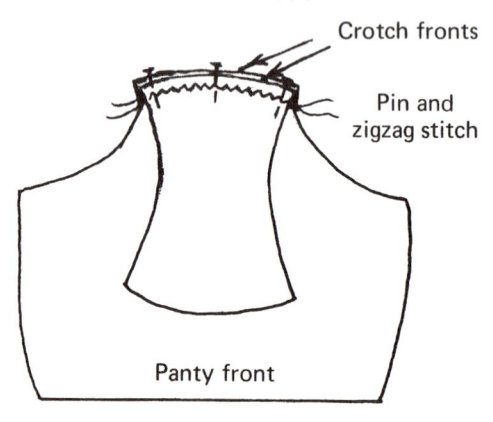

Crotch fronts

Pin and zigzag stitch

Panty front

Panties 129

4. Sew the panty front and the two crotch pieces as positioned in Step 3. Using a 1/8-inch seam and a medium zigzag width with a short stitch length, keep the needle on the fabric at all times. Do not overcast the seam.

5. Lay the panty back and front right sides together. Bring the inside crotch piece (crotch lining) across and pin the right side of this crotch piece to the wrong side of the panty back. Next, bring the outside crotch piece down around the entire panty and pin the right side of the crotch to the right side of the panty back. Stitch the three pieces (panty back and the two crotches wrong side out) together with a medium zigzag. It is not necessary to trim these seams.

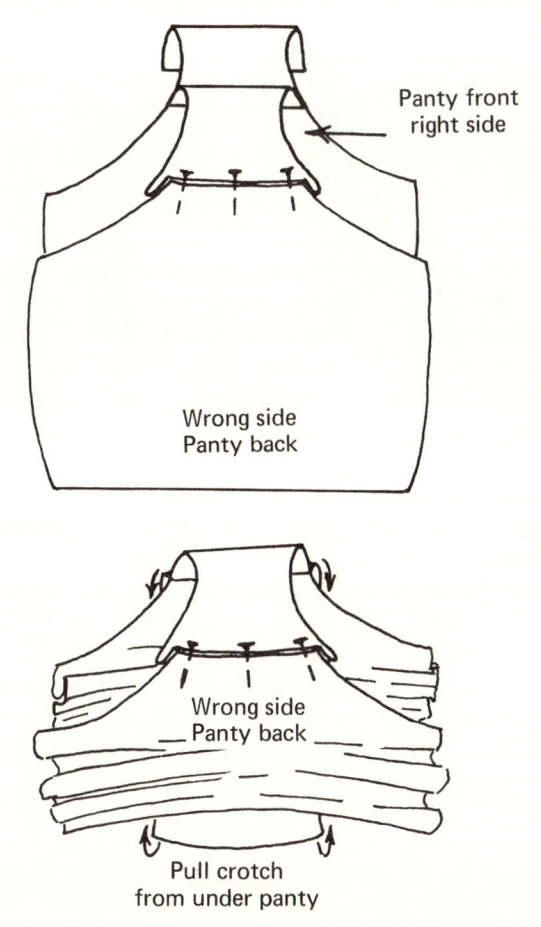

Pin to back crotch—zigzag seam

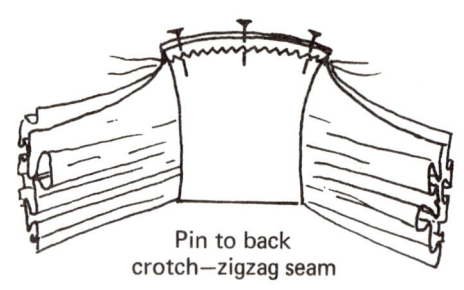

Pull panty out from between crotches

6. Pull out the panty back and front from between the two crotches. All seams should now be hidden between the two crotches.

7. Sew the side seams with the panty back and front right sides together. Use a medium zigzag and a short stitch length. Do not overcast this seam. Trim the seam close to the zigzag.

8. Join the ends of the elastic by machine using any method. Quarter the elastic by marking each quarter with a pin. These pins will mark where the elastic should meet the center front and back and the sides.

9. Notch the panty slightly at center back and center front. Use the side seams as the other quarter marks.

10. With panty right side out, lay joint of elastic on the wrong side of the fabric at the center back notch with the top scalloped edge or picot edge facing down on the wrong side of the fabric. Place a small piece of satin ribbon between the elastic joint and the tricot. Zigzag close to the picot edge with a regular length stitch and a small zigzag width. Use the pin quarter marks on the elastic to match the elastic to the side seams and the center front notch. Keep the fabric well under the elastic in order to have a good seam. Do not let the needle extend beyond the edge of the elastic onto the fabric.

11. Turn the garment wrong side out and turn the elastic to the right side. Cut the joint cover ribbon to the necessary length to tuck the bottom edge under. Using the widest zigzag, stitch around the bottom edge of the elastic; let the needle go into the elastic, then over the elastic edge into the tricot. Be sure that the needle is overcasting the elastic onto the tricot. This will prevent the elastic from stretching out of shape. Try to keep the needle from cutting the large elastic threads that run through the elastic, as this weakens it.

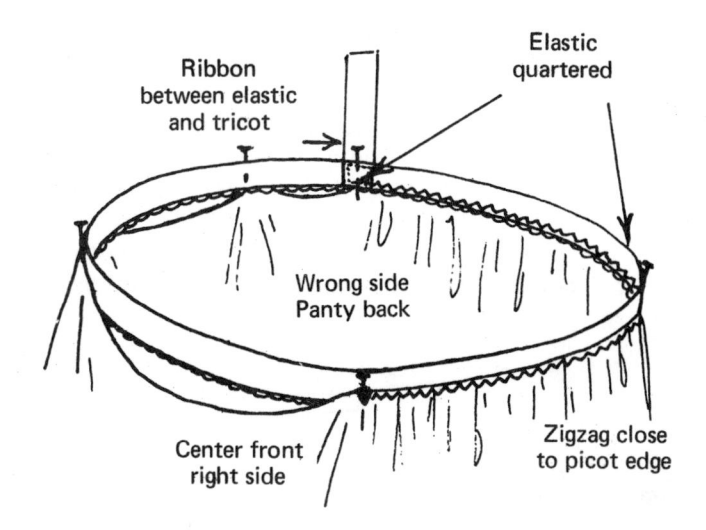

Panties

Ribbon between elastic and tricot

Elastic quartered

Wrong side Panty back

Center front right side

Zigzag close to picot edge

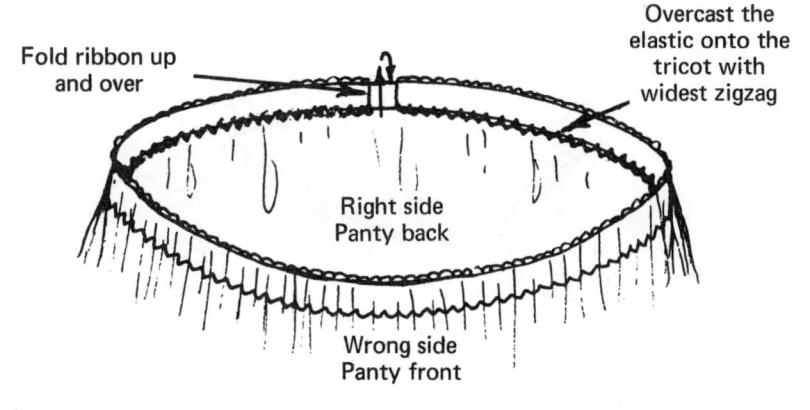

Fold ribbon up and over

Overcast the elastic onto the tricot with widest zigzag

Right side Panty back

Wrong side Panty front

12. Straight stitch around all four sides of the ribbon as it is tucked over the elastic joint. Be sure to lock these threads well by stitching a couple of stitches with the stitch length at "0" both at the beginning of the straight stitching and when finishing.

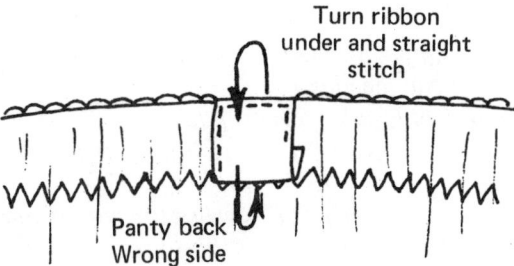

Turn ribbon under and straight stitch

Panty back Wrong side

13. Cut necessary length of leg elastic (usually 18 inches for sizes 5 and 6). Overlapping the elastic a half inch, join the ends by either straight stitch or zigzag.

14. Place the joint of elastic at side seam on the right side of the tricot. Use the widest zigzag and a regular stitch length to sew the elastic to the right side of the fabric. Be sure the picot or scalloped edge extends beyond the panty leg material. Let the needle go into the elastic, then swing back into the fabric beyond the elastic. Continue zigzagging in this fashion around the panty leg.

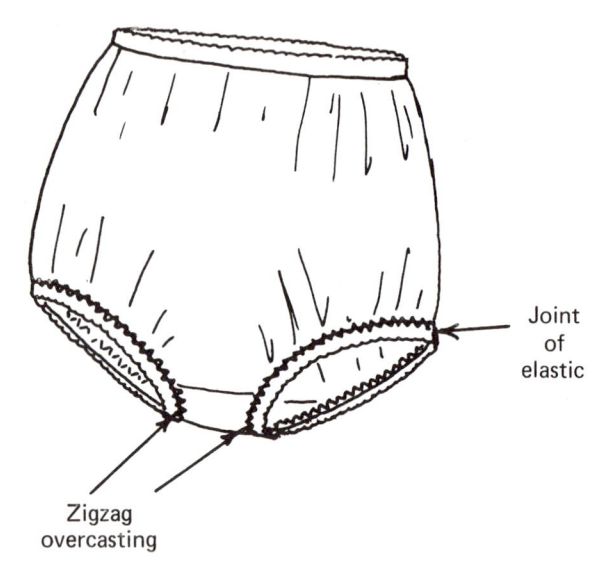

Joint of elastic

Zigzag overcasting

15. Sew the elastic around the other panty leg in the same manner as in Step 14.

16. Press panties with a warm temperature iron.

LADIES BAND-LEG PANTY

Materials Needed:

Pattern—the same as brief-type panty may be used by omitting the leg elastic.
½-yard tricot (will make several pairs)
½-inch wide top elastic 2 inches shorter than waist measurement
4-inch wide strip of tricot cut across the top of material
1½ inches of ½-inch wide satin ribbon

Panties 133

Step-by-Step:

1. Follow Steps 1 through 6 of the instructions for the ladies brief-type panties.

2. Fold the 4-inch strip of tricot in half. Starting at one side seam edge, lay the folded binding against the wrong side of the panty leg section with the raw edges together. Sew a ¼-inch seam using a zigzag around the leg of the panty.

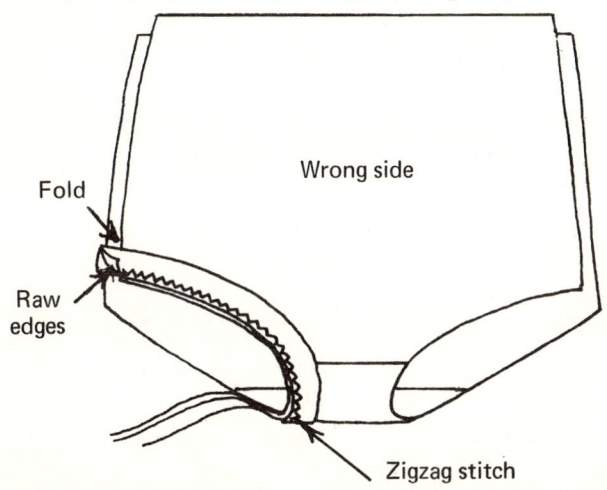

3. Turn the folded edge of the binding to the right side of the panty leg and zigzag by overcasting the edge of the binding directly over the edge of the first seam.

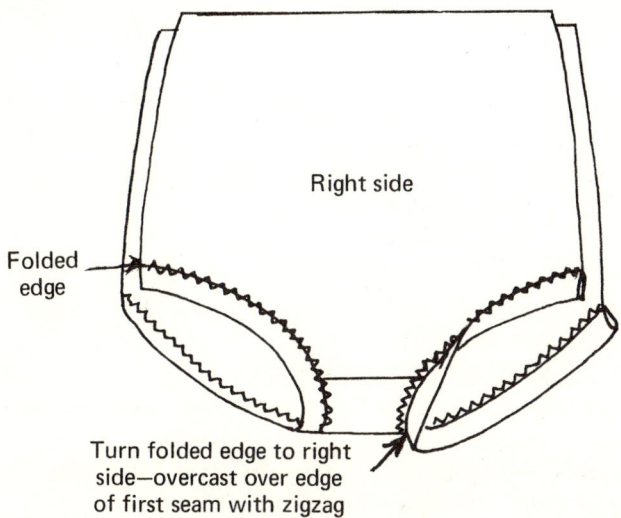

4. Sew the binding around the other leg by using the same method.

5. Finish the panty by using Steps 7 through 12 of the ladies brief-type panty instructions.

LADIES BIKINI PANTIES

Bikini panties may be made by cutting 2½ to 3 inches off the top of a pair of regular panties or a regular panty pattern and then finishing the panty by the same method as other panties. A sufficient amount of elastic for the top of the panty is the hip measurement minus three inches. There are some ladies bikini panty patterns available in the pattern books, and they are usually included in the chemise slip patterns.

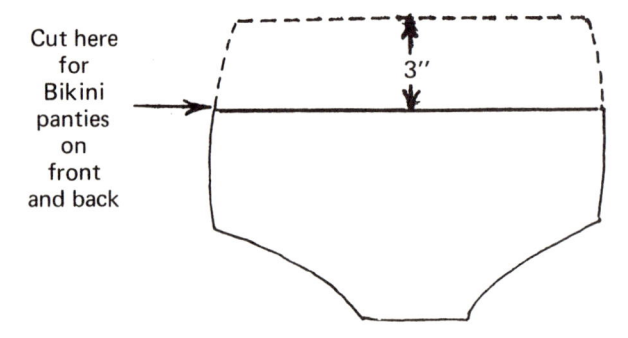

Cut here for Bikini panties on front and back

3"

In making the bikini panty, use the same methods as making the ladies brief-type panty. If you wish to make bikini panties from old panties, especially those with worn-out top elastic, simply cut 2½ inches to 3 inches from the top of a regular pair of panties. Then apply the new elastic to the top edge as you would any other panty. Many ladies prefer to wear the bikini panty under a panty girdle, because it makes less bulk at the waistline where the more rigid elastic is found.

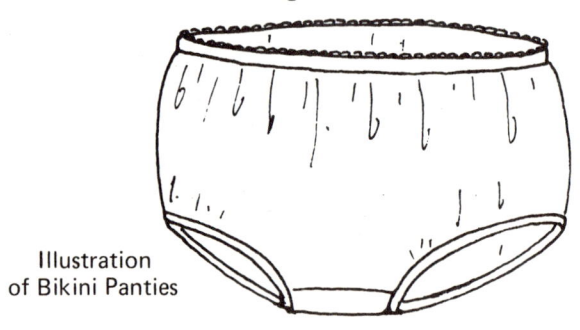

Illustration of Bikini Panties

LADIES LOOSE-LEG PANTY

Materials Needed:

Pattern can be ordered from any pattern book.
½ yard of nylon tricot (will make several pairs because of the width)
1½ inches of ½-inch wide satin ribbon
Lace as desired

The loose-leg panty may be made by using Steps 1 through 12 of the instructions for making the ladies brief-type panties. The legs of the loose-leg panty should be hemmed by the same method as a slip, either by edging with lace or turning up a hem and stitching with a decorative stitch. Refer to Step 12 of the overall lace bodice slip instructions, Step 5 of the ladies chemise slip instructions, and to the tailored slip instructions.

PETITE PANTIES

Materials Needed:

½ yard of nylon tricot
Pattern (available in all pattern books)
Waist elastic as per other panties
Lace as desired

Petite panties should be constructed in the same manner as the half-slip, except a crotch reinforcement is zigzagged in the crotch area on the wrong side of the garment. Pant-slip patterns are also available and may be constructed in the same manner as the ladies chemise.

Illustration
of Petite Panties

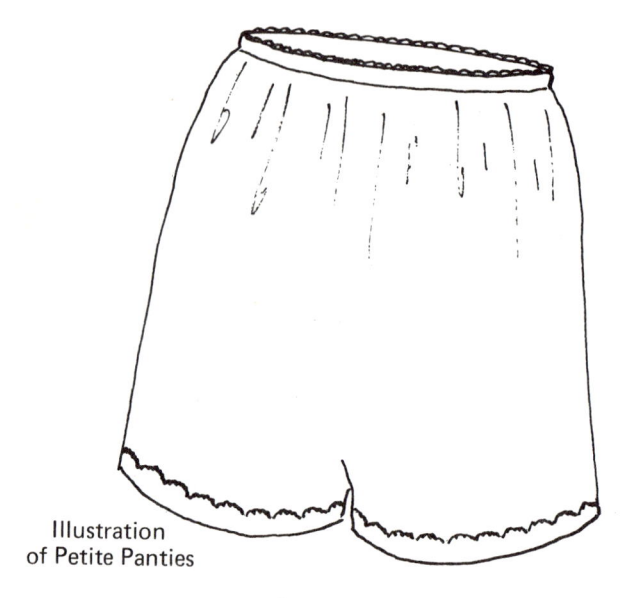

CHILDREN'S PANTIES

Materials Needed:

Patterns are available in pattern books.
1/3 yard of nylon tricot (will make several)
½-inch wide waist elastic 2 inches shorter than the waist measurement
¼-inch wide leg elastic 1 inch shorter than thigh measurement (enough for each leg)
1½ inches of satin ribbon
Lace as desired

Step-by-Step:

1. Decorate the seat of small children's panties with strips of lace zigzagged across the back of the panty. This lace can be either flat and attached on both sides, or slightly gathered and sewed at the top edge of the lace where it is gathered. All decorations other than the leg lace should be applied before the crotch seam is made.

Styles of Little Girl's Panties

2. Follow Steps 1 through 15 of the ladies brief-type panties instructions.

3. Zigzag any desired lace onto the top edge of the leg elastic, stretch the elastic just enough to get the fullness out of the fabric. Be sure to allow the needle to go through the elastic and then onto the tricot as the lace is sewed. The leg lace should be flat, rather than gathered, since the elastic will make gathers in the lace.

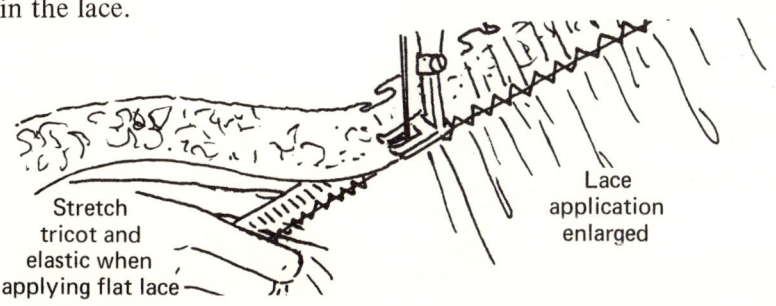

Stretch tricot and elastic when applying flat lace

Lace application enlarged

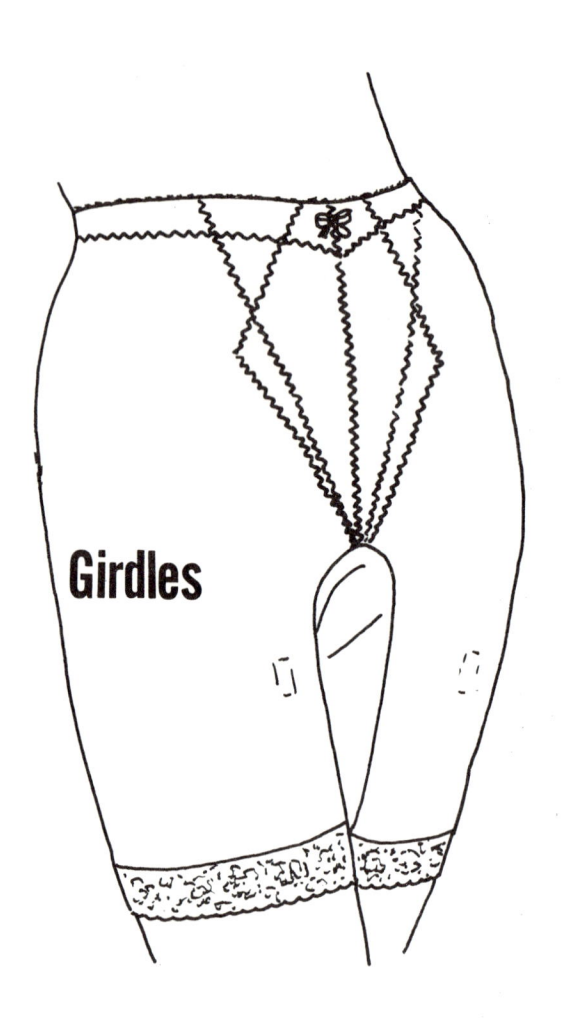

Girdles

CHAPTER IV

GIRDLES

Pre-cut girdle kits may be purchased at most lingerie fabric shops at a fraction of the cost of a ready-made girdle. A pattern, however, may be taken from a favorite girdle by using the foil method discussed in the Slip Chapter (II), or you may take an old girdle apart and use it for a pattern. Girdle fabric is available at most lingerie fabric stores.

Every stitch on a girdle must be zigzagged with nylon thread to allow for stretch. If your machine does a three-step zigzag stitch similar to this /\/\/\/\ , you may prefer to use it for top stitching on the girdle instead of the plain zigzag. This stitch holds better than the regular zigzag and tends to eliminate the skipping of stitches. The ballpoint sewing machine needle is excellent for sewing the girdle, too, and helps prevent stitch-skipping.

Regular needle   Ballpoint needle

In cutting the girdle, the length or straight of the material should go around the body. The larger elastic cords in the fabric run lengthwise in the girdle material. The pattern length should be placed crosswise on the fabric so that the large elastic threads will extend around the body. Most girdles have these pieces or are similar to the following:

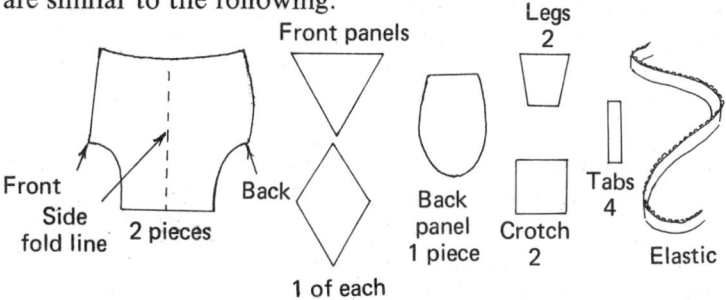

Front Side fold line — Back 2 pieces
Front panels 1 of each
Back panel 1 piece
Legs 2
Crotch 2
Tabs 4
Elastic

Materials Needed:

Two-thirds of a yard of girdle material in the 72-inch width will make any size.

1-inch wide nap-back elastic with one picot edge for top edge, waist fabric measurement minus 1-inch

Elastic lace or elastic the same as the top for the girdle legs, leg fabric measurement minus ½ inch on each leg

Two 6-inch squares of nylon tricot for center crotch section

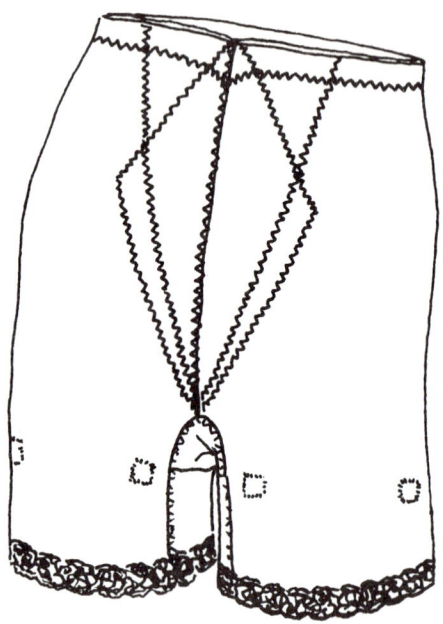

Step-by-Step:

1. Sew center front with a ¼-inch seam by using a narrow zigzag width and a regular stitch length. Start this seam at the waistline and sew down toward the crotch. Be sure to lock the stitch by sewing two stitches with the stitch length set at "0" at the beginning of the seam. All seams should be locked in this manner both at the beginning and the end of the seam. This prevents raveling.

2. Pivot the material on the needle at the crotch and turn the fabric around with the fabric between you and the machine. Open the girdle sections and turn the seam to the right. (Since this seam has been zigzagged, it cannot be pressed open.) Now the two sections are flat on the machine before you with the crotch end of the center front seam under the needle.

Girdles

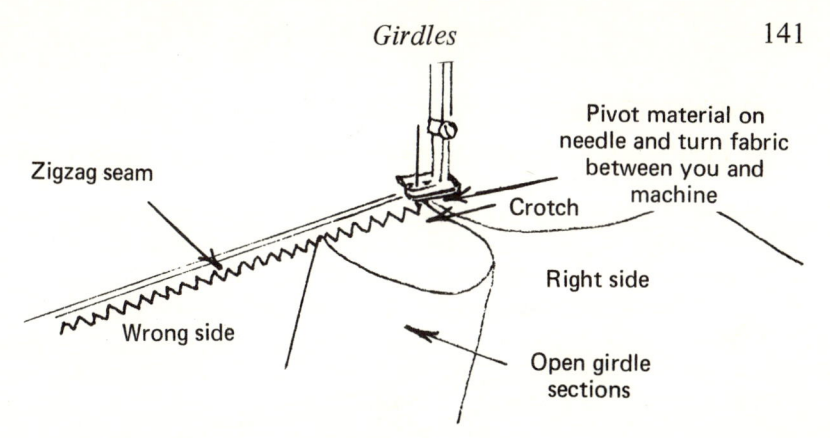

3. Pin the front panel pieces together with the diamond piece on top. Put the pins on the diamond side so they will not end up in the inside of the girdle.

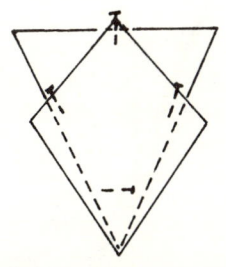

4. Center the two front panels under the center seam with the long point against the needle. Be sure the triangle panel is sandwiched between the diamond and the outside pieces so the pins will not be inside.

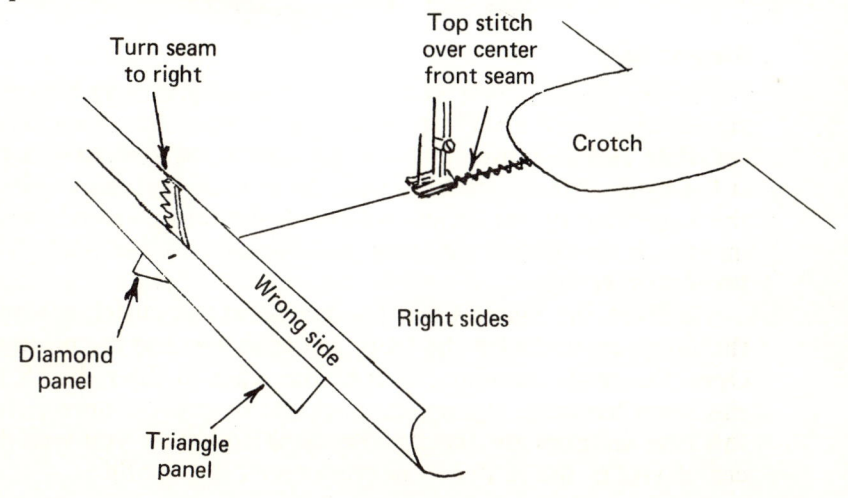

5. Set the machine on the widest zigzag or the three-step zigzag, whichever you prefer, and a regular stitch length and top stitch over the center front seam. Go through all three layers from the crotch to the top. A prettier seam is obtained by allowing the needle to go slightly beyond the left side of the seam. Then overcast the seam to the right of it.

6. Reduce the zigzag width to one-half or medium width and zigzag with a regular zigzag or the three-step zigzag around each edge of the front panels. A neater job may be done by sewing from the right side of the garment.

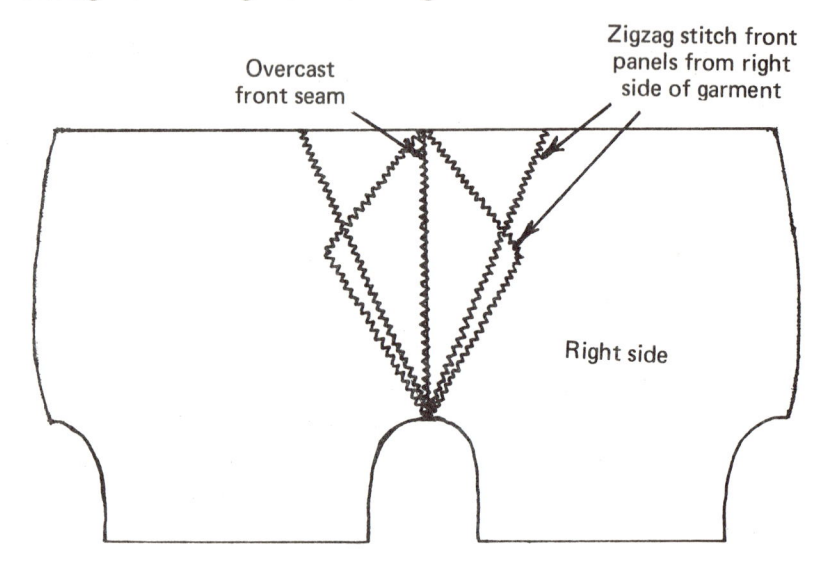

Overcast front seam

Zigzag stitch front panels from right side of garment

Right side

7. Cut the two crotch pieces so that the stretch of the tricot is going front to back, or the straight of the fabric is going from one leg piece to the other. This is important because the crotch must stretch from front to back for comfort.

8. Place the leg piece between the right sides of the crotch pieces with the straight of the tricot fabric against the large end of the leg section. Sew these three pieces at the large end of the leg section with a ½-inch seam and using a medium zigzag and a regular stitch length. Be sure to lock the seams well at either end of the seam by sewing a couple of stitches with the stitch length set at "0".

Girdles

Stretch of tricot goes from front to back

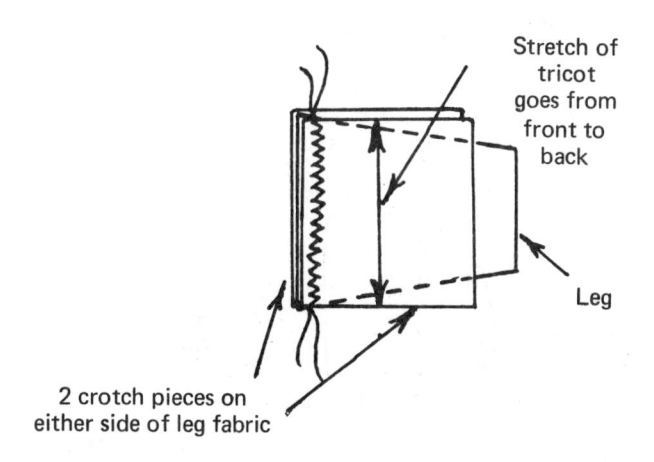

Leg

2 crotch pieces on either side of leg fabric

9. Fold the just-sewed leg spandex piece between the tricot crotch, and repeat Step 8 with the other spandex leg piece by sandwiching the second leg piece between the right sides of the tricot crotch. Sew this seam with a zigzag as in Step 8. Then turn right side out so that the raw seams are inside the crotch section and the elastic leg pieces extend out on either side of the crotch pieces.

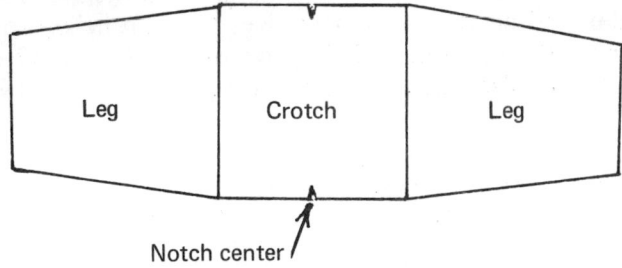

Leg | Crotch | Leg

Notch center

10. Notch the center of the crotch on both front and back. Place the right side of the crotch against the right side of the girdle front with the notch against the center front seam. Zigzag the crotch-leg section to the girdle front from the center front to the leg edge; then zigzag back to the center front and over to the edge of the other leg.

11. Open or flatten the center front and crotch-leg section. Turn the seam to the right and top stitch this seam with the widest zigzag and regular stitch length. Either a regular zigzag or the three-step zigzag may be used. This top stitching strengthens the crotch-leg-front section seam and makes a neater garment.

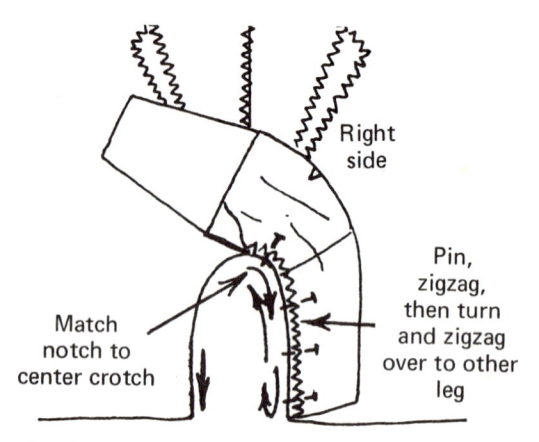

12. Fold the leg-supporter tabs in thirds and zigzag over the raw edge. Sew through all layers. Finish all four in the same manner.

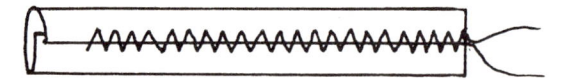

13. Fold the leg supporters in half and zigzag in place. The best location is one inch from the seam of the leg-crotch-front section with the raw ends of the tab in line with the seam of the leg spandex and crotch tricot. This gives the right height for the supporter on the leg, and is slightly on the inside of the leg for comfort. It will also not show through tight-fitting skirts when seated.

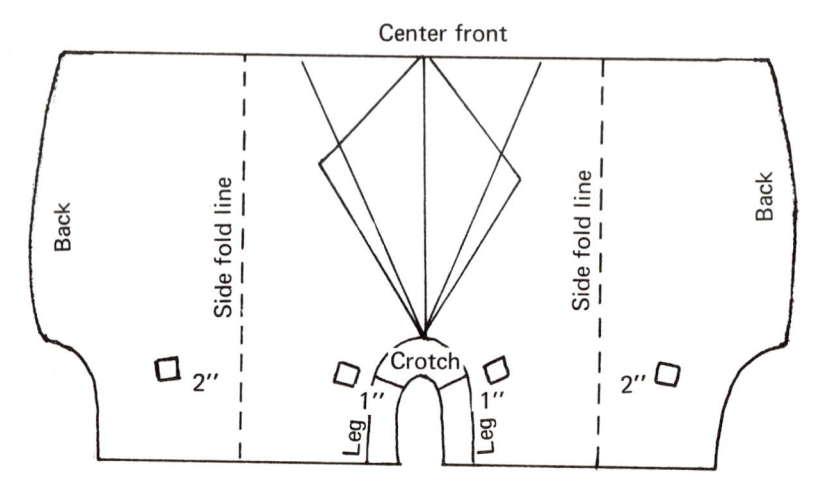

Girdles

14. If three support tabs per leg are desired, place a tab on the leg-crotch-front seam, a tab on the exact side-center of the girdle, and a tab on the leg-crotch-back seam.

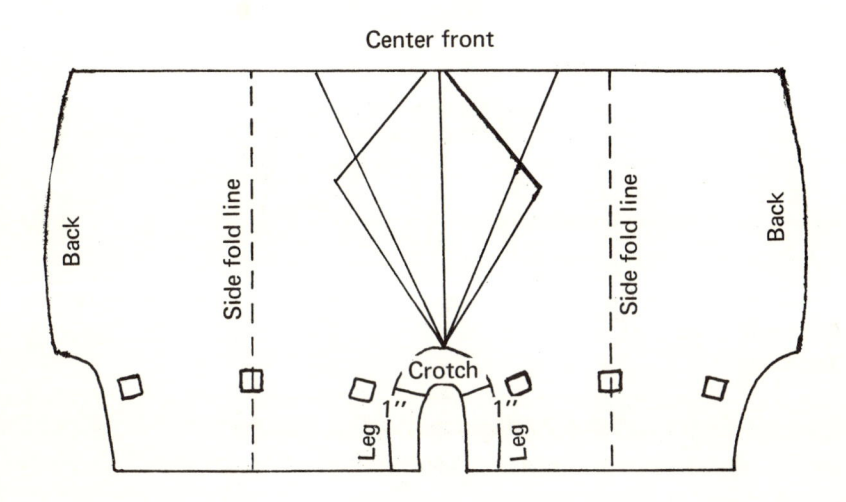

15. If elastic lace is used for the bottom of the legs, zigzag it around the bottom of each leg section. If the plain elastic is being used for the legs, though, it should be applied after the back seam is sewed.

16. Place the right sides of the back section together and zigzag the center back seam from top to bottom. Then pivot the material on the needle and flatten the two pieces before stitching in the same manner as the front seam. Center the back panel on the back seam on the wrong side of the girdle back section. Then stitch from the needle position at the crotch up the center seam to the top. This should be a top stitch sewed with the widest zigzag and a regular stitch length overcasting the center back seam, or use the three-step zigzag stitch.

17. Reduce the zigzag width to medium and stitch around the edge of the back panel. Allow the needle to overcast the edge in the same manner as the front panels. This will look better if stitched from the right side of the girdle, even though the panel is underneath the fabric.

18. Turn the girdle inside out and place the right side of the

leg-crotch section against the right side of the girdle back. Position the center of the crotch against the center back seam. Zigzag this seam in the same manner as the front crotch seam. Then turn the seam toward the crotch section and top stitch with the widest zigzag or three-step zigzag. Overcast the edge of the seam as you stitch.

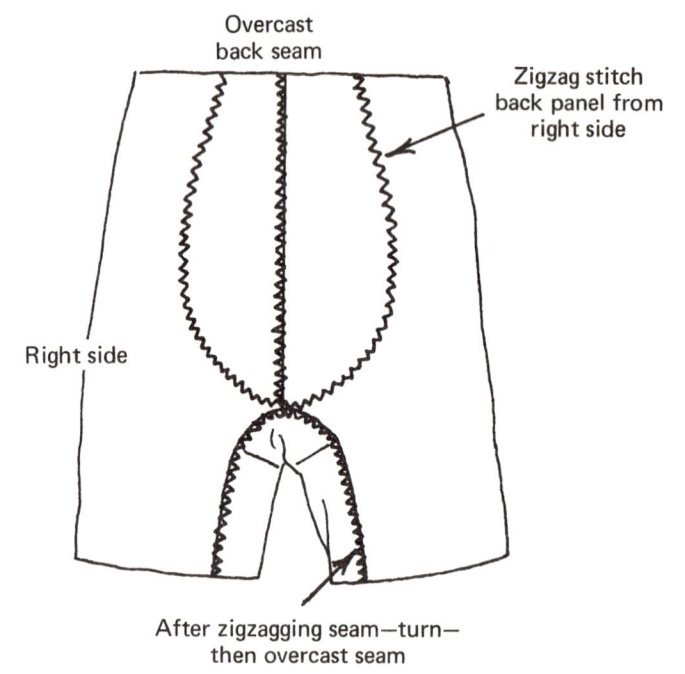

Overcast back seam

Zigzag stitch back panel from right side

Right side

After zigzagging seam—turn— then overcast seam

19. Lay the wrong side of the girdle center front seam on the machine. Place the waist elastic against the right side of the girdle with the nap side toward you. The elastic should be at a right angle to the girdle top and positioned so that the picot edge is right on the center front seam and extending about three-fourths of an inch above the waistline. Zigzag three stitches from the picot edge of the elastic and then back three stitches to the picot edge. Then place the elastic around the girdle top with the girdle spandex extending almost to the top of the elastic.

Zigzag the elastic around the top of the girdle close to the picot edge. Use a medium zigzag and a regular stitch length. Do not let the needle extend beyond the picot edge.

Girdles 147

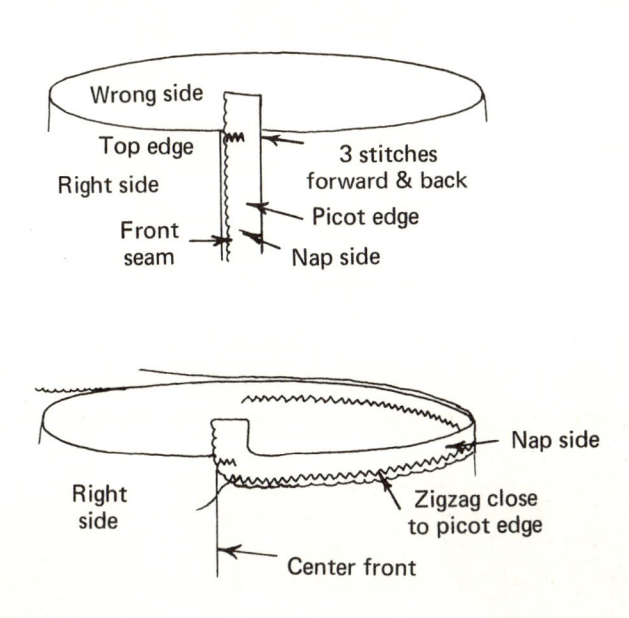

[Diagram: top elastic attachment showing Wrong side, Top edge, Right side, Front seam, 3 stitches forward & back, Picot edge, Nap side]

[Diagram: elastic attached around girdle showing Right side, Nap side, Zigzag close to picot edge, Center front]

20. When completing the elastic at the center front, bend the end of the elastic around so that it overlaps the first end and the curves match. This will make a decorative V at the center front.

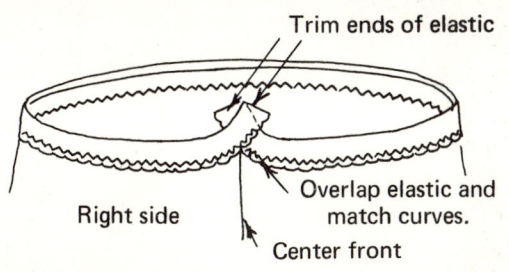

[Diagram: Trim ends of elastic, Right side, Overlap elastic and match curves, Center front]

21. Turn the elastic to the wrong side or inside of the girdle, and sew with the widest zigzag and regular stitch length. Be very careful to overcast the bottom edge of the elastic by allowing the needle to extend beyond the elastic into the girdle fabric, then overcast back into the top elastic.

22. If leg elastic is used, apply in the same manner as the top elastic, except that it should be overlapped at the joint instead of making a point or V as in the top center front. The joint of the elastic should be zigzagged securely from edge to edge several times for strength.

Turn elastic to inside—zigzag overcasting

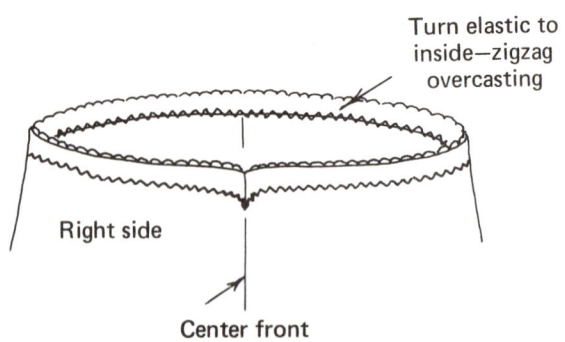

Right side

Center front

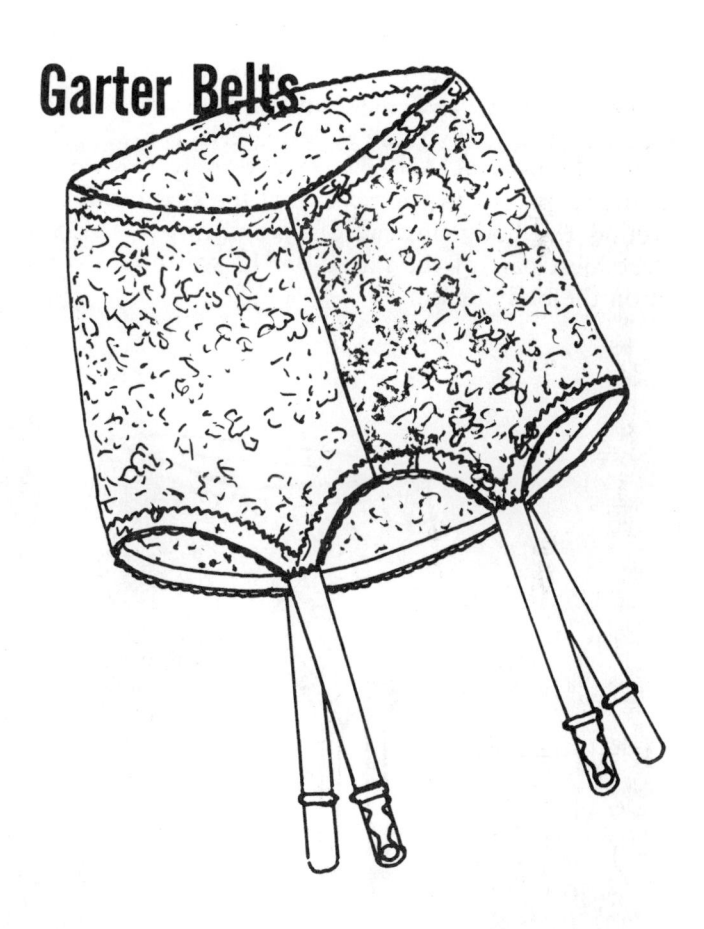

Garter Belts

CHAPTER V

GARTER BELTS

Garter belts may be made from the same material as the girdle or from any medium to heavy weight non-stretchy material. If a non-stretch type material is used, a bra-type hook should be used in the back. If a stretchy type material is used, as the lycra, cut the fabric so that the straight of the fabric goes around the body, instead of up and down. This will make the stretchiest part of the fabric on the width of the body, instead of on the body length.

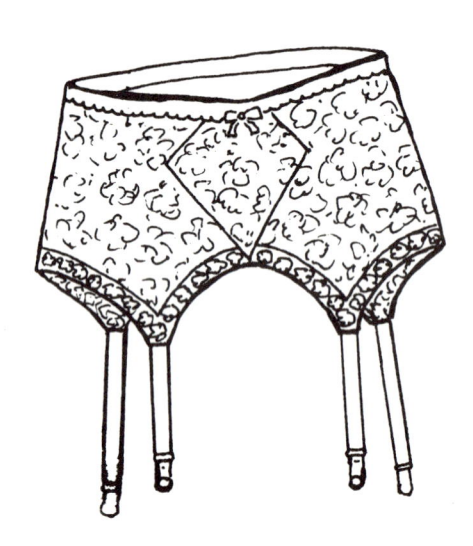

If lycra or a stretchy material is used, elastic should be applied at the top and bottom of the garter belt in the same manner as at the waist and legs of the girdle. The long supporters may be purchased at any lingerie fabric store. Garter belt patterns are available in most pattern books, or a pattern may be made from an old garter belt. Since the straight of the fabric goes around the body, material required to make a garter belt would be the measurement of the hips. If you wish to conserve fabric, put a seam on either side of the garter belt. In this way the material needed would be only one-half of the hip measurement. The side seams should be zigzagged with a normal stitch length and a medium zigzag width. Then the seam should be folded to the right and top-stitched with a wide zigzag, overcasting the seam. For more instructions on the method of sewing the side seams, refer to the girdle front and back seam instructions in Chapter IV.

Bras

CHAPTER VI

BRAS

Brassieres or bras may be made very inexpensively—$1.00 to $1.50 at most. They are more time consuming than the slip or girdle, because there is more tedious work. Bra patterns may be bought; however, it is much better to take your pattern from a very expensive bra. A good bra costs more money, but will last longer, give the proper support, and be more healthy in that it allows good circulation and cuts down on breast cysts. A cheap bra will cost about the same as it costs to make a good bra; therefore, a cheap bra is not worth the time involved. A good bra will improve the muscle tone of the breasts and chest cavity. It will not deform the shoulder or collar bones by pulling them down into a sloping position, and will increase the size of the breasts by improving the muscle tone. A good bra is engineered to uplift without the straps. The straps merely stabilize. Since it takes the same amount of time, approximately, to make a good bra as a cheap one, why settle for an inferior product?

One big advantage of making your own bras is that you may make matching sets of bras, slips, panties, and girdles. The bras of the matching sets may be made from leftover scraps from the other garments in the set. The only additional thing needed would be the straps and back hooks.

To take a bra pattern from another bra, use aluminum foil and spread the bra on a padded surface (a quilt or a blanket spread on a table or an ironing board). Spread the bra flat on the padded surface. Starting at the back hook section, place the foil over the end section. Press the finger down on the foil at the bra edge of this section and rub it along the edges and down the seam. Then cut the foil along the indented lines made by the finger. Mark the cut-out pieces as to what it is, the fabric from which it is to be cut, and to what it is to be sewed. Then repeat this foil process on each flat piece of the bra, one piece at a time. Be careful to cut and mark each piece as it is made.

Next, spread a piece of foil against the padded surface and place the right side of the lower section of the bra cup against the foil. Rub the index finger along the seams of this lower cup section. Then cut and mark as before. The next step is to make the upper cup section of the bra pattern. This is the most difficult, and four hands or two people are useful. Again place the foil on the padded surface. Place the upper cup section against the foil. Again rub the seams and the edges of this section with the index finger. This piece is curved and should be started at the center front half, then worked back to the underarm section. The top cup section from the middle to the underarm seam is not difficult to mark if someone helps hold the bra stationary while you rub the seams for the foil indentations. Then cut the foil on the indented marks and identify the pieces as before.

After the cup pieces are cut, try on the bra and measure the cup foil pattern pieces to the bra cup. If the foil bottom cup section is too short, the bra will have a downlift instead of an uplift. If the top foil cup section is too long, it will also cause problems. At this point, adjust the foil in any manner necessary for a perfect fit.

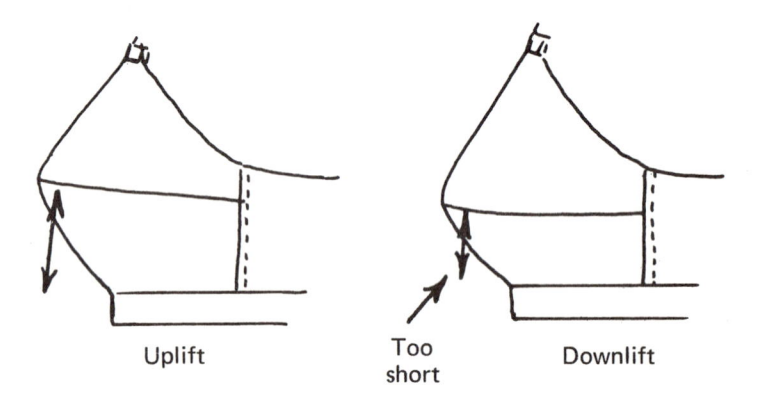

Uplift   Too short   Downlift

Next, place the foil pattern on plain paper. Cut out around the foil pattern one-fourth of an inch from the foil edge. This will give a ¼-inch seam allowance for the paper pattern. Be sure to mark the paper pattern pieces well so that it will be perfectly clear what kind of material to use for each piece and what seams should be sewed together. The paper pattern should look like this:

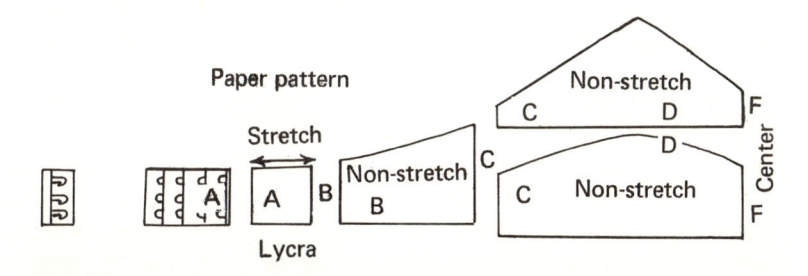

Bras

Paper pattern
Stretch
Lycra
A A B
Non-stretch B
Non-stretch C D F
C
Non-stretch C D F Center

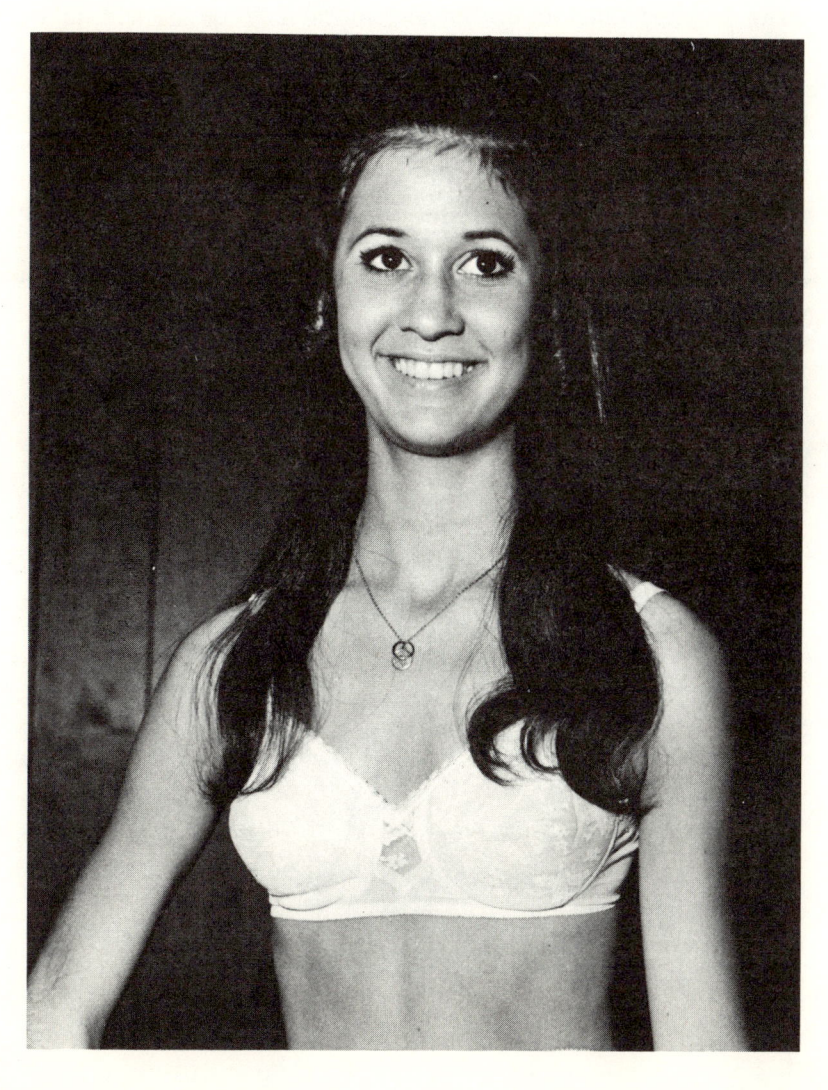

If the bra you are copying has inside support pieces, you can get a foil pattern from these in the same method used for the other bra sections.

In cutting the bra materials, the lycra section should be cut so that the stretch or straight of the fabric extends from side to side or around the body. All other pieces may be cut in any direction. All elastic seams should be zigzagged to allow stretch. All other seams are straight stitched. If you are copying a bra, sew all seams in the same manner as the bra you are copying. Bra edgings and all of the finishings may be bought at the lingerie supply store.

In sewing your bra together, bind all of the seams with a sheer strip of nylon. The best way to do this is to sew a ¼-inch seam, flatten the seam out either to the left or to the right, not opened, and zigzag down the middle of it. Then fold a 1-inch strip of sheer nylon the length of the seam to be bound, and straight stitch each edge of the sheer strip over the seam with the raw edges against the bra. If the seam to be bound has ragged edges, it should be trimmed smooth.

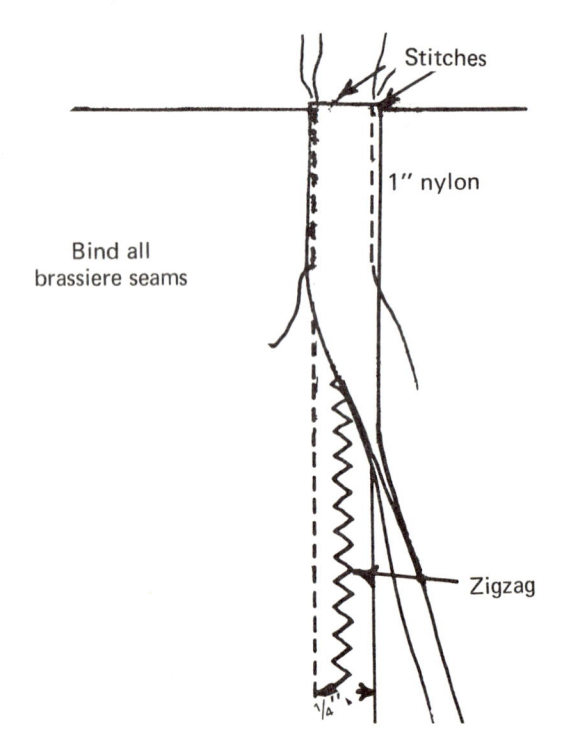

All outer edges of the bra should be edged with some sort of edging. Bra edging may be purchased at lingerie stores, or other edgings may be found at fabric stores that will be suitable. The nylon or cotton part of the bra, usually the cup sections, should be bound with nylon or cotton. The elastic portions should be bound or edged with elastic edging similar to the type used at the bottom and top of panties. To edge the bra, place the edging material wrong side against the right side of the bra with the picot or scalloped edge of the edging toward the center of the bra. Then stitch the edging close to the picot or scalloped edge. Next, turn the edging to the wrong side of the bra and stitch the bottom edge down. Remember to use a zigzag stitch on the stretchy portions of the bra and a straight stitch on the cotton or nylon portions. Again, it is important to lock all seams at the beginning and the end by sewing a couple of stitches with the stitch length set at "0." This will secure them so that there will be no raveling nor mending.

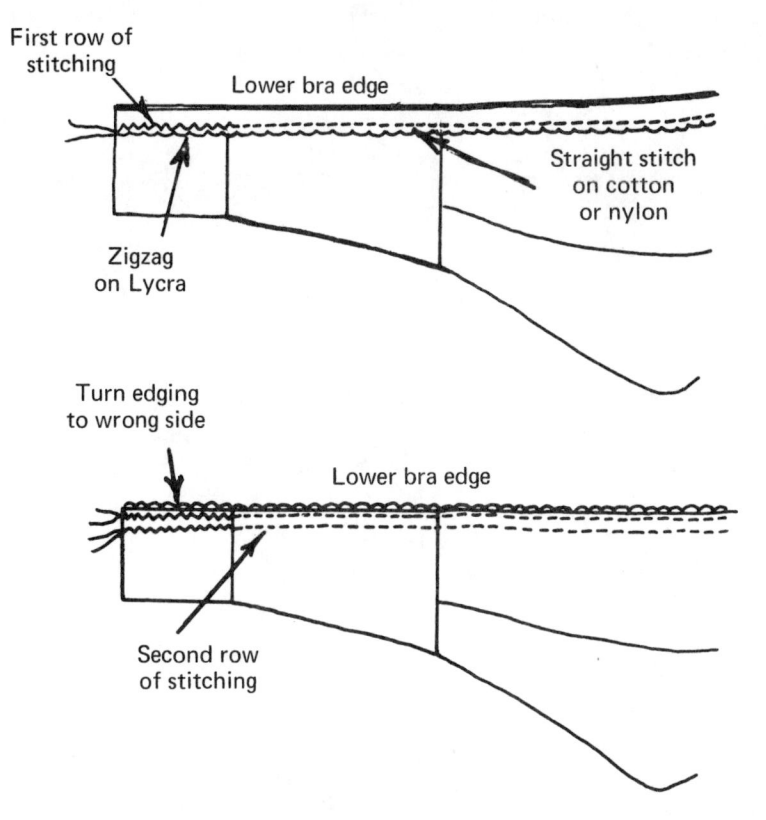

First row of stitching

Lower bra edge

Straight stitch on cotton or nylon

Zigzag on Lycra

Turn edging to wrong side

Lower bra edge

Second row of stitching

Gowns

CHAPTER VII

GOWNS

Probably the most fun that can be had in sewing is making a luscious gown and robe set. These gorgeous sets may be made for less than one-third of the cost of a ready-made set. Inherent in each of us is a desire to create beauty. When the beautiful object has both an artistic and a useful purpose, it gives an inexhaustible source of joy. It is both aesthetic and therapeutic, as well as a durable, practical thing. Women, like little girls, love frilly, feminine things. Creating these inherently feminine garments gives great pleasure and deep satisfaction. This is truly a form of art, and has a great emotional therapy that leaves the person uplifted and refreshed. Frilly, feminine lingerie is every woman's dream that can now be had with the added benefit of being able to say, "I made it myself."

Gown and robe patterns are no problem, because the manufacturers are beginning to recognize the lingerie market and have met the demand with a multitude of styles and pattern designs. Many dress patterns may be used for a gown and robe, also, especially one with a yoke or straight lines and open down the front.

Since the materials are 96 inches to 108 inches wide and sometimes even wider, you cannot use the yardage instructions on the back of the patterns. The only way to accurately determine the amount of material to purchase is to decide on the length of the garment, then measure the width of the hem or bottom of each piece. One length of material may be sufficient if only a gown or a robe is being made. However, if both are being made, two lengths of material will probably be necessary. It is better to be sure that you have enough than need more material and it not be available. The excess can always be used for making slips, panties, scuffs, bras, or crotch pieces for girdles and swimsuits.

The easiest design to make is one with a front and back yoke covered with all-over lace. One-half of a yard of all-over lace that is 45 inches wide will make yokes for a gown and robe set. Some laces are even three yards wide, so a 9-inch length of material of this width would suffice. Edging laces may be used instead of hems and facings. The amount of edging lace needed can only be determined by measuring the pattern or garment. A much more beautiful garment is made with the edging lace, and it is much easier to sew and less time consuming.

The same general principles discussed in Chapter I apply to the gown and robe made of tricot. All pattern pieces are cut on the straight of the fabric.

SLEEVELESS TRICOT GOWN WITH ROUND OVER-ALL LACE YOKE WITHOUT LACE EDGING

Materials Needed:

Refer to opening remarks in this chapter.

Step-by-Step:

1. Place the pattern on the straight of the fabric. Cut the larger garment pieces first; then use the smaller, leftover pieces for the yoke, bindings, etc.

2. Place the cut yoke and pattern pinned together on the lace and cut the lace.

3. Cut a 2-inch wide strip of tricot on the crossgrain of the fabric. This will be used as a double-fold binding around the neck, armholes, and any top openings where edging lace is not desired. The easiest way to cut this binding strip is to fold the fabric lengthwise many, many times until it is only about three or four inches wide. Pin the top section together so that all of the edges are even. Then trim the top edges so that all of them are straight and even. Measure 2 inches down from the edge of the fabric and mark by laying a straight edge across the 2-inch mark. Then cut along the straight edge at the 2-inch mark.

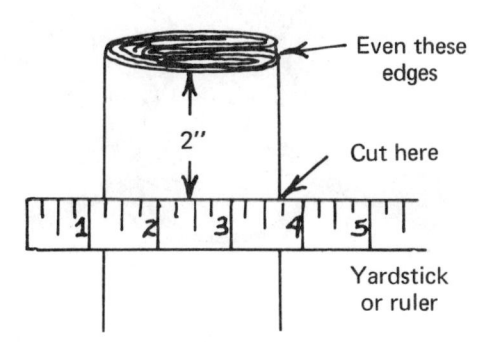

4. Stay stitch the lace and tricot yoke pieces together with a straight stitch very close to the fabric edges.

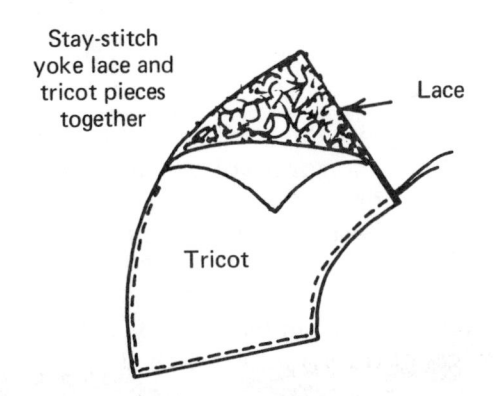

5. Fold the cut double-fold binding right sides out with th edges together at the top.

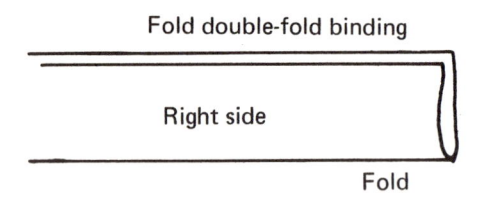

Fold double-fold binding

Right side

Fold

6. Sew the shoulder seams with a straight stitch and overcast with a very short stitch length and the widest zigzag.

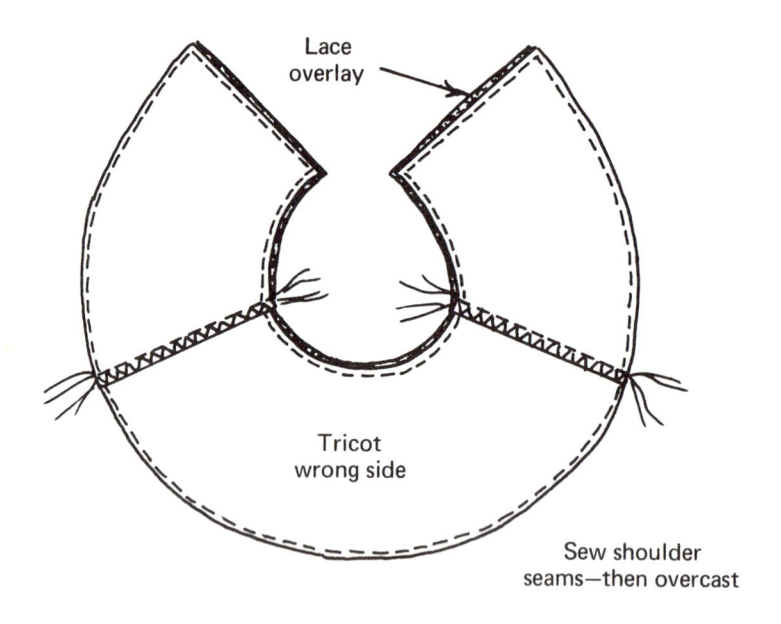

Lace overlay

Tricot wrong side

Sew shoulder seams—then overcast

7. Place the raw edges of the double-fold binding of Step 5 against the right side of the gown yoke with the raw edges of the gown and binding together at the section to be bound. (Probably the neck or perhaps the front opening.)

8. Straight stitch one-fourth of an inch from the raw edges around the neck binding.

9. Flatten the binding away from the garment.

10. Fold the raw edges of the seam toward the binding.

Gowns

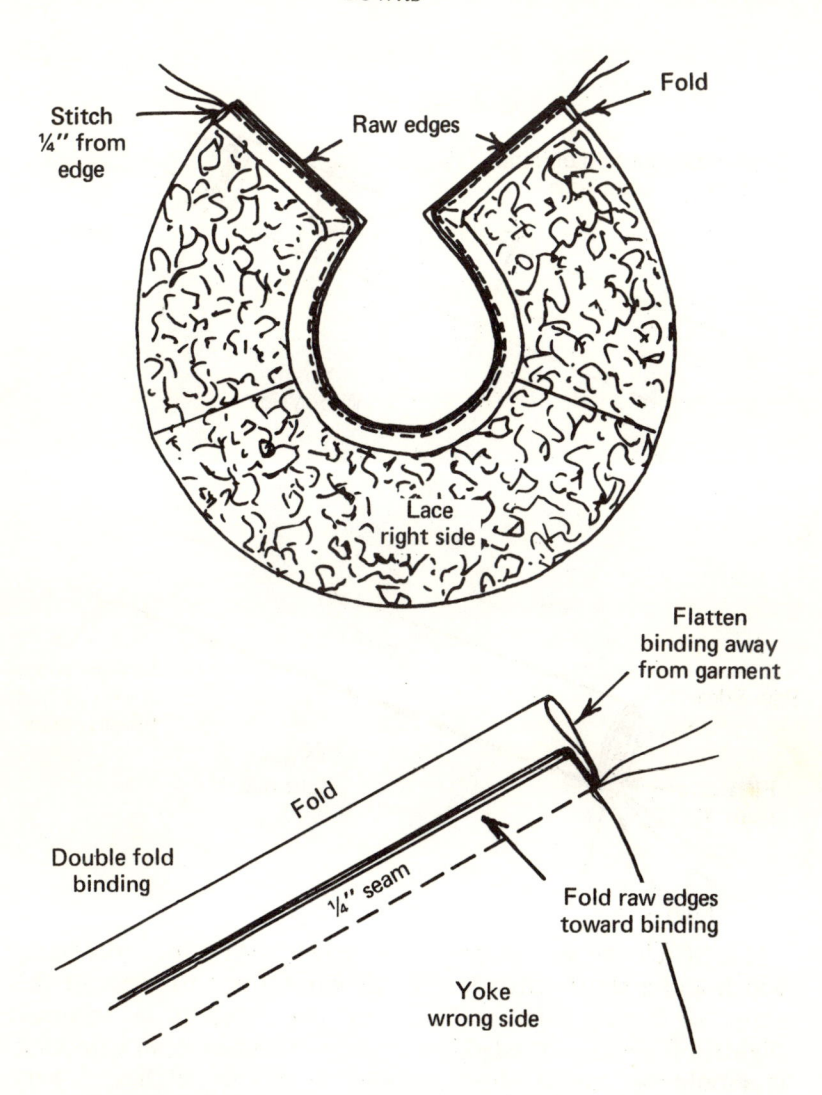

[Figure: Lace neckline binding with labels — Stitch ¼" from edge, Raw edges, Fold, Lace right side]

[Figure: Double fold binding application with labels — Double fold binding, Fold, ¼" seam, Flatten binding away from garment, Fold raw edges toward binding, Yoke wrong side]

11. Fold the folded edge of the double-fold binding over the raw seam edges to the wrong side of the garment. Hold the binding tightly so that the folded edge will extend slightly below the first seam.

12. From the right side of the garment, straight stitch in the crack or well of the first binding seam very close to the binding right side, but do not sew up on the right side of the binding. This seam will secure the binding to the wrong side of the garment, but will be attractive on the right side, also.

164   Sewing The Unusual

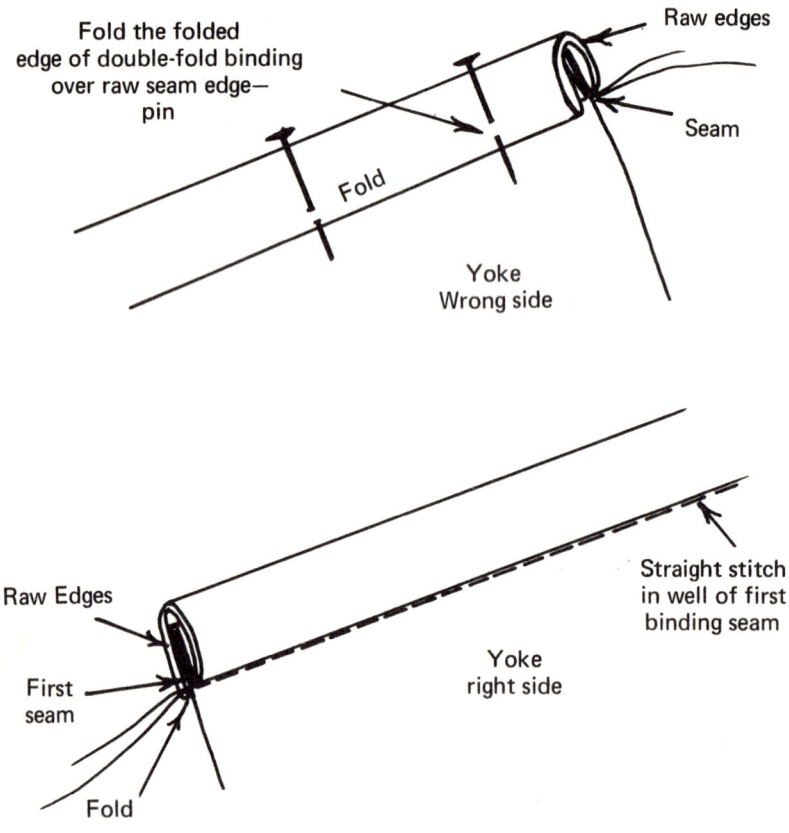

Fold the folded edge of double-fold binding over raw seam edge— pin

Raw edges

Seam

Fold

Yoke Wrong side

Raw Edges

First seam

Fold

Yoke right side

Straight stitch in well of first binding seam

13. Stitch the side seams of the gown with a medium zigzag width and a short stitch length. Be careful not to overcast this seam, or it may pucker. This seam may need to be trimmed slightly, if rough, cut edge is unsightly or too wide; in trimming, it should be cut as close as possible to the stitches. A very narrow seam allowance—about the width of the zigzag stitch —looks very professional. If a sheer overlay is used, it should be sewed in the same manner as the tricot side seams, but should be sewed separately. The sheer overlay should be pre-shrunk before sewing, because it sometimes shrinks in length. The only places the sheer overlay is sewed into the seam with the tricot are at the armholes and the yoke.

14. Stay stitch the sheer to the tricot at the armholes and across the top if a sheer overlay is being used.

Stay stitch sheer to tricot

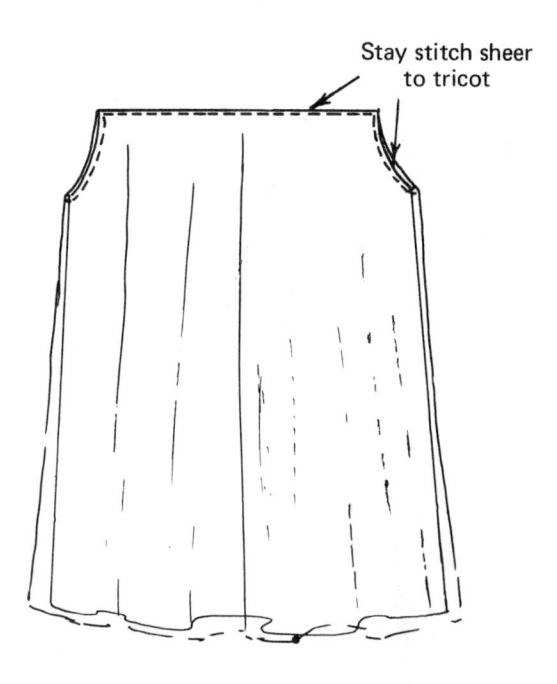

15. Stitch two rows of gathering stitches across the top front and back of the gown where it will be attached to the yoke.

16. Ease the fullness of the front and back to equal the width needed to fit the yoke. Straight stitch the gathered gown skirt section to the yoke with right sides together. Then trim this seam as close as possible to the stitches. Be VERY careful not to trim through the stitches and cut a hole in the yoke and front sections.

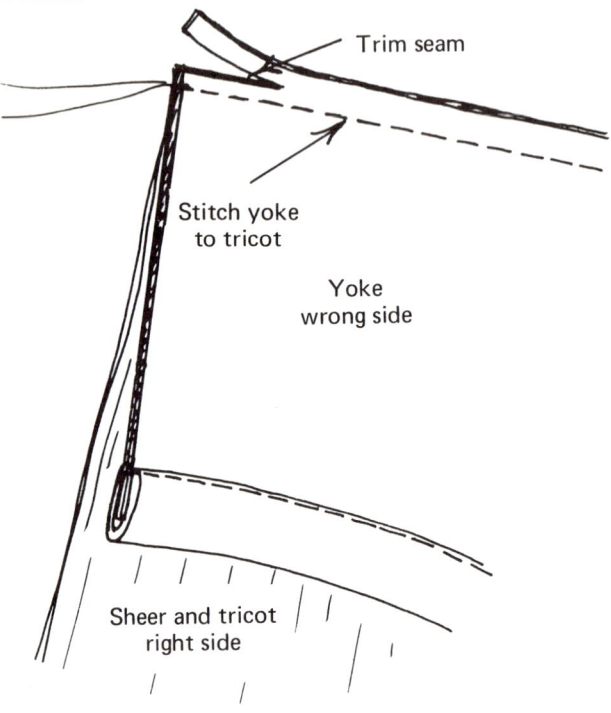

17. Bind the armholes with a double-fold binding in the same manner as the neck was bound. The double-fold binding should be overlapped at the underarm seam and the raw edge tucked under.

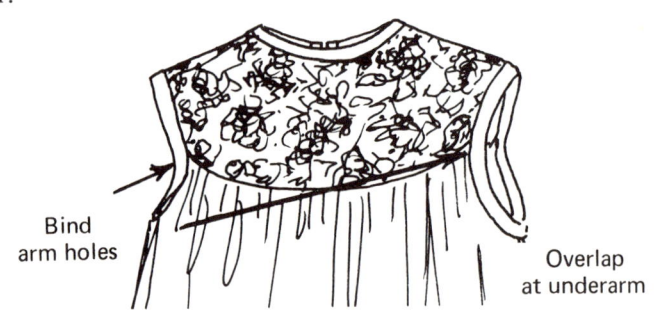

18. Finish the hem by zigzagging lace on the bottom of the skirt. Place the lace (any width) on the right side of the garment close to the edge and zigzag along the top of the lace. It usually looks better not to overcast the top of the lace, but let the needle come close to the top. If sheer overlay is being used, it should be edged with lace in the same manner as the tricot underskirt. It is better to edge both the tricot and the sheer overlay with lace rather than hemming one in another manner. The sheer overlay is attached to the tricot only at the yoke and armholes (not at the side seams nor the hem), and falls free over the tricot in a cloud-like effect.

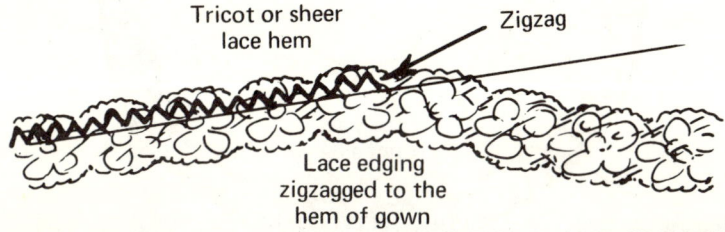

GOWN WITH LACE-EDGED ROUND YOKE AND SLEEVES

Materials Needed:

Refer to the opening remarks in this chapter.

Step-by-Step:

1. Follow Steps 1, 2, and 3 of the sleeveless tricot gown instructions.

2. Gather or pleat 1-inch wide lace for edging the yoke.

3. If you are using lace overlay on the yoke, straight stitch the shoulder seams of the lace and then overcast the seams with a zigzag. Next, repeat this process on the shoulder seams of the tricot yoke.

4. Stay stitch the edging lace to the right side of the lace yoke with the right sides and bottom edges together.

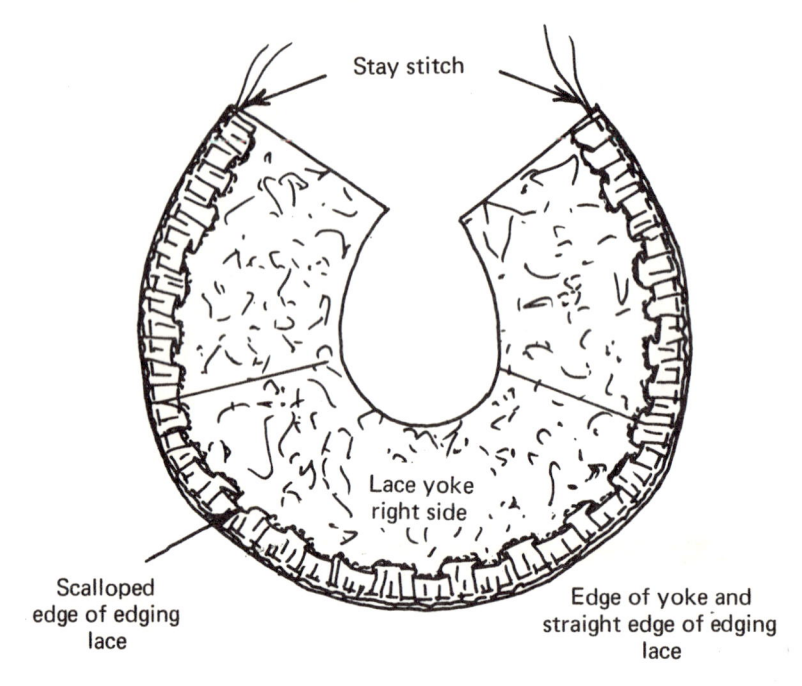

Labels on figure:
- Stay stitch
- Lace yoke right side
- Scalloped edge of edging lace
- Edge of yoke and straight edge of edging lace

5. Zigzag lace edging to the bottom edge of the sleeve by placing the lace just above the tricot edge as in Step 18 (finishing the hem) of the sleeveless tricot gown instructions.

6. Cut 1/8-inch wide elastic to fit the measurement of the arm at either wrist or upper arm, depending on the sleeve length used.

7. Run a gathering stitch one-half of an inch from the top edge of the sleeve edging lace where it is attached to the tricot, and stitch across the sleeve and from side seam to side seam. Then gather the sleeve until it is about 3 inches longer than the unstretched elastic.

8. On the wrong side of the sleeve, place the elastic at the side seam on the gathering stitch. Lock the thread by placing the needle through the elastic and the tricot; then sew a couple of stitches with the stitch length at "0."

9. Set the machine on the regular stitch length and a wide enough zigzag to overcast the elastic without stitching through it. Stretch the elastic along the gathering stitch to the end of the sleeve edge. Overcast the elastic in position with the zigzag; then lock the end of the elastic at the sleeve edge in the same manner as at the beginning of the seam.

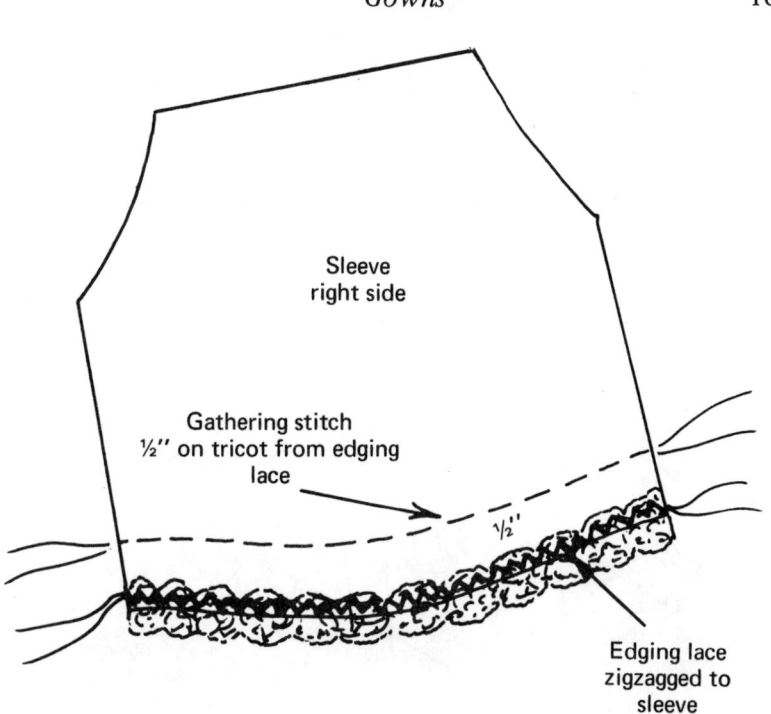

Gowns

169

Sleeve
right side

Gathering stitch
½" on tricot from edging
lace

½"

Edging lace
zigzagged to
sleeve

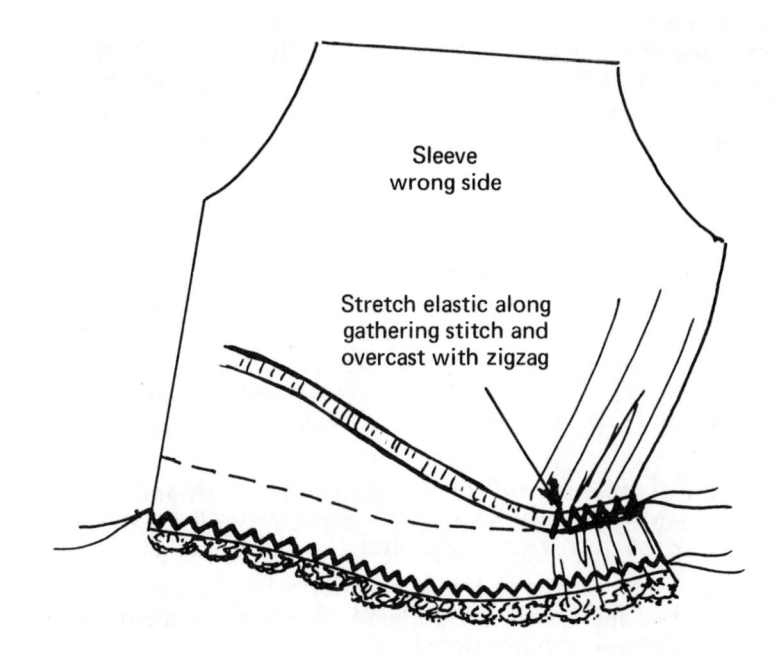

Sleeve
wrong side

Stretch elastic along
gathering stitch and
overcast with zigzag

10. Zigzag the underarm seam of the sleeve with a medium width zigzag and a short stitch length. Do not overcast this seam, or it will pucker. Then trim the selvage close to the stitches.

11. Sew the skirt side seams in the same manner as the sleeve underarm seams.

12. Place the right sides of the sleeve and gown skirt section together and straight stitch; then trim the seam and overcast it with a zigzag.

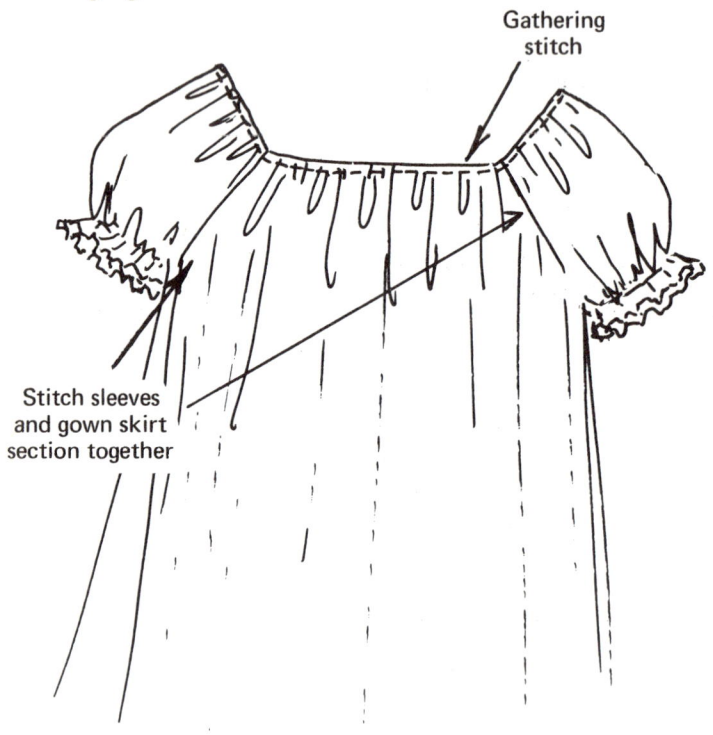

Gathering stitch

Stitch sleeves and gown skirt section together

13. Since a round yoke gown is being made, sew a gathering stitch around the entire top of the gown skirt and sleeve sections.

14. Gather the skirt and sleeve sections to fit the yoke.

15. Sandwich the gathered sleeve-skirt sections between the wrong side of the tricot yoke and the right side of the lace overlay. Check to see that the gathers are even.

16. Straight stitch the yoke pieces to the skirt-sleeve section with two rows of stitches one-eighth of an inch from the fabric

edges. Check to see if the edging lace is properly placed before sewing this seam; then check the position of the edging lace in the seam periodically as you stitch.

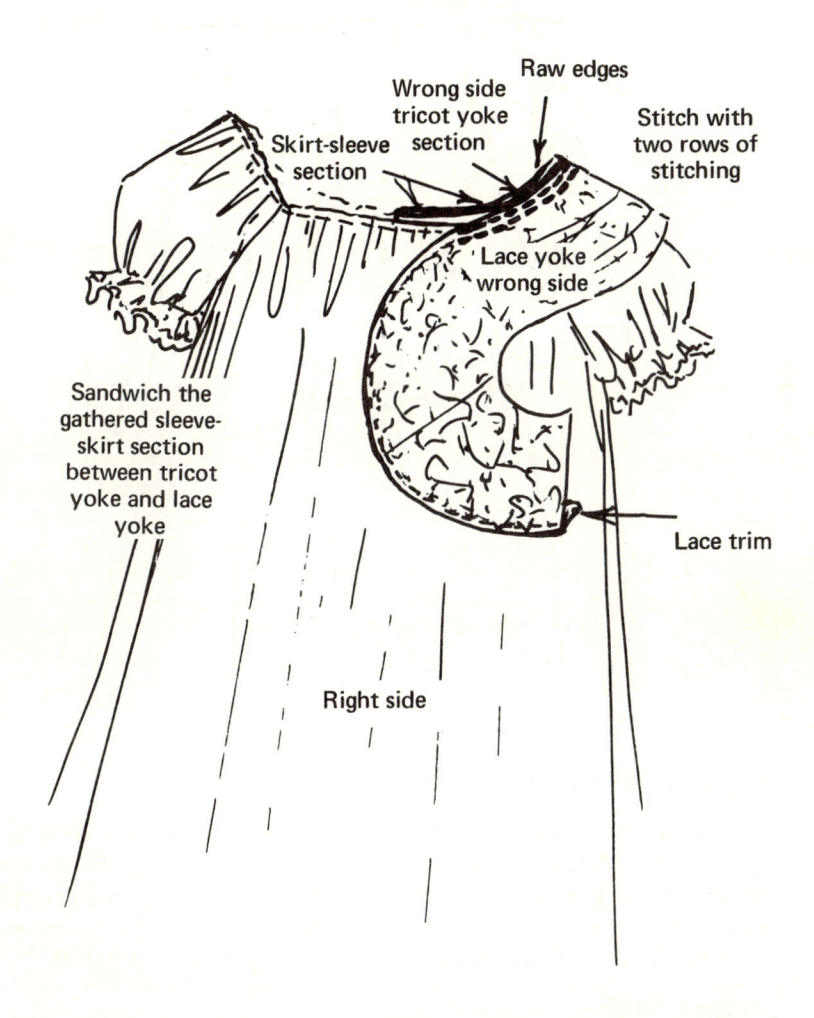

17. Bring the two yoke (tricot and over-all lace) neckline edges together and bind the top edge with a double-fold binding as in Steps 7 through 12 of the sleeveless tricot gown instructions given previously.

18. Edge the hem of the gown with lace by the same method used in edging the sleeve.

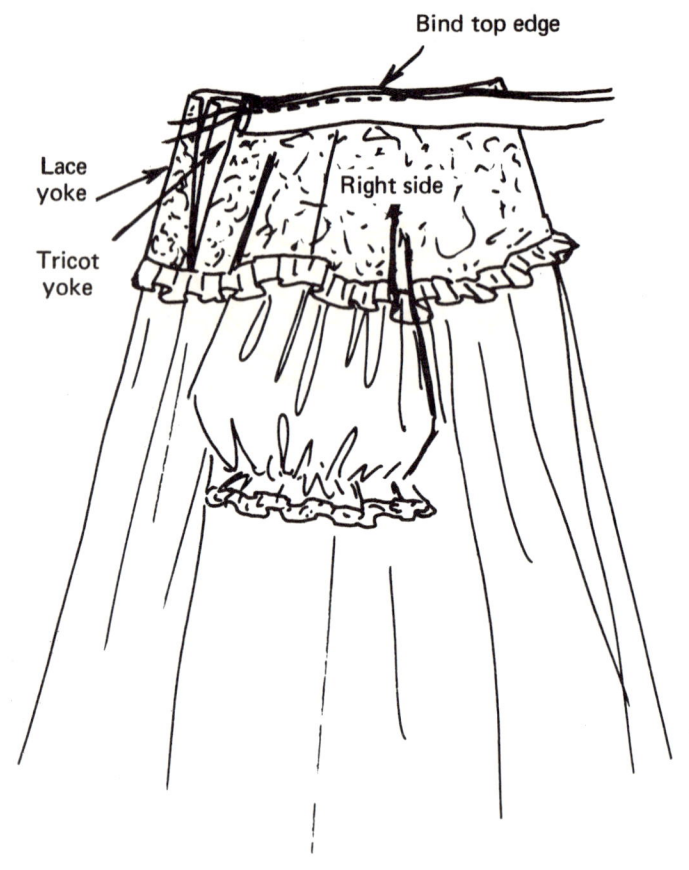

Diagram labels: Bind top edge; Lace yoke; Tricot yoke; Right side

SPAGHETTI STRAPS

Sometimes a tiny, thin, covered string is desired for shoulder straps, tiny bows, button loops, or gathering ties. These can often be bought at lingerie shops, but may be made from tricot, satin, or most any other fabric. Be sure that your chosen material is as washable and durable as the garment material.

Step-by-Step:

1. Cut 1-inch wide strips from the length of any type fabric. These should be cut from the length of the fabric so that they will have as little stretch as possible.
2. Fold in half with right sides together.
3. Attach a piece of string securely at one end and lay it inside along the fold. Allow a portion of the string to hang out

Illustration of
Gown with lace-edged round yoke
and sleeves

the bottom of the tricot or fabric strip.

4. Sew about one-fourth of an inch from the fold with a short length straight stitch. Then trim the seam.

5. Turn the fabric right side out by pulling the string.

Gowns

BUBBLE TRIM

The bubble trim is another decorative touch to a gown or robe. It gives a slightly different effect from the lace, and helps lend variety to your garments.

Step-by-Step:

1. Make a tube of sheer tricot by folding the material in half and making a small, straight-stitched seam down the raw edge side. Then turn the piece inside out so that the seam raw edges are inside the tube.

2. Gather the tube at intervals, even or uneven for a novel effect. It is better to hand gather the tube, rather than use the machine. It should also be attached to the garment by hand.

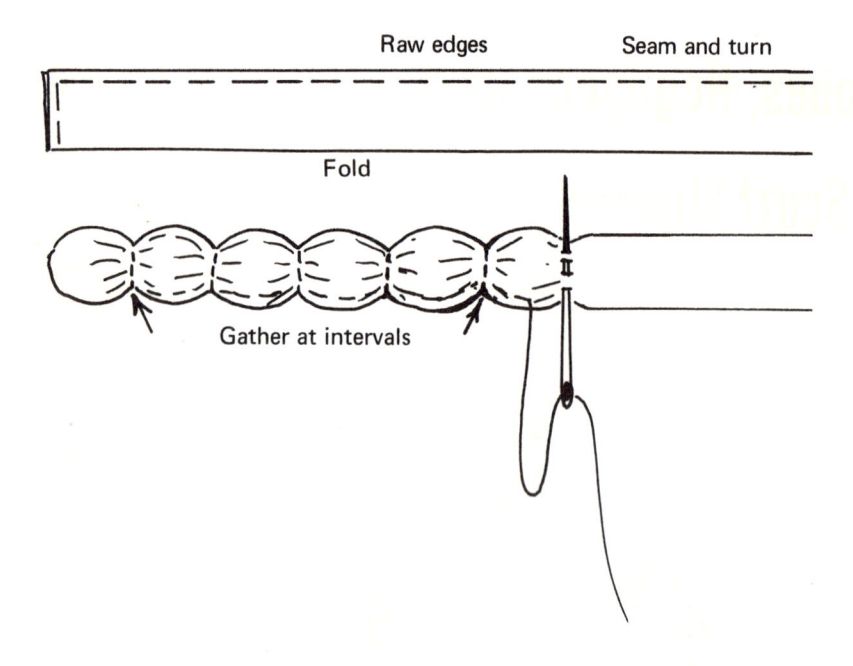

Any style gown may be made by combining any of the methods given in these gown styles. Many gown patterns are available in pattern books. With imagination, the industrious woman may make anything available in the ready-mades or design her own originals.

Robes, Negligees, and Scuff Slippers

Sewing The Unusual

CHAPTER VIII

ROBES, NEGLIGEES, AND SCUFF SLIPPERS

The same patterns used for gowns may be used for robes and negligees simply by cutting open the front and edging the opening with lace. A double-fold binding may be used to edge the front openings, too, if lace is not desired. The double-fold binding should be cut 4 inches wide, instead of the 2 inches used for neck openings on gowns. Many robe patterns are available in pattern books, and the same general sewing instructions apply to robes as any other tricot garment. Facings are not necessary, usually, because lace edging or a double-fold binding is much prettier and easier. Often gown and robe sets are made from the same fabric and the same pattern; merely cut the front open for the robe. The robe should have sleeves, also, whereas the gown may or may not have sleeves. The sleeves should be set in with a straight stitch and overcast with a zigzag. It is suggested that Chapter VIII be read carefully.

Loops for buttons in both tricot and satin may be bought in most lingerie supply stores. Small satin and tricot buttons in most colors are also available, or you may cover your own. If the loops of satin or tricot strings are not available in the right color, make your own by using the spaghetti strap instructions given in Chapter VIII. Buttonholes may be made using a tricot facing and a heavier interfacing. These are quite serviceable, even though the tricot is very stretchy. Just be sure to use a non-stretch interfacing.

Beautiful negligees may be made from regular tricot or sheer. The main difference between a negligee and a robe is that a negligee is fancier, frillier, and more feminine; whereas, the robe is simply a serviceable garment. Negligees are much more fun to make, because it is so easy to zigzag yards and yards of lace onto a beautiful work of art. These beautiful, feminine garments can transform any Cinderella into a fair princess. On the negligees, you should never use buttonholes—they are too plain.

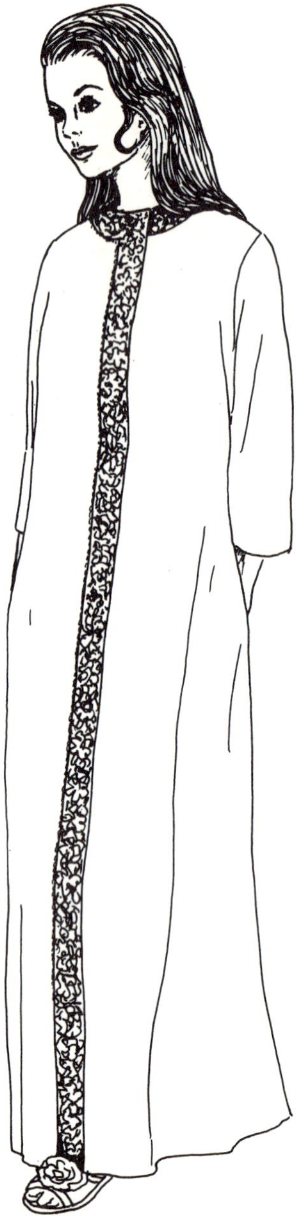

Robes, Negligees, and Scuff Slippers 181

Instead, use satin loops, satin spaghetti string ties, ribbon ties, or snaps covered with flower appliqués. Go to your most exclusive lingerie shop and get ideas; then go home and copy them for pennies. The sheer or tricot pom-pon ruffles are beautiful for edging sleeves, hems, or necklines. These are very inexpensive and easy to make, yet no one will ever imagine that the garment was not professionally made.

POM-PONS AND POM-PON RUFFLES

Materials Needed:
1½-inch wide or 2-inch wide sheer strip binding four or five times the length of the edge to which it is to be attached

Step-by-Step:
1. Purchase the desired width of sheer (usually 1½ inches - 2 inches). Machine-cut sheer tricot is available in lingerie stores and may be purchased by the yard like lace. If it is not available to you, you may cut your own from sheer fabric. Buy four or five times the measurement of the edge to which it is to be attached. Twenty-five yards is usually required for a knee-length negligee with a full skirt and full sleeves if the ruffle is to go around the neck, down the front, around the skirt, and around the sleeves. This sheer is extremely inexpensive, so it will not make the cost of the negligee exorbitant even though quite a few yards are needed.
2. Run a gathering stitch down the exact center of the sheer strip the entire length of the fabric.
3. Gather the fabric very, very tightly.

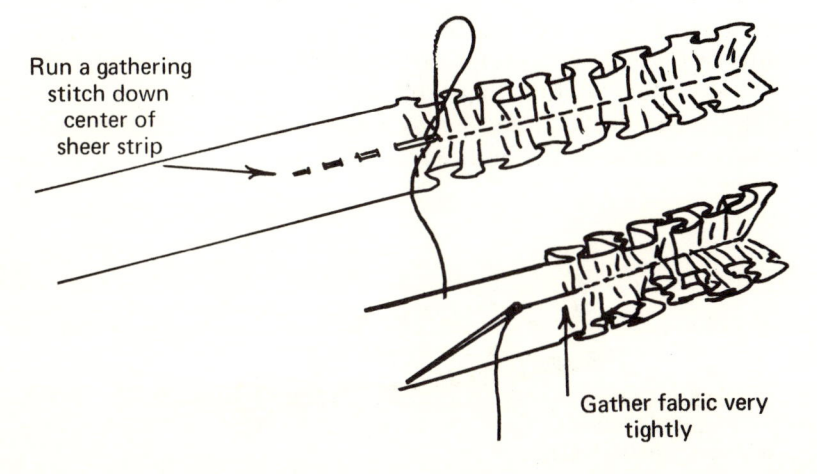

Run a gathering stitch down center of sheer strip

Gather fabric very tightly

4. If a ball-type pom-pon is needed, tie the strings at each end and tack the ball onto the tie ends or wherever needed for decoration.

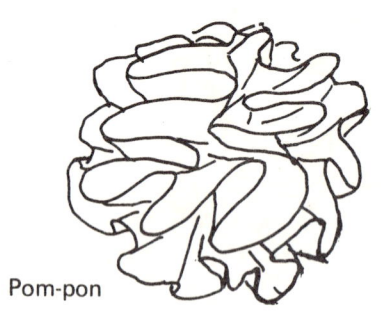

Pom-pon

5. If a pom-pon ruffle is desired, place the pom-pon on the right side of the negligee's edge with the gathered stitch about one-fourth of an inch from the negligee's edge. Straight stitch along the gathering stitch. Be sure that the pom-pon ruffle is not being sewed too close to the fabric edge nor too far up on the garment.

QUILTED NYLON ROBE

Quilted fabric should be cut on the straight grain as any other material. It is better to avoid as many seams as possible; therefore, choose a simple pattern and place the center back seam on the fold of the material so that no seam will be necessary there.

The fiberfill of the fabric must be sealed inside, so overcast the edges of each piece with a zigzag before doing any sewing of seams or darts. If you prefer to slit the darts to cut down on the bulk, slit them at this time and zigzag these raw edges before stitching the darts. If the seams are properly sealed, there will be no separating of the quilting.

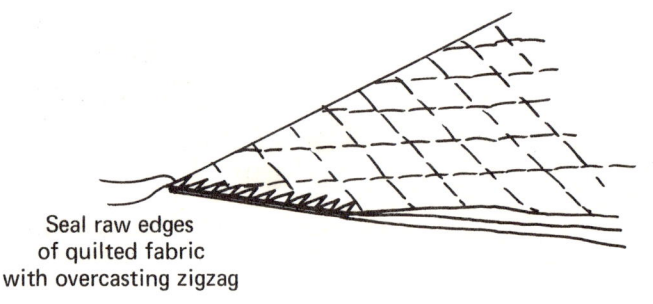

Seal raw edges
of quilted fabric
with overcasting zigzag

Quilted Nylon
Robe

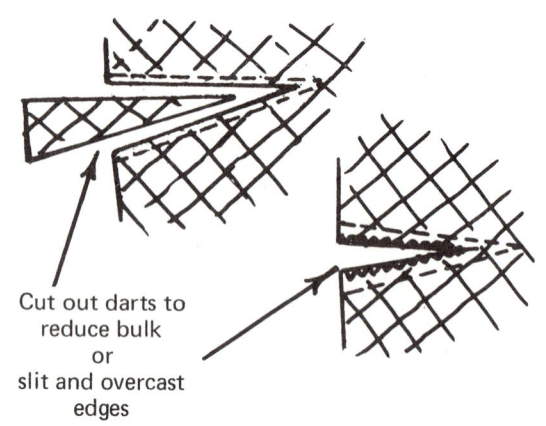

Cut out darts to
reduce bulk
or
slit and overcast
edges

Quilted material should be sewed with a straight stitch and a 5/8-inch seam as you would any other fabric. Because the fabric is bulky, collars and cuffs are not too desirable, but nylon accordian-pleated ruffles or lace ruffles are an excellent decorative replacement.

There are many ways to finish the front edges and the sleeves of a quilted robe. Self-fabric facings may be used with or without a lace edging, but a tricot facing in a matching color is much less bulky. A tricot double-fold binding may also be used to face the front. This is very attractive, non-bulky, and serviceable.

Any type buttonholes may be used on a quilted fabric. If bound buttonholes are used, however, they should be made with a matching color of tricot instead of the quilted fabric. Regular machine-made buttonholes are very successful in this fabric, especially if you stitch around the buttonhole three or more times.

BRUSHED NYLON FLEECE ROBES

The robes made from brushed nylon fleece are warm, lightweight, easy to care for, and easy to sew. These robes may be straight stitched with a 5/8-inch seam or a 1/8-inch seam and overcast with a zigzag. If the 1/8-inch seam is used, it should be considered when cutting the pattern. Usually, by purchasing a size smaller pattern than usual, you can compensate for the 1/8-inch seam, or you can cut closer to the seam instead of following the cutting line.

The instruction sheet of a pattern chosen can be followed explicitly in sewing a robe from the brushed nylon. If button-

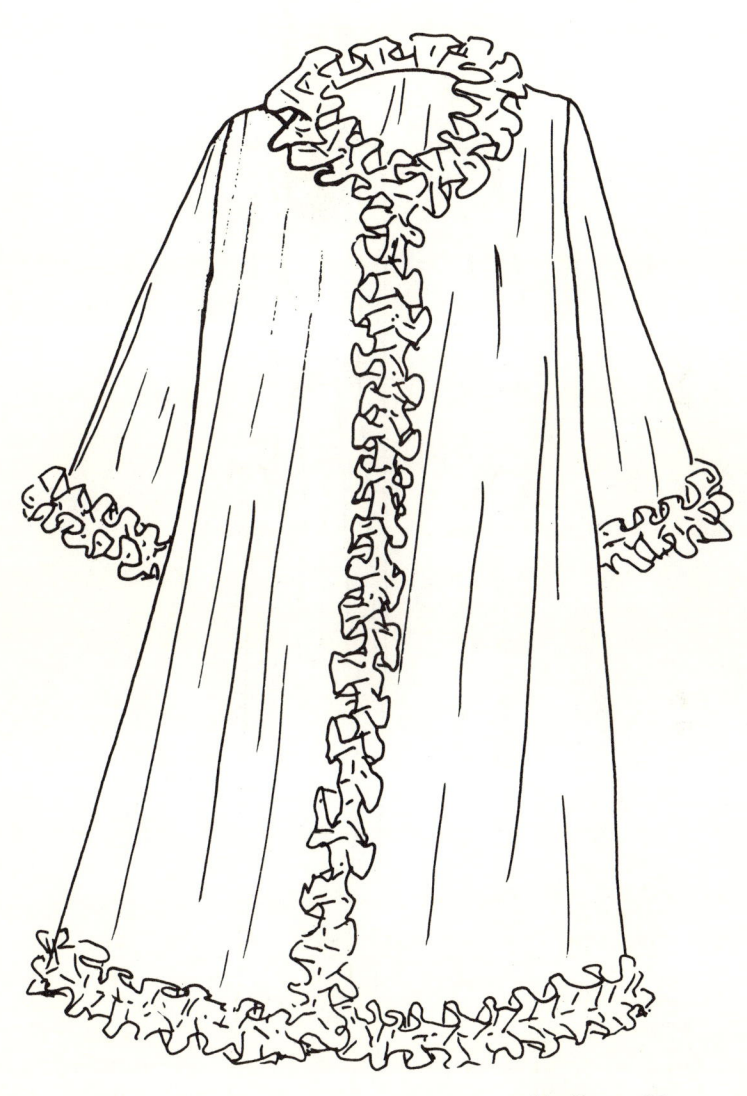

Negligee with pom-pon ruffle

Brushed Nylon Fleece Robe

holes are desired, use a pellon interfacing to give rigidity to the front. Loops may also be used very effectively on this type material. For decoration, try lace or appliqués. These can be very becoming on this type of material and help make an ordinary robe into a lavish creation at little expense.

SCUFF SLIPPERS

Attractive little scuffs are very easy to make, and certainly add much to a gown and robe set. They can be made from tricot scraps left from the other garments, yet help give a very professional look to any set.

Materials Needed:

12-inch x 24-inch strip of tricot, or two 5-inch x 12-inch strips and four 6½-inch x 8-inch strips of tricot
Two 28-inch strips of double fold tricot binding (see Chapter VIII) 2¼ inches wide cut on the stretch of fabric (across the top of fabric)
Two 10-inch strips of double fold tricot binding
Two 5-inch strips of double fold tricot binding
Two 5-inch x 12-inch pieces of vinyl upholstery material or scuff soles, if they are available. Baby puddle pad material or quilted fabric may also be used for soles
12-inch x 24-inch strip of art foam, fiberfill, or other padding
Decorative lace, appliqués, pom-pons, etc., as desired

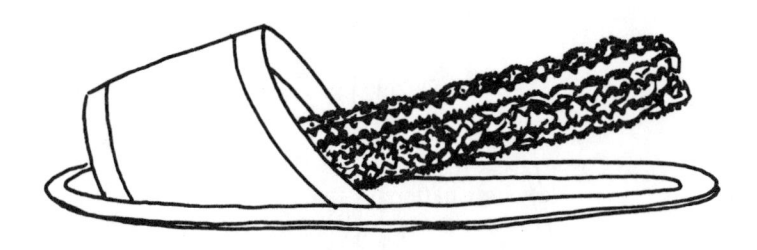

Scuff with elastic sling

Scuff Slipper Pattern

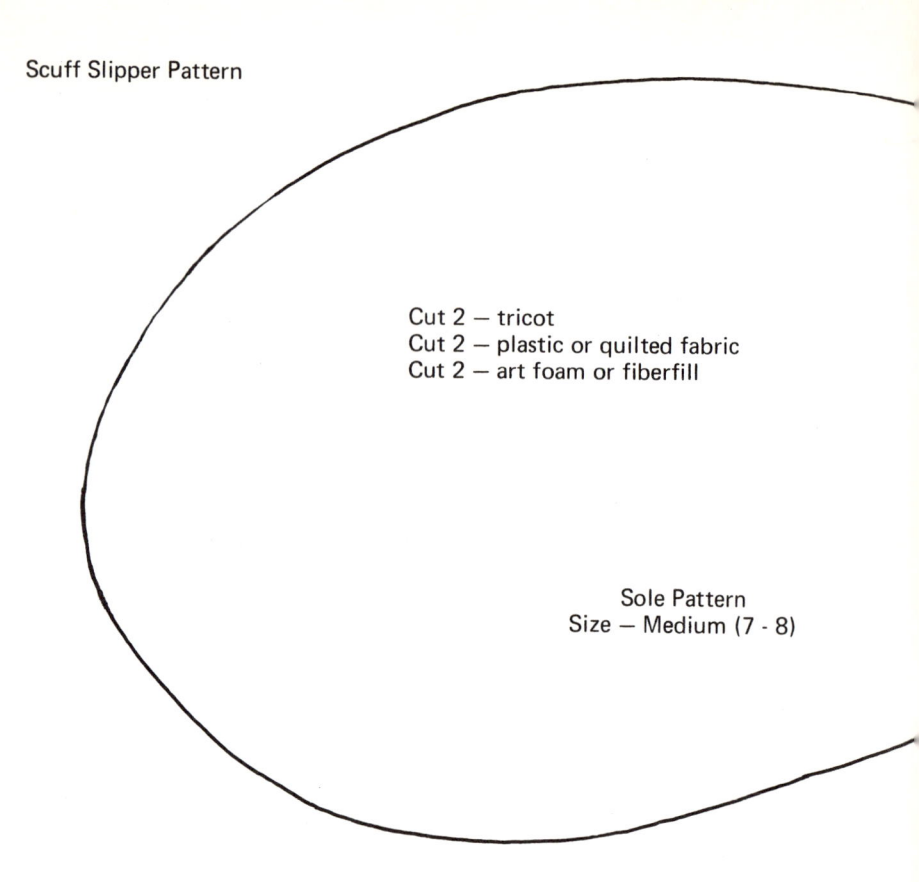

Cut 2 — tricot
Cut 2 — plastic or quilted fabric
Cut 2 — art foam or fiberfill

Sole Pattern
Size — Medium (7 - 8)

Trace pattern on a piece
of tissue paper and tape
sole pieces together for
accurate pattern

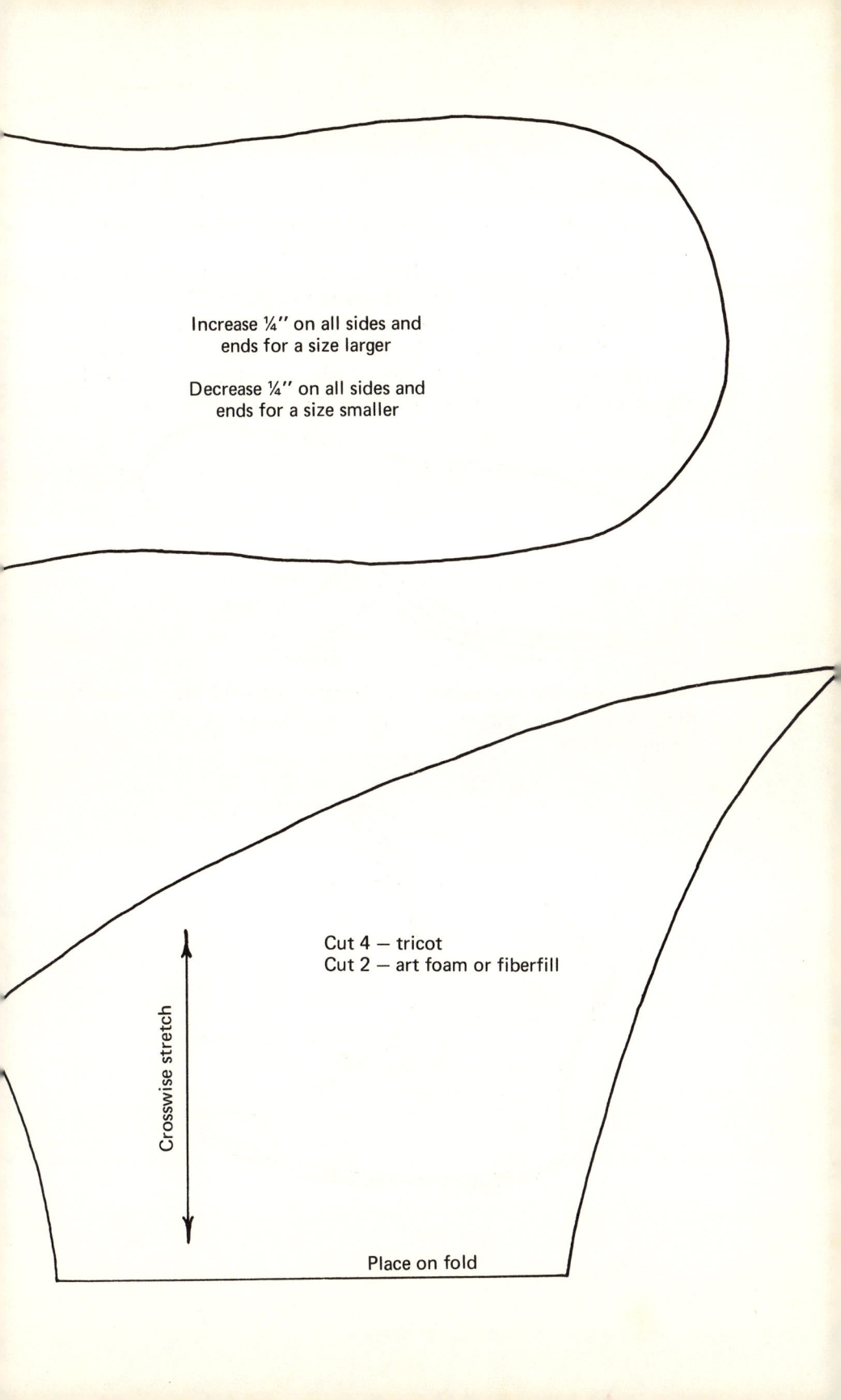

Increase ¼" on all sides and ends for a size larger

Decrease ¼" on all sides and ends for a size smaller

Cut 4 — tricot
Cut 2 — art foam or fiberfill

Crosswise stretch

Place on fold

192   *Sewing The Unusual*

Step-by-Step:

1. Cut all necessary pieces from the proper fabric as listed on the pattern pieces on the previous page.

2. Cut the double-fold binding strips following the instructions given in the gown instructions in Chapter VIII.

3. Place the piece of plastic on the bottom; then sandwich the art foam or fiberfill between the tricot and the plastic bottom piece. Stay stitch these three pieces into position by straight stitching close to the edge all around the sole.

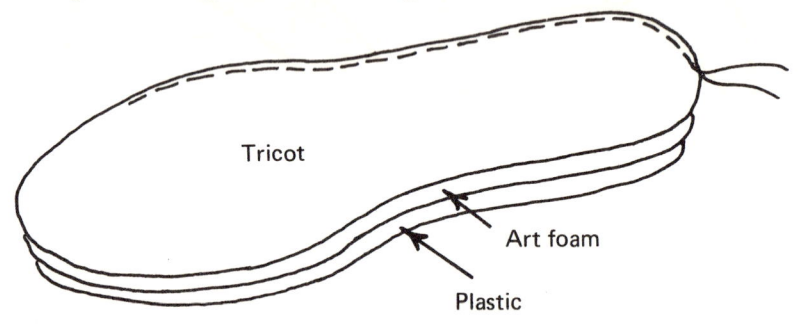

4. Sandwich the instep art foam or fiberfill piece between two instep tricot pieces and stay stitch along the edges to hold them in place.

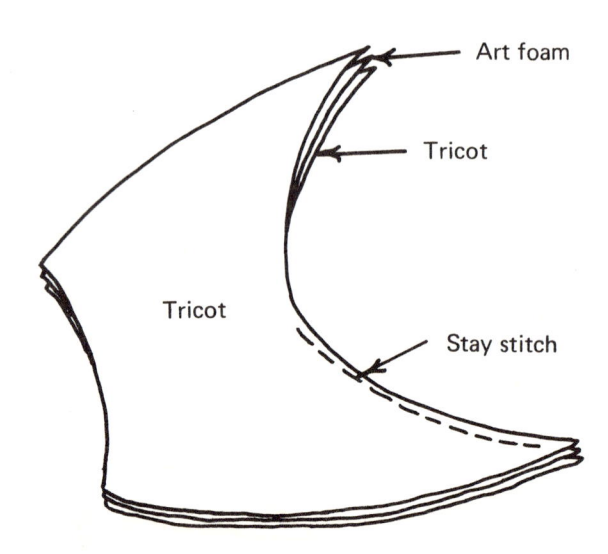

Robes, Negligees, and Scuff Slippers

5. Zigzag any lace, appliqués, or other decorations onto the instep. Roses or other decorations that are applied by hand should be applied later.

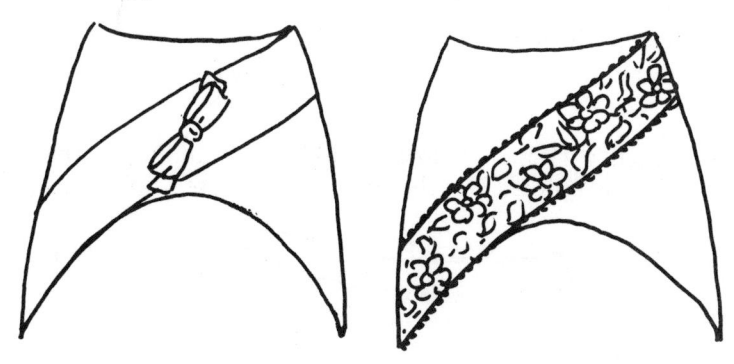

6. Fold the 5-inch strip of double-fold binding in half wrong sides together so that it will be 1 inch wide, approximately. Place the double-fold binding on the top section of the instep on the right side of the piece with the raw edges together. Straight stitch this binding across the toe section edge with a 1/8-inch seam. Trim this seam very close; then turn the binding to the wrong side of the instep until the fold is just covering the line of stitching.

7. Straight stitch this folded edge of the double-fold binding in place by sewing from the right side in the well of the seam. (See Chapter VIII)

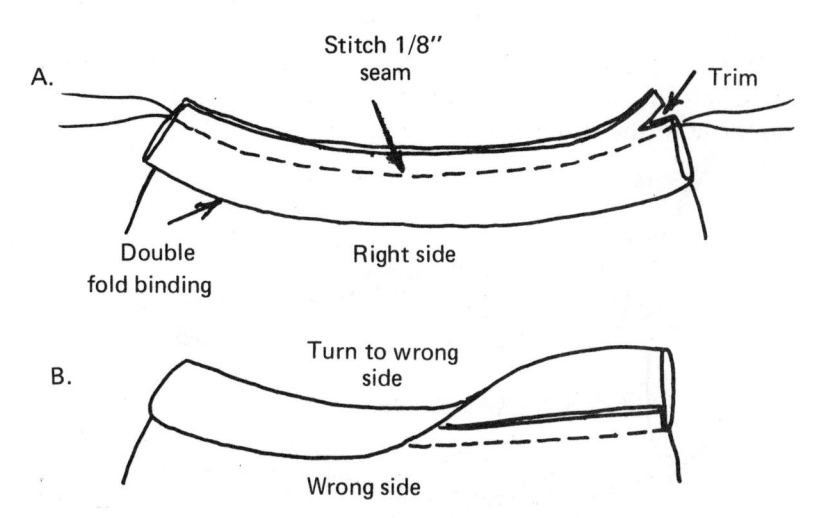

Sewing The Unusual

C.

Right Side

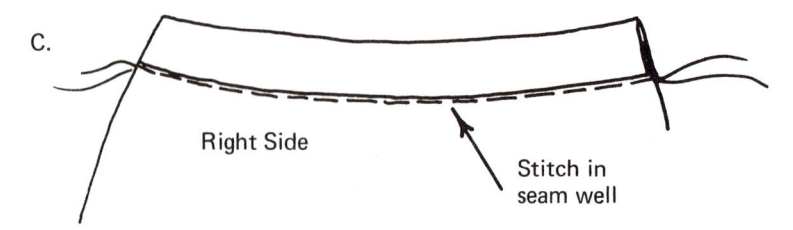

Stitch in seam well

8. Attach a 10-inch strip of double-fold binding to the top edge of the instep piece by the same method used on the toe.

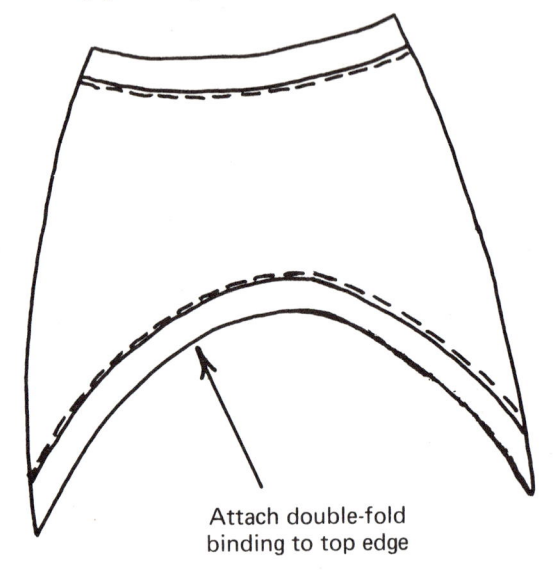

Attach double-fold binding to top edge

9. Place the instep piece on the sole in the correct position and stitch in place with a 1/8-inch seam. Then trim this seam very close to the stitches in a smooth line.

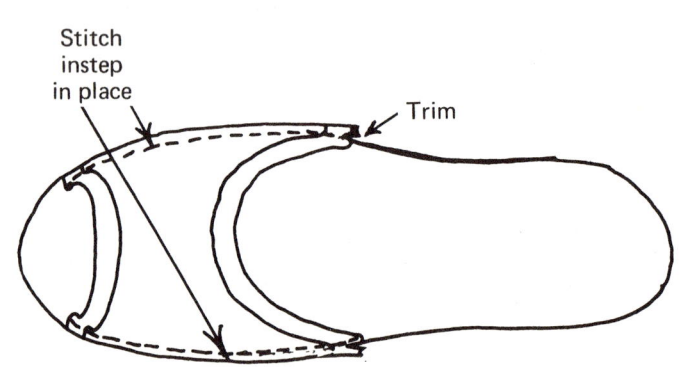

Stitch instep in place

Trim

Robes, Negligees, and Scuff Slippers

10. Finish the sole edges with a double-fold binding by placing the doubled binding on the bottom of the sole with the raw edges together. With the seam beginning at the inside instep, stitch a 1/8-inch seam all the way around the sole. Trim this seam smooth. Then turn the folded edge of the binding over the raw edges and top stitch the binding in place by sewing very close to the folded edge on the top of the shoe sole.

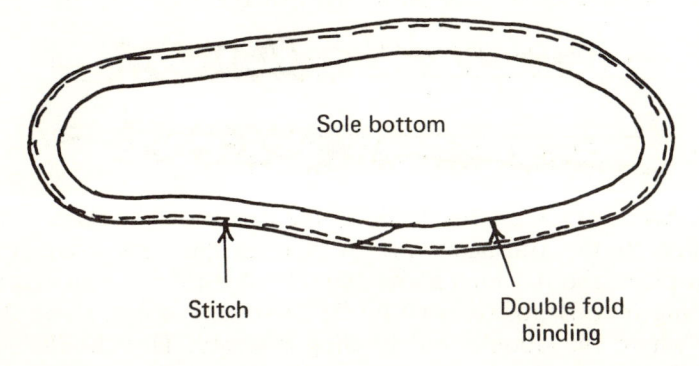

Sole bottom

Stitch   Double fold binding

11. If you desire a rose or other large ornament that should be handsewn or tacked onto the scuff, stitch this securely at this time.

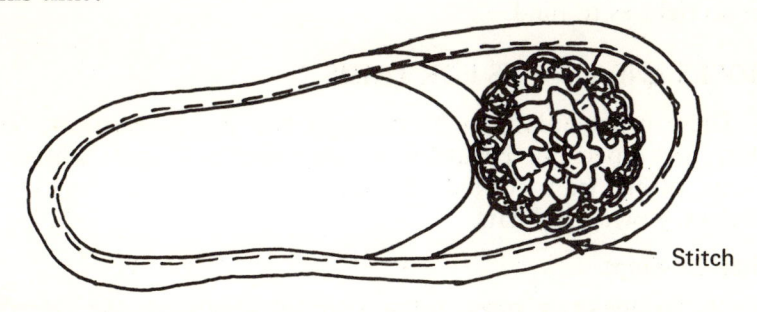

Stitch

12. Some people have difficulty keeping the little scuffs on their feet, or do not like the feel of the sole flip-flopping as they walk. If you like the scuffs with an elastic sling going around the heel, simply get a piece of ½-inch wide elastic and a piece of ¾-inch wide lace. Measure the elastic to go from the scuff instep edge, about an inch from the sole, around the heel to the same point on the other side of the instep piece. Stretch the elastic slightly so that it will fit snugly and hold the scuff in place, but will not bind. Cut the lace 1 inch longer than the measurement from the point it is to be attached around the heel to the other

196   Sewing The Unusual

point where it will be attached. Then center the elastic on the wrong side of the lace, and zigzag the elastic onto the lace by allowing the needle to overcast the edge of the elastic onto the lace and then swing back onto the elastic. Be sure to stretch the elastic until it is the same length as the lace. This will gather the lace very attractively. The stitches at either end of the zigzag seams should be locked by setting the stitch length on "0" for a couple of stitches. Zigzag both edges of the elastic to the lace.

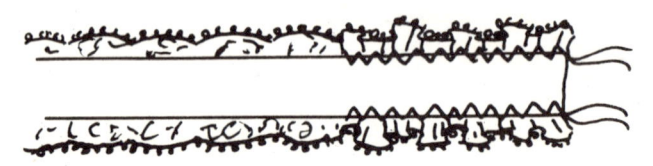

13. After attaching the elastic to the lace, tack the elastic and the lace to the finished scuff by placing the ends inside the instep piece about 1 inch above the sole. Another way to attach the sling in this position would be to straight stitch along the seam where the double-fold binding is sewed. This should not show if you are very careful to sew directly over the seam in the well of the double-fold binding. This sling is very comfortable, because the elastic is all that is touching the foot. It should not be so tight as to bind.

ROSES AND LEAVES FOR TRIMS

These ornaments may be used on any sort of garment, but they are especially beautiful on negligees and scuff slippers. They often trim formal dresses, wedding dresses, cocktail dresses, gowns, and hats.

Step-by-Step:

1. To make a rose, cut a strip of tricot on the stretch (crosswise of the fabric) or a piece of satin on the bias. For a 1½-inch deep rose, cut the strip 3¼ inches wide.

2. Fold the strip in half with the wrong sides together. Then hand gather this folded strip along the raw edges for several stitches. Next, pull the thread tight and secure; this makes the center for the rose. Make a few more stitches, then pull to gather and secure to the center of the rose. Continue around the center in this way until the rose is as large as you desire. The length of the strips will depend upon the size of the rose you desire.

Fold

Gather and pull thread tight

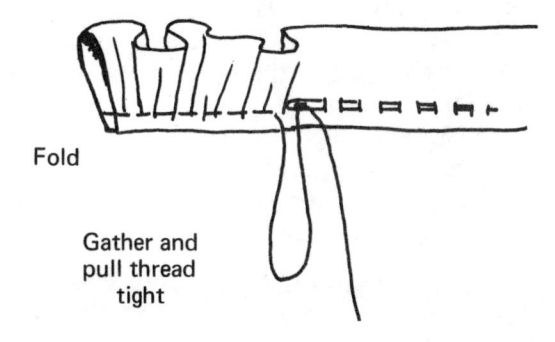

3. To make the rose show up better, gather a piece of lace around the bottom of the rose. The lace is usually more flattened out and makes a pretty background or cradle for the rose.

4. To make a leaf, use a smaller strip of tricot or satin. Fold the strip to make a triangle. Then make a few tiny gathering stitches at the base of the triangle and pull them slightly. Secure the base of the triangle in this gathered position. The leaves should correspond in size to the rose.

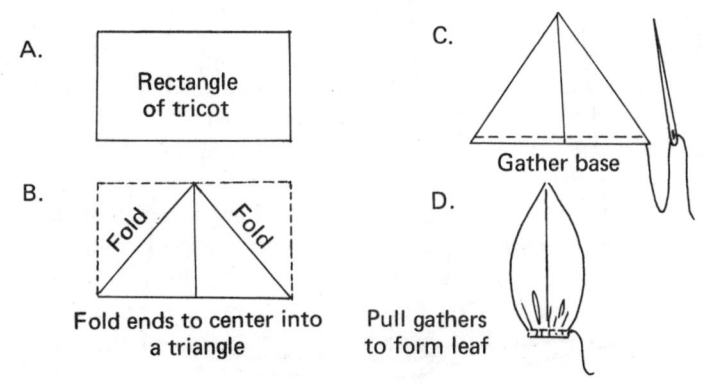

A. Rectangle of tricot

B. Fold ends to center into a triangle

C. Gather base

D. Pull gathers to form leaf

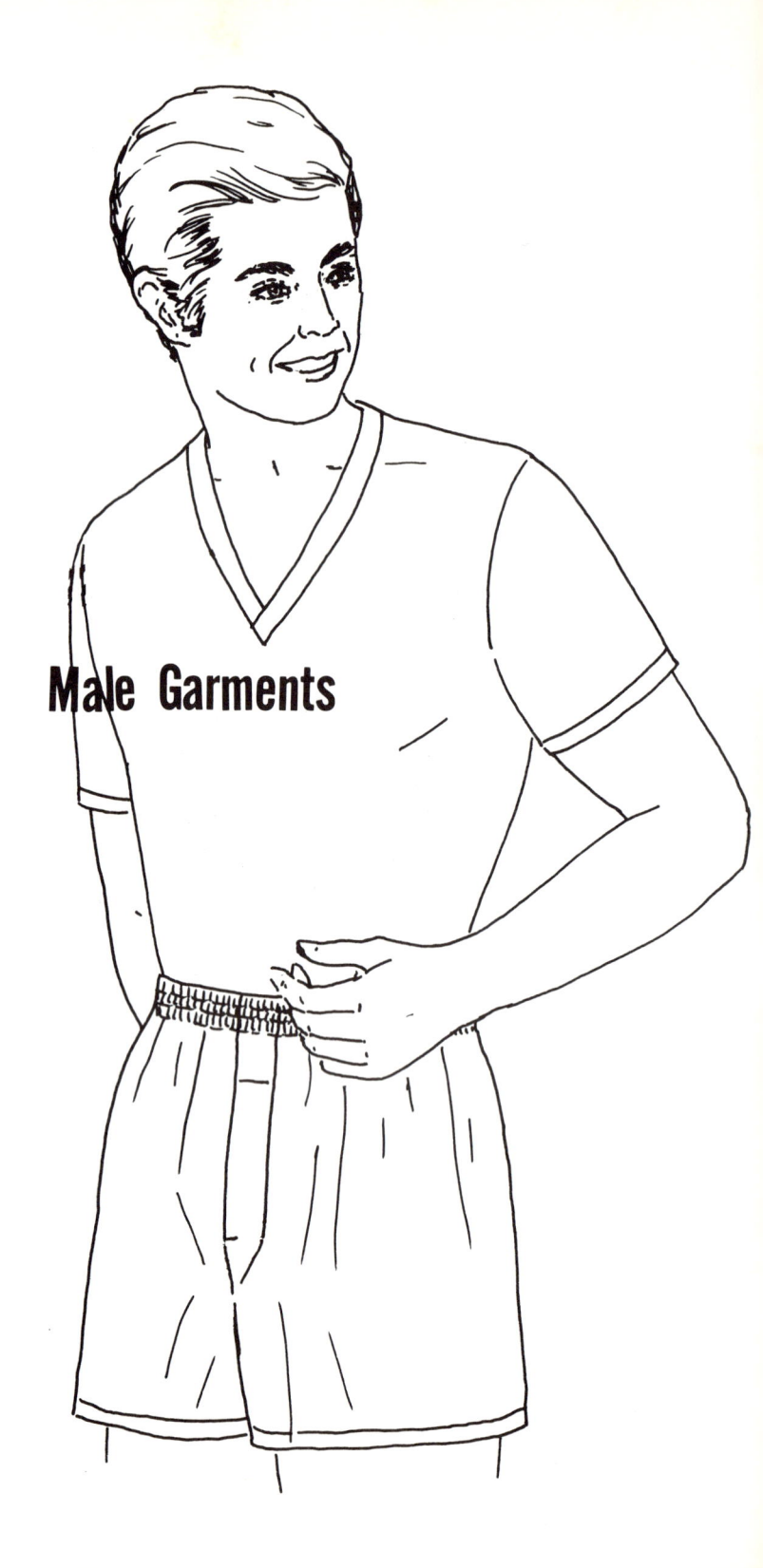

Male Garments

CHAPTER IX

MALE GARMENTS

Although tricot is more widely used in women's garments, it is just as practical and versatile for men's things. Nylon tricot underwear for men is sold in only the most exclusive stores at extremely high prices. They are certainly worth more, however, because they outlast cotton garments threefold. By sewing the garments yourself, you can make the tricot underwear for less than the cost of ready-made cotton garments.

Knit shirts have always been popular with males and females alike, and now they can be sewed at home at a fraction of the cost of the ready-mades. Design your own; make them long-sleeved or short. Pick out an expensive one in your local men's shop, then copy it. Sleeve ribbing may be purchased at most department stores, or you may make the popular three-quarter sleeve with a hemmed edge. The newly revived tank-top, which is the latest in knit shirts, is very easily made. Three tank-tops may be made for the price of one ready-made. In this chapter you will find many garments for males, both large and small, and the possibilities for other garments are limitless.

T-SHIRTS OR KNIT SHIRTS WITH A ROUND NECK

Materials Needed:

1 yard of 108-inch nylon tricot will make one shirt and a pair of shorts in most sizes.

Step-by-Step:

1. Obtain a pattern by either purchasing a sport shirt pattern or by cutting up an old T-shirt. If you cut the old T-shirt carefully at the seams, it will not be necessary to make a seam allowance when making the pattern. Place the shirt pieces on a piece of paper, flatten them carefully, and pin them to the paper. Then cut a pattern for a permanent T-shirt pattern.

T-shirt to knit shirts with a round neck

2. Place the pattern on the straight of the tricot fabric, and cut out the garment.

3. Next, cut a 4-inch wide strip of tricot across the fabric (the stretchy way) for a neck binding.

4. Straight stitch a 1/8-inch seam across one shoulder; then overcast this seam with a wide zigzag set on a short stitch length.

Straight stitch then overcast

5. Fold the 4-inch neck binding in half, and place it on the right side of the fabric on the neck at the shoulder with the raw edges together and the folded binding edge away from the neck.

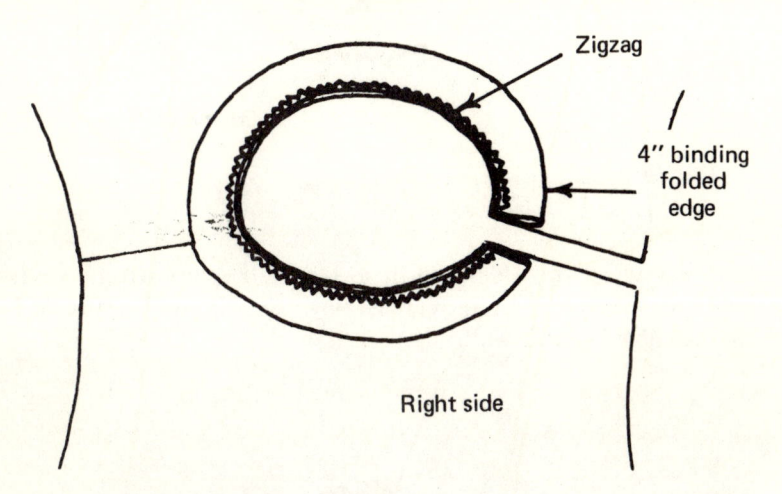

6. Stitch this binding to the neck with a medium width zigzag and a regular stitch length.

7. Sew the other shoulder seam and binding ends together in the same manner as the first shoulder seam.

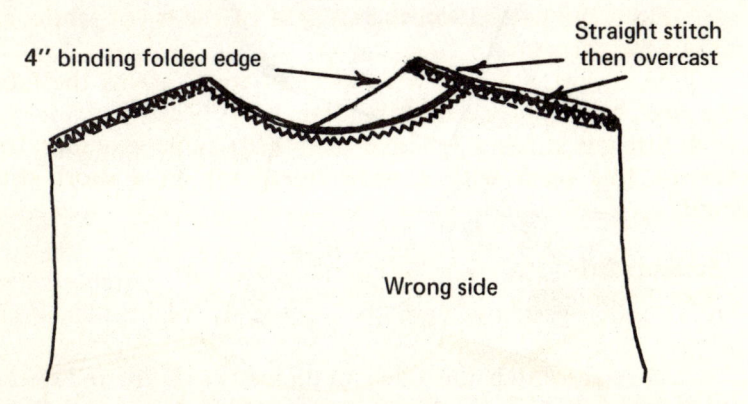

8. Turn the folded edge of the binding to the wrong side, and stitch it to the top of the shirt with a wide zigzag and a regular stitch length. Stitch this from the right side of the garment; let the needle go into the binding, then overcast the binding edge and go into the garment.

Folded binding edge turned to wrong side

Overcast

Right side

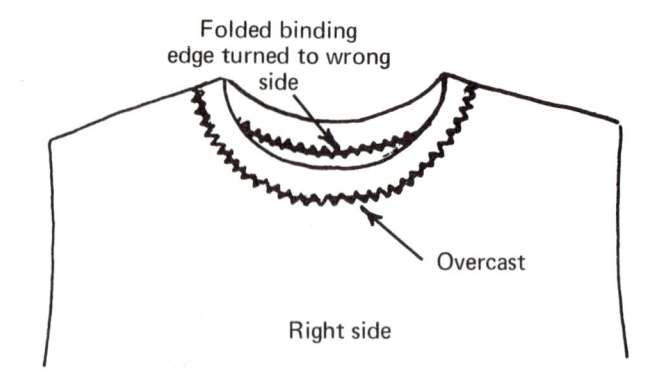

9. Sew in the sleeve with a 1/8-inch seam stitched with a straight stitch and then overcast with the zigzag. Be sure to lock all zigzagged seams well.

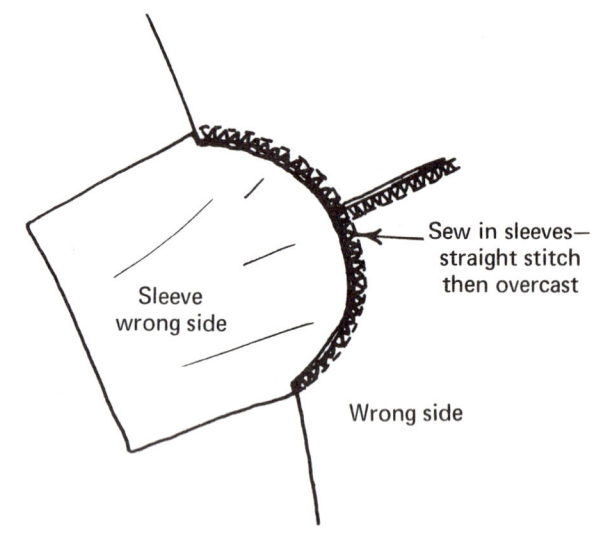

Sleeve wrong side

Sew in sleeves— straight stitch then overcast

Wrong side

10. Stretching the fabric slightly so that the stitches will not break under pressure, hem the sleeves with a regular straight stitch.

11. Straight stitch the side and underarm seams, and overcast them with a zigzag.

12. Hem the shirt bottom in the same manner as the sleeves.

13. This shirt may be used as an undershirt or a knit outer garment. Any color fabric may be used, and the heavier, brush-type nylon tricots are nice for winter wear.

T-SHIRTS WITH A V-NECK

Materials Needed:

1 yard of 108-inch nylon tricot will make two shirts in smaller sizes

2 yards of 108-inch tricot will make three shirts in large sizes

T-shirts with V-neck

Step-by-Step:

1. Follow Steps 1 and 2 of the instructions for a T-shirt with a round neck, except cut the front neck opening into a V.

2. Straight stitch a 1/8-inch seam across each shoulder; then overcast these seams with a wide zigzag set on a short stitch length.

3. Sew in the sleeve with a 1/8-inch seam stitched with a straight stitch, and then overcast with a zigzag. Be sure to lock all zigzagged seams well.

4. Cut a 2-inch wide strip of tricot across the fabric (the stretchy way) for a neck binding.

5. Fold the 2-inch neck binding in half lengthwise, and place it on the right side of the fabric on the neck with the end at the V and the raw edges together. The folded binding edge will be away from the neck.

6. Straight stitch the binding to the neck with a 1/8-inch seam.

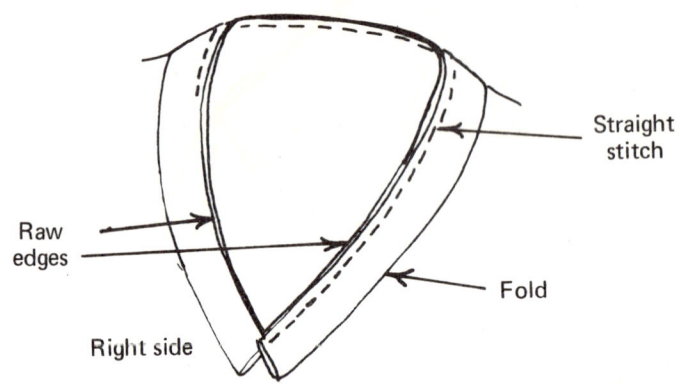

7. At the V, straight stitch the raw edges of the ends into the seam on the other side of the V. One binding edge will be stitched into each side of the V. Stitch the binding edges into the opposite edge seam as they would naturally go; do not stretch or pull the binding.

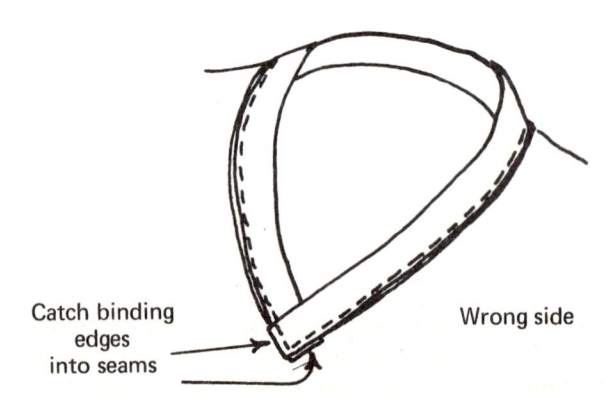

8. Overcast the binding edge seam with a zigzag. Be sure to lock the seam at the beginning and the end with a couple of stitches sewed with a "0" stitch length. Since the ends of the binding are tucked into the V on the opposite side, the binding will stand up so that the seam attaching it to the shirt will not show.

Male Garments

Overcasting zigzag

Right side

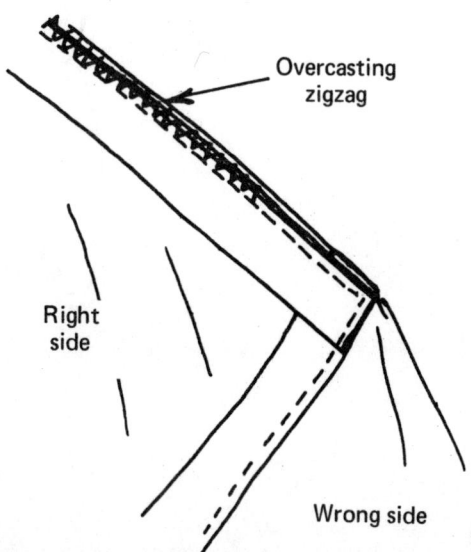

Wrong side

9. Stretching the fabric slightly so that the stitches will not break under pressure, hem the sleeves with a regular straight stitch.

10. Straight stitch the side and underarm seams, and overcast them with a zigzag.

11. Hem the shirt bottom in the same manner as the sleeves.

12. This method of making a V-neck may be used in any type garment—pajamas, dresses, bathing suits, shells, and many others. It is much easier to apply a V-neck in this manner than any other, and the results are just as good.

SLEEVELESS UNDERSHIRT

Materials Needed:

1 yard of 108-inch tricot will make two shirts

Step-by-Step:

1. Follow Steps 1 through 8 of the T-shirt instructions given previously (round-neck type). Cut more 4-inch binding so that you will have enough for the armholes as well as the neck.

2. Sew the armhole bindings in the same manner as the neck binding.

3. Next, straight stitch the side seams; then overcast them with a zigzag.

4. These shirts are excellent for undershirts or summer sport shirts.

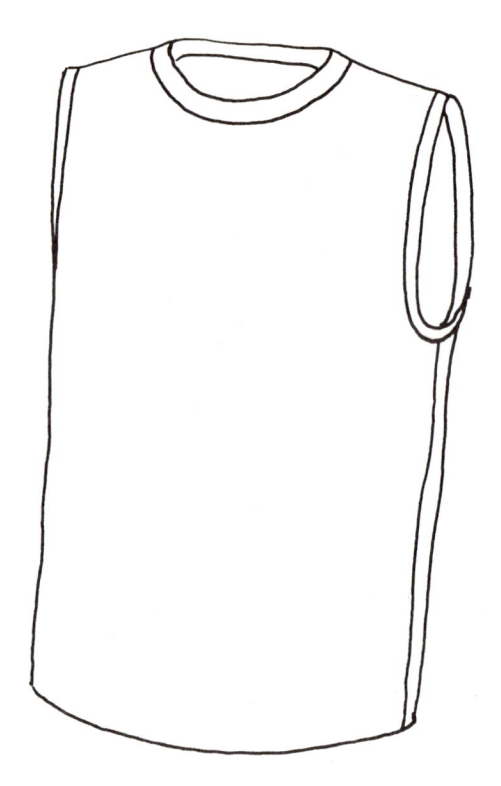

VEST-TYPE UNDERSHIRT OR TANK-TOP

Materials Needed:

1 yard of 108-inch wide fabric will make three undershirts

Step-by-Step:

1. Cut a pattern from an old undershirt. Then cut the fabric on the straight of the material.
2. Straight stitch one shoulder seam, and overcast the seam with a zigzag.
3. Cut a 3½-inch wide strip of tricot across the fabric (on the stretch) for neck and sleeve bindings.
4. Fold the binding strip in half, and place it on the garment right side at the neck with the raw edges together and the folded edge away from the neck. Beginning at the unsewed shoulder seam, zigzag the binding to the garment neck with a 1/8-inch seam.
5. Sew the other shoulder seam and neck binding ends together with a zigzag.

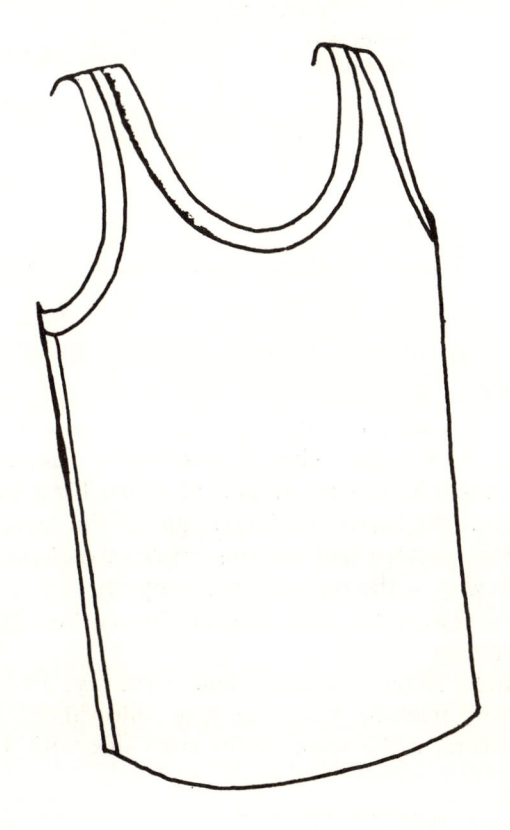

6. Bind the armholes in the same manner as the neck.

7. Straight stitch the side seams; then overcast them with a zigzag.

8. Stretching the fabric slightly so that the threads will not break easily, hem the bottom of the undershirt with a straight stitch.

BOXER UNDERSHORTS

Materials Needed:

Three-fourths of a yard of 108-inch wide nylon tricot (will make two pairs in smaller sizes)

Waist elastic enough for the waist measurement minus 1½ inches

Pattern (either a boxer shorts pattern or shorty pajamas pattern)

208 *Sewing The Unusual*

Right side fly facing

Front and side back

Side

Cut 2

Double seat or back panel

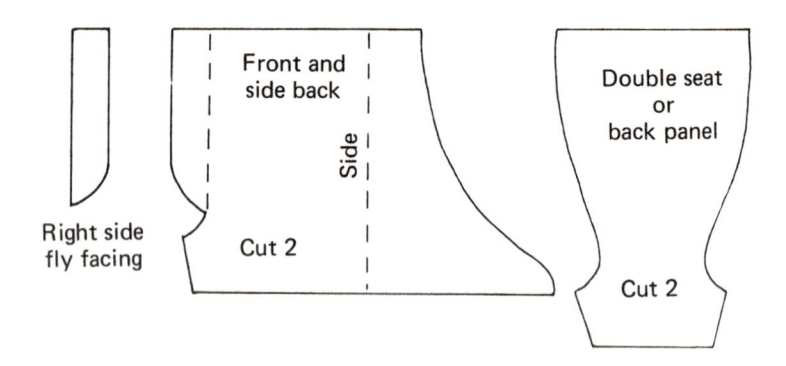

Cut 2

Step-by-Step:

1. Choose a pattern with a double panel in the back, instead of a center back seam. This is much more comfortable. If no pattern is available, use an old pair of shorts for a pattern.

2. Cut out the fabric on the straight of the material.

3. Follow pattern instructions, or construct the undershorts in the same way as the pair you are copying.

4. Begin sewing the shorts on the fly section. This should be straight stitched.

5. Straight stitch the seam below the fly. Then flatten the seam on the machine with the seam allowances going to the right, and overcast the seam on the right side with a zigzag.

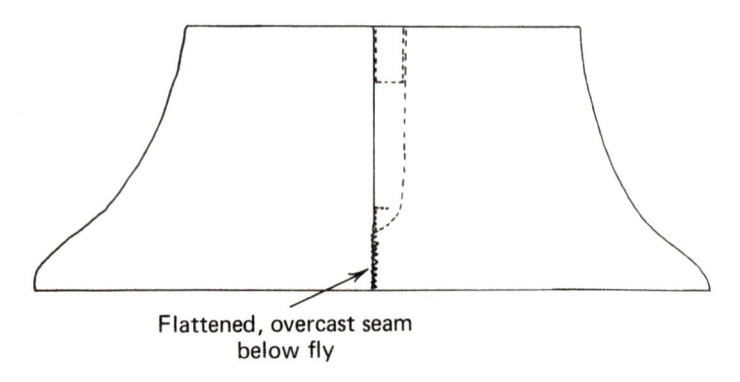

Flattened, overcast seam below fly

6. Sandwich the front-sideback panel between the right sides of the back panels, and straight stitch them in this position. Then stitch with a medium zigzag and a fine stitch length close to the straight-stitched seam on the seam allowance to reinforce the seam and reduce the bulk.

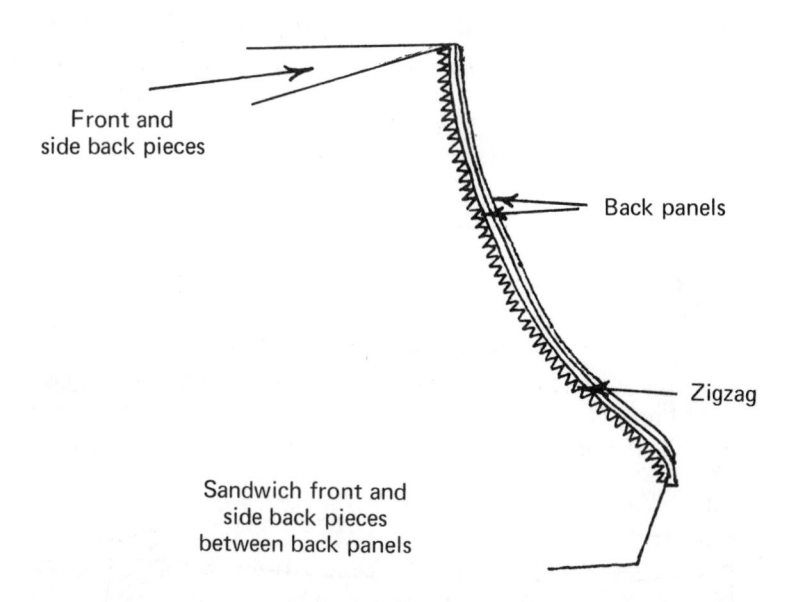

Male Garments

Diagram labels: Front and side back pieces; Back panels; Zigzag; Sandwich front and side back pieces between back panels

    7. Sandwich the other front and side back panel between the right sides of the back panels, and straight stitch into position as before. Then finish the seam in the method used on the other back panel seam.

    8. Turn the shorts right side out. The raw edges of the double-seat seams should be enclosed between the two seat pieces.

    9. Notch the center of the back panels at the crotch.

    10. Match the crotch seam with the notch on the back panel, and position the right sides of the front and back together. Straight stitch this stride seam, and then overcast it with a zigzag.

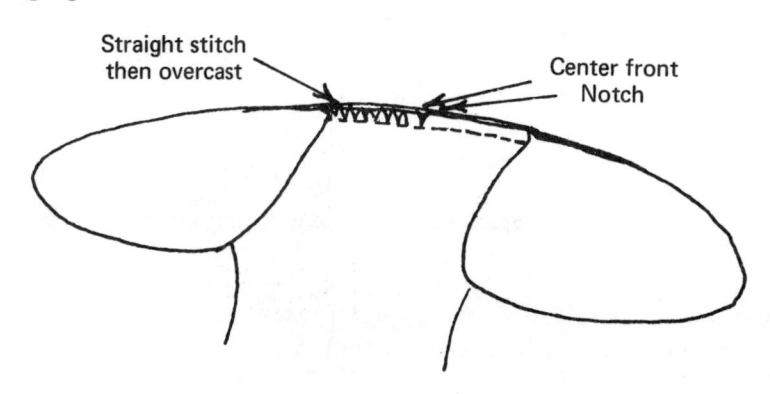

Diagram labels: Straight stitch then overcast; Center front Notch

210   *Sewing The Unusual*

11. Make a 1-inch hem on the legs with a straight stitch. If the machine skips stitches, place a narrow piece of sheer tricot (may be bought at lingerie shops in narrow strips) inside the tucked under part, and sew through this.

12. Join the elastic and quarter it. Mark the quarter marks with pins.

13. Quarter the shorts at the waist; then mark the sides, center front and center back.

14. Match the elastic quarter marks to the shorts quarter marks.

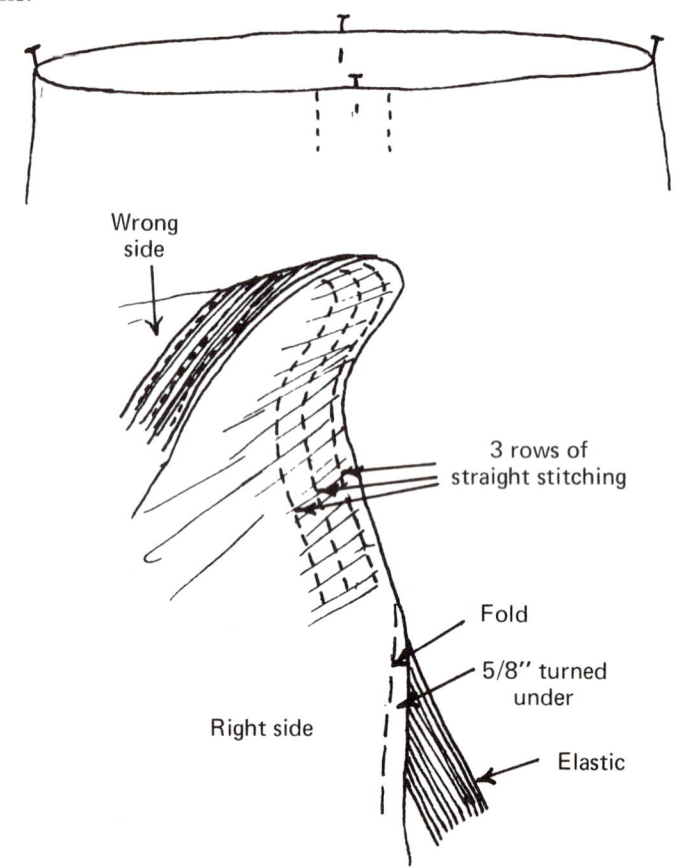

Wrong side

3 rows of straight stitching

Fold

5/8" turned under

Right side

Elastic

15. Turn the shorts inside out, and place the elastic against the machine. Place the wrong side of the shorts against the elastic, and turn the raw top edge under about five-eighths of an inch. Stretching the elastic to match the quarter marks, straight stitch the shorts to the elastic at the top edge. Then straight stitch the elastic to the shorts at the middle and bottom edge.

JOCKEY SHORTS

Materials Needed:

One-half yard of nylon tricot in the 108-inch width will make two pairs.
Waist elastic sufficient for the waist measurement minus 1½ inches

Jockey Shorts

Sewing The Unusual

Step-by-Step:

1. Cut up an old pair of jockey shorts in the correct size to use for a pattern.

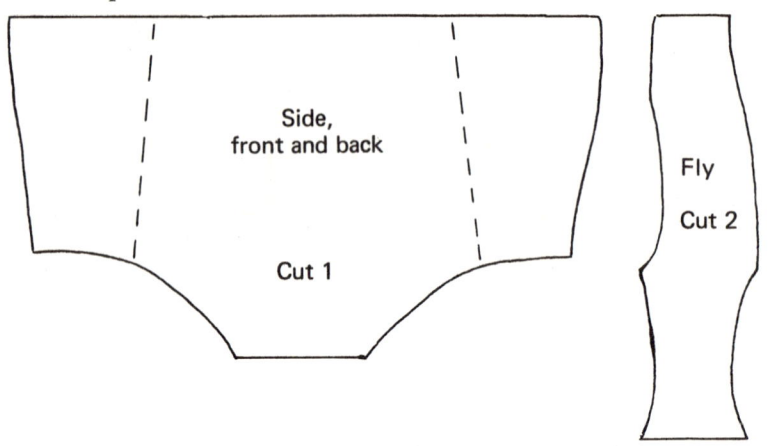

Side, front and back — Cut 1

Fly — Cut 2

2. Construct the shorts in the same manner as the pair being used as a pattern.

3. Cut a 2-inch wide strip 12 inches long across the fabric (stretchy way) for the fly facings. Cut a 3-inch strip 55 inches long for the leg facings (across the top of the fabric, also).

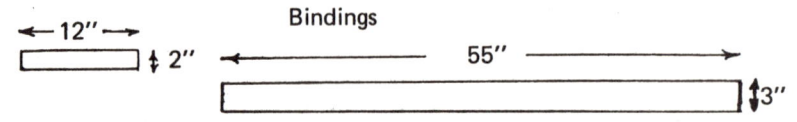

Bindings — 12" × 2"; 55" × 3"

4. Fold the 2-inch binding in half, and place the raw edges against the right side of the fly opening raw edge. Straight stitch the binding in this position with a ¼-inch seam; then flatten the binding away from the garment, and fold the raw edges of the seam toward the binding.

5. Fold the folded edge of the binding over the raw seam edges to the wrong side of the garment. Hold the binding tightly so that the folded edge will extend slightly below the first seam.

6. From the right side of the garment, straight stitch in the crack or well of the first binding seam very close to the binding right side, but do not sew upon the right side of the binding. This seam will secure the binding to the wrong side of the garment but will be attractive on the right side, also. For more details on applying the double-fold binding, see Chapter VIII.

Male Garments

7. Apply the 2-inch double-fold binding to all edges of the fly opening.

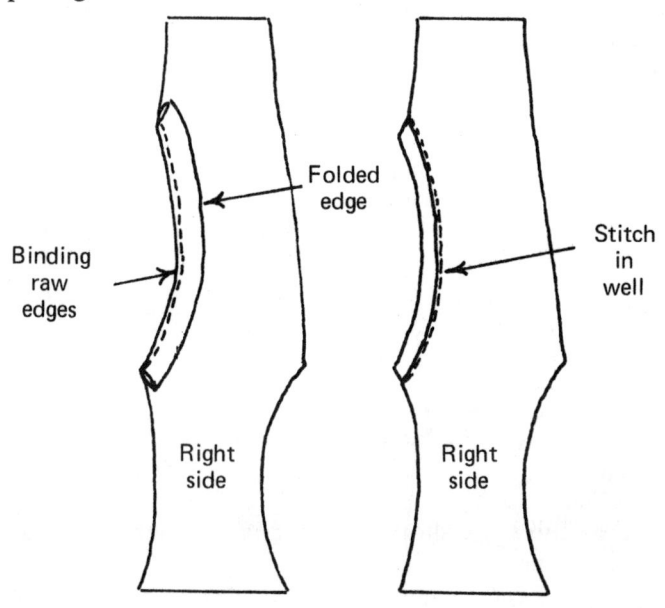

8. Lap the left fly over the right one, and stay stitch together on the outside edges.

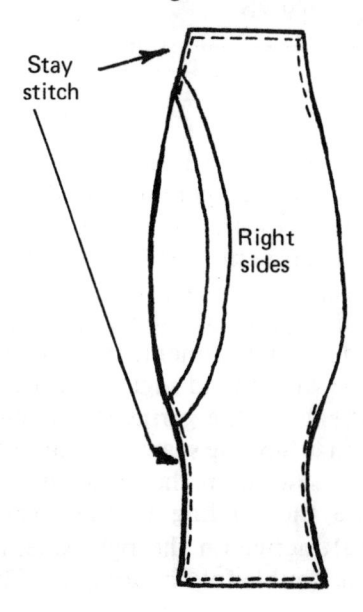

9. Sew the fly front crotch seam to the back crotch with a straight stitch. Then overcast the seam with a zigzag.

10. Sew the fly side seams to the side-back panel in the same manner.

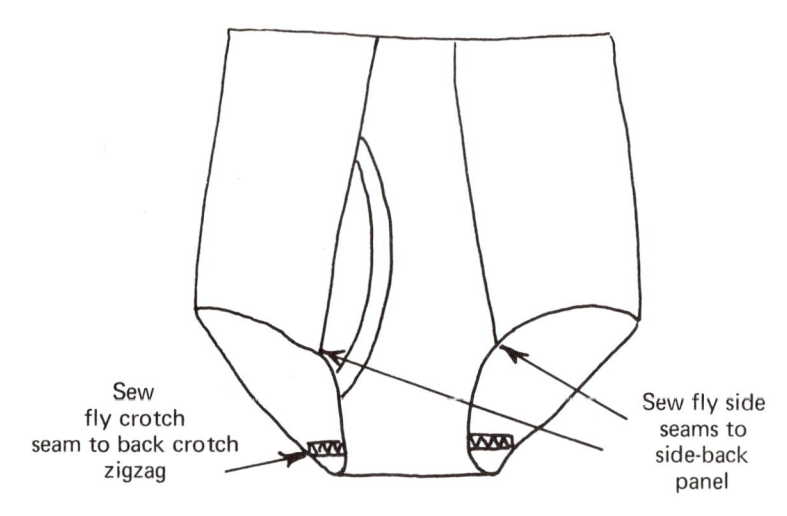

Sew fly crotch seam to back crotch zigzag

Sew fly side seams to side-back panel

11. Fold the 3-inch leg binding in half, and place it on the right side of the fabric on the leg at the front-back seam. With the raw edges together and the folded binding edge away from the leg opening, stitch the binding in place with a medium width zigzag and a regular stitch length.

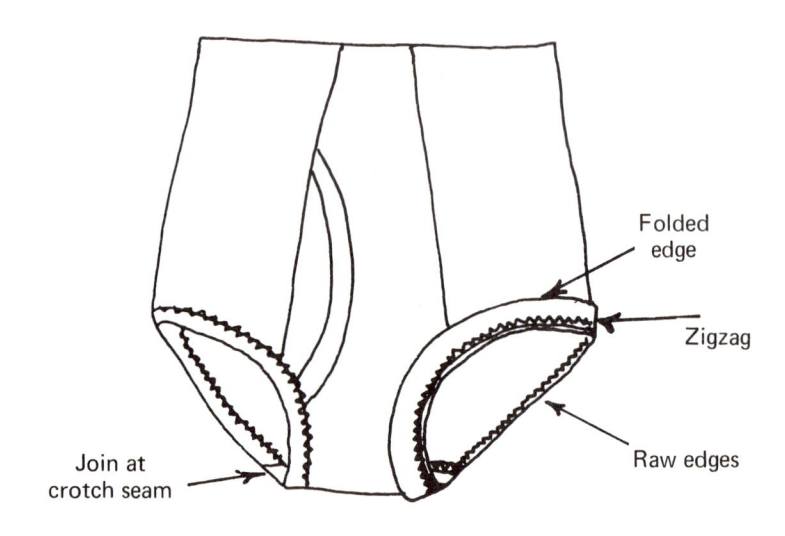

Folded edge

Zigzag

Raw edges

Join at crotch seam

Male Garments 215

12. Straight stitch the binding ends together at the crotch seam.

13. Turn the folded edge of the binding to the wrong side, and stitch it to the leg of the shorts with a wide zigzag and a regular stitch length. Stitch this from the right side of the garment, and let the needle go into the binding; then overcast the binding edge and go into the garment.

14. Bind the other leg in the same manner.

15. Apply the elastic to the top by following Steps 12, 13, 14, and 15 of the boxer shorts instructions given previously in this chapter.

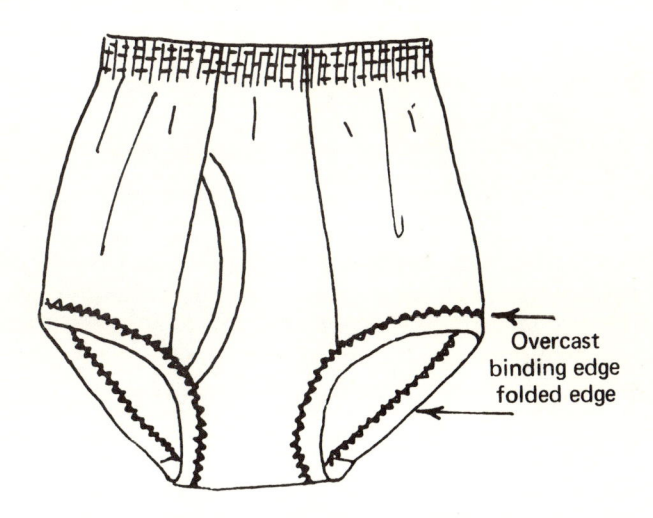

Overcast
binding edge
folded edge

PART III
HOUSEHOLD ITEMS

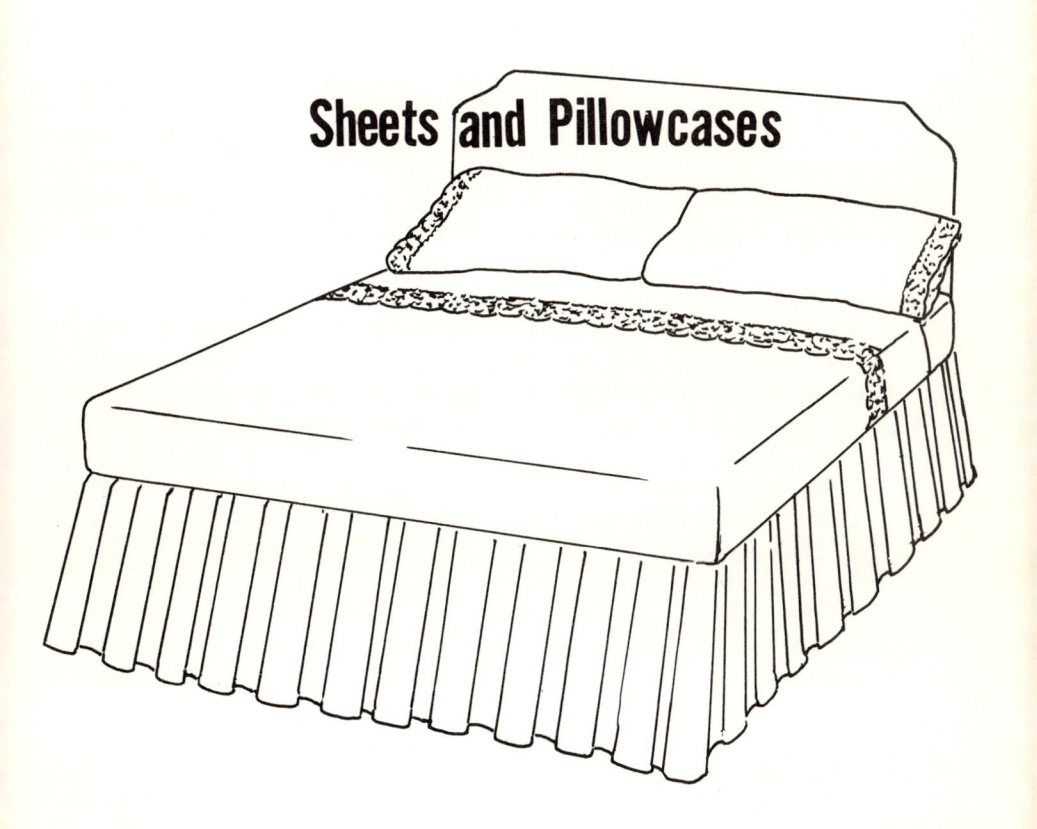

Sheets and Pillowcases

CHAPTER I

SHEETS AND PILLOWCASES

Nylon tricot sheets and pillowcases are the latest thing in elegance. They are quite expensive to buy but very inexpensive to make. They are not very time consuming to construct, and outlast cotton or satin sheets threefold. It is better to use the heavier weight tricot—either the antron or the satin finish; and again, the nylon thread and nylon lace should be used.

Nylon sheets are much more comfortable for sleep than cotton, because they are so smooth. It is surprising how much easier it is to turn over in bed on tricot sheets. After becoming accustomed to nylon sheets, the cotton ones seem to scratch and rub the skin almost like an abrasive. This is especially a boon to elderly people and invalids, who are prone to have tender skin and develop bedsores so easily. The nylon sheets are so easy to launder and dry so fast that you will not need as many sheets as before.

The nylon tricot pillowcases are extremely easy to make; they are especially good because they are slick and do not mess the hair by catching the individual hairs and matting them. Often a woman will find that she no longer needs to protect her coiffure with a net or protective covering if she uses a nylon tricot pillowcase.

For the trousseau, nothing makes a bigger hit than a set of nylon tricot sheets and pillowcases in a gorgeous color if they are decorated lavishly with lace. This is the ultimate in a wedding gift and is always appreciated. The range of colors available covers the entire spectrum, and lace in matching or blending colors is available in all widths. The wider the lace, the more expensive-looking the set.

STANDARD-SIZE BED TOP SHEET

Materials Needed:

3 yards of 96-inch or wider tricot (If wider tricot is used, a

Sheets and Pillowcases

pair of pillowcases may be made from the excess.)
Lace for trimming and edging, if desired
Elastic, if fitted top sheet is being made

Step-by-Step:

1. All top sheets should be cut on the straight of the fabric with the straight going from the top or head to the foot or bottom of the bed. Cut the fabric 86 inches wide and 108 inches long.

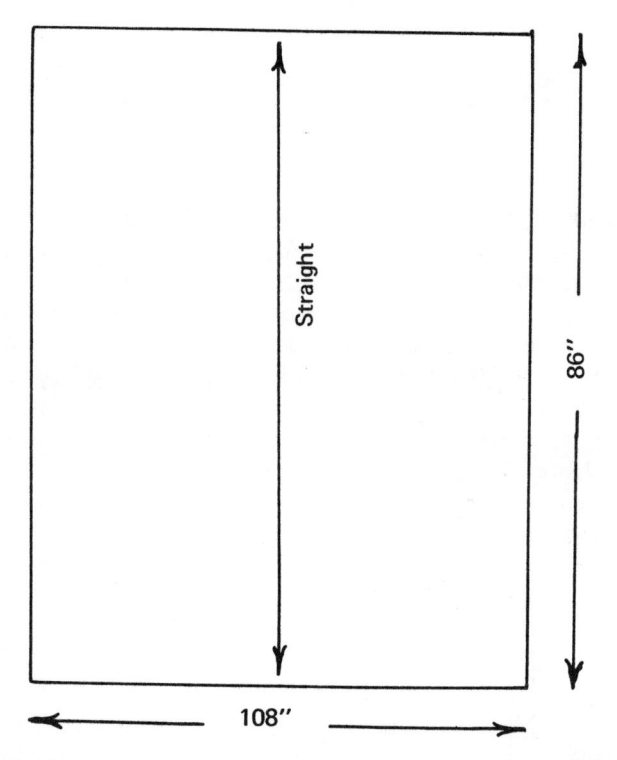

2. Finish the edges of the sheet either by zigzagging lace along the end of the sheet or hemming the edges by folding a 2-inch hem, tucking under the raw edge, and straight stitching it down. If the machine begins to skip stitches when hemming, insert a narrow strip of tricot sheer inside the tuck-under to make the material more stable. Lace is almost always used across the top of the sheet, and the wider lace (1½ inches or wider) adds elegance at very little expense. Be sure to use nylon thread and nylon lace. A very narrow lace is used across the

bottom of the sheet. This is just a little easier to do than hemming the bottom, but is not very expensive. The wide lace at the top of the sheet may be applied in various ways. Probably the best way is to hem the top of the sheet with a 2-inch hem; then zigzag the lace onto this hem as an overlay.

Sheer tricot strip folded in hem to stabilize

Lace overlay at top of sheet

Narrow edging lace at bottom of sheet

3. If a fitted sheet is desired, use the following instructions for making the fitted bottom sheet. Only the bottom end of the top sheet should be fitted, however. In applying the elastic, tack it in the hem about a foot above the corner seam and stretch it through the end hem. Then tack it in the same position on the other side of the sheet. Usually, the fitted top sheet is not necessary, because a generous amount of fabric is allowed for tuck-under.

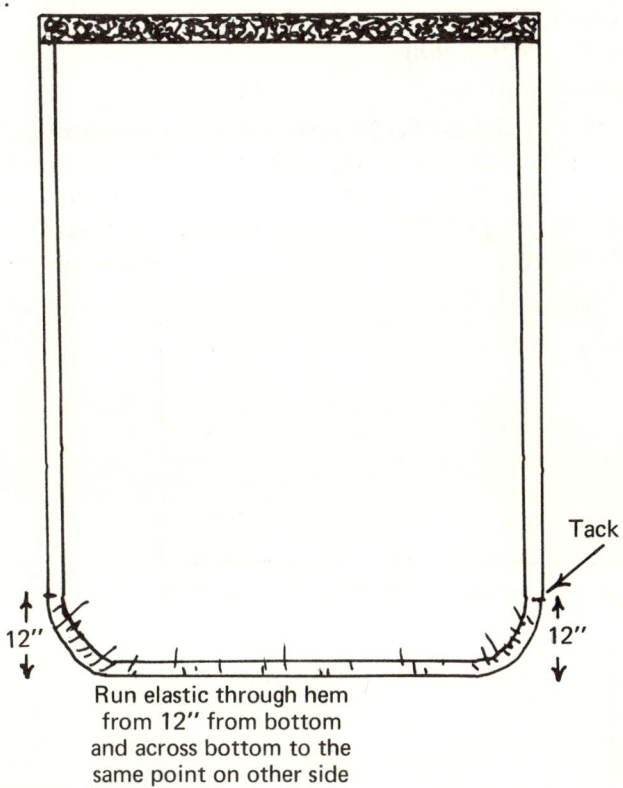

Tack

12"   12"

Run elastic through hem from 12" from bottom and across bottom to the same point on other side

KING-SIZE BED TOP SHEET

Materials Needed:

*3 1/3 yards of 108-inch wide tricot
Elastic, if fitted top sheet is desired
Lace, as desired*

Step-by-Step:

With a piece of fabric 108 inches wide and 120 inches long, follow the instructions for making a standard-size top sheet.

TWIN-SIZE TOP SHEET

Materials Needed:

3 yards of 96-inch wide tricot or 108-inch wide tricot (The waste on the 96-inch wide tricot is so narrow that it is not very usable. Fabric 108 inches wide is recommended so that the excess on the sides may be used for pillowcases, slips, panties, etc.)
Elastic, if a fitted sheet is desired
Lace for trimming

Step-by-Step:

1. Cut the fabric 76 inches wide by measuring 76 inches on one end. Then cut up the side at the 76-inch mark and fold the cut-off edge back over the uncut portion with the selvages even. Use the cut portion for a straight edge so that the cutting line will be even.

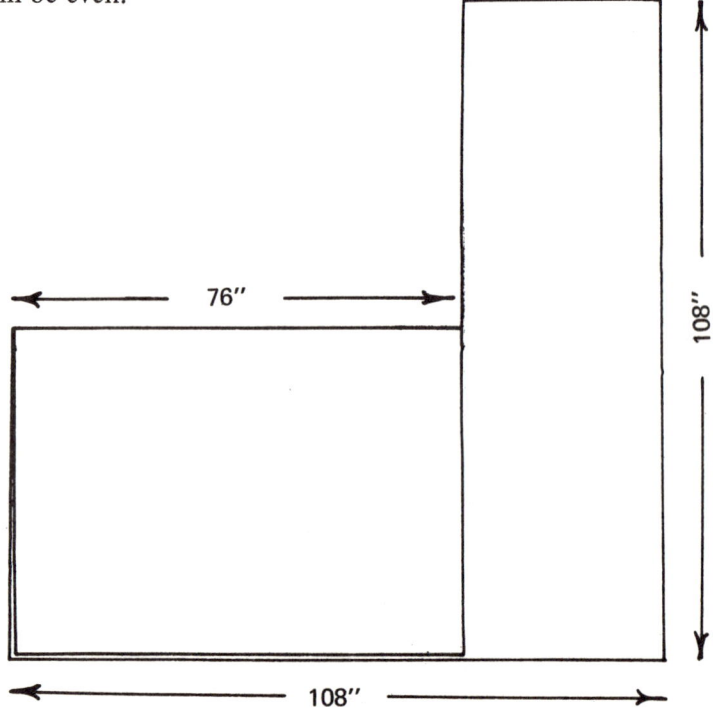

2. Make a 2-inch hem by sewing with a straight stitch around all four sides of the sheet, or edge with lace in the desired width. A very beautiful sheet is made by hemming the

sheet, then zigzagging the lace on the hem as an overlay. Refer to the instructions for making a top standard-size sheet.

STANDARD-SIZE FITTED BOTTOM SHEET

Materials Needed:

2¾ yards of 96-inch or wider tricot for an 8-inch deep mattress
2 2/3 yards of 96-inch or wider tricot for a 6-inch deep mattress
2½ yards of 96-inch or wider tricot for a 4-inch deep mattress
2¾ yards of ¼-inch to ½-inch wide elastic

Step-by-Step:

1. Although all top sheets should be cut on the straight of the material so that they will not be so stretchy when you turn over in bed, the bottom sheets may be cut with the straight going either way. Consider the width of the material, and figure which way would require less fabric. Pillowcases, slips, panties, etc., may be made from the excess material from the very wide fabrics. It is probably more economical to purchase the wider material, even if it does cost more, since the excess may be used in so many ways. In figuring your yardage, measure the mattress length, the depth at each end, and add 4 inches for tuck-under at each end. (This will be 8 inches total for tuck-under.) In figuring the width of the sheet, measure the width of the mattress, the mattress depth, and 4 inches for tuck-under on either side (8-inches tuck-under in all).

2. After deciding whether it would be more economical to have the straight going from side to side or head to foot, cut the tricot the proper width by measuring across one end and begin cutting at this point. Then cut along this measurement line 3 inches, fold the excess material over the uncut material and use the selvage edge as a straight edge. This assures a good, straight edge, and makes it easier to cut the side edge of the sheet the proper width without too much measuring.

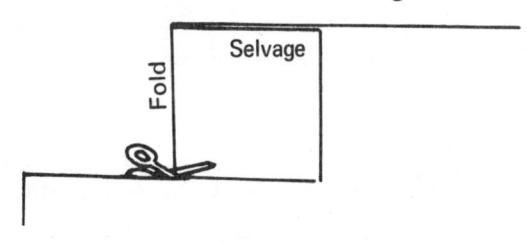

3. Lay the bottom sheet flat on the floor and fold it into fourths so that all four outside corners are together. Then cut a square from the outside corners equalling the mattress depth and the 4-inch tuck-under.

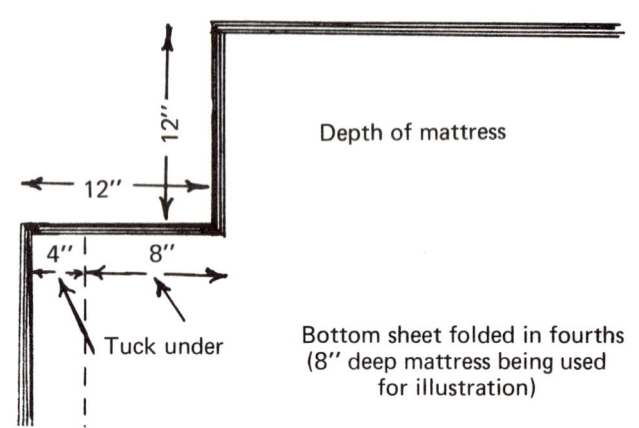

Depth of mattress

Tuck under

Bottom sheet folded in fourths
(8" deep mattress being used for illustration)

4. Unfold the sheet and place the right sides of the cut edges of the corner together. Sew these pieces together with a straight stitch; then overcast the seam with a zigzag set on a short stitch length. Repeat on all four corners of the bottom sheet.

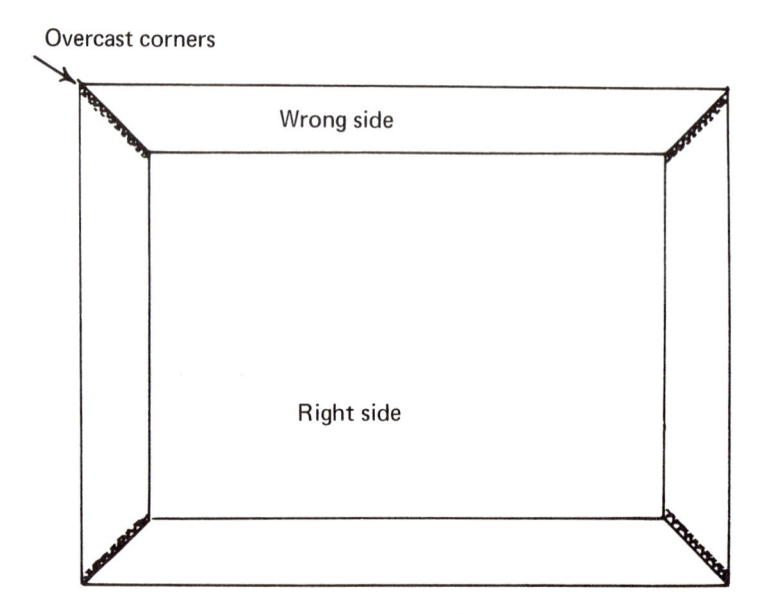

Overcast corners

Wrong side

Right side

Sheets and Pillowcases

5. Hem the edges of the sheet with a straight stitch. Make a ¾-inch hem with the raw edge tucked under. If the machine begins skipping stitches while sewing across the stretchy ends of the fabric, place a narrow strip of sheer tricot against the wrong side of the fabric edge; then tuck under the raw edge over the sheer. This sheer strip will not show, but will stabilize the seam so that it will sew smoothly.

6. Insert the elastic in the hem by placing a large safety pin on the end of the elastic and pushing it through the hem. Then secure the elastic ends with a zigzag stitch in a square shape down the three ends and across the middle of the elastic overlap.

FITTED BOTTOM SHEET FOR KING-SIZE AND QUEEN-SIZE BEDS

Since the king-size and queen-size beds vary in size so much, it is impossible to give exact fabric amounts required for these sheets. Mattress depths vary greatly, as well as the length and widths. The safest way to determine the amount of fabric to purchase is to measure the length of the mattress and the depths of the two ends and add four inches of tuck-under for each end; then total these measurements to get the amount of material to purchase. Fabric 108 inches wide is required for the width of the bed. On the queen-size bed, you will have to cut some from the side. Simply follow the standard-size bed instructions after measuring your mattress width, depth, and adding 4 inches on either side for tuck-under to give you the proper sheet width.

Three and one-fourth yards of ½-inch wide elastic is required for the fitted king-size sheet; however, two and three-fourths yards of elastic will suffice for the queen-size sheet.

After purchasing the fabric and elastic, follow the instructions for making a fitted standard-size bottom sheet. Since oversize linens are so expensive to purchase ready-made, a great savings may be realized by making your own.

TWIN-SIZE FITTED BOTTOM SHEET

Purchase 63 inches of tricot in the 108-inch width and 2½ yards of ½-inch wide elastic for the twin-size bottom sheet. Then follow the instructions for making the fitted standard-size bottom sheet.

PILLOWCASES

Materials Needed:

1 yard of 108-inch wide fabric will make three pillowcases.
2 yards of 108-inch wide fabric will make three pairs of pillowcases.

Step-by-Step:

1. Spread the 108-inch wide fabric on the floor folded in half crosswise (the way it comes off the bolt). Then measure 18 inches from the folded edge at the top and bottom of the fabric. Lay a yardstick to connect the two measuring marks, and draw a straight line between the two. Then carefully cut along this line.

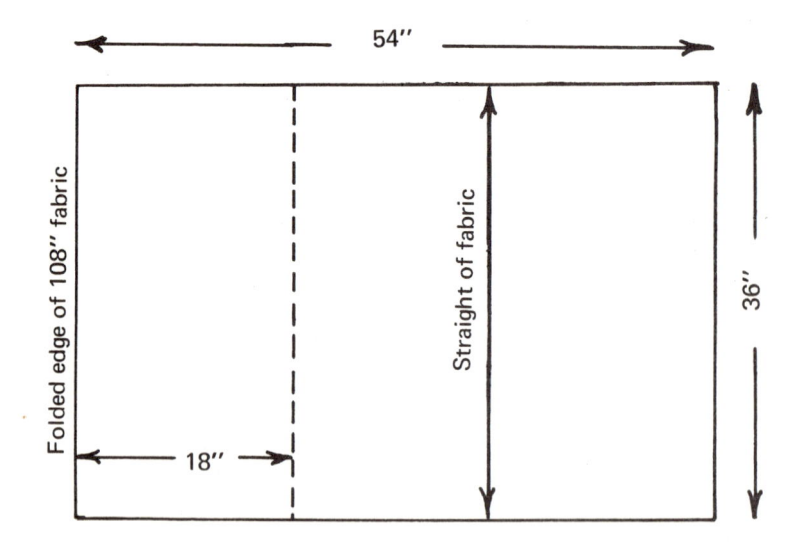

2. Take one of the 1-yard square pieces of tricot and fold it in half so that the straight of the fabric goes the length of the pillow (open end to sewed end).

3. If you want a hem, straight stitch a 1/8-inch seam across the end of the pillow and down one side; then overcast this seam and the fabric edge with a medium zigzag and a short stitch length.

4. Next, turn a 2-inch hem at the open end, tuck under the raw edge, and straight stitch along the edge of the tucked under edge.

Sheets and Pillowcases 229

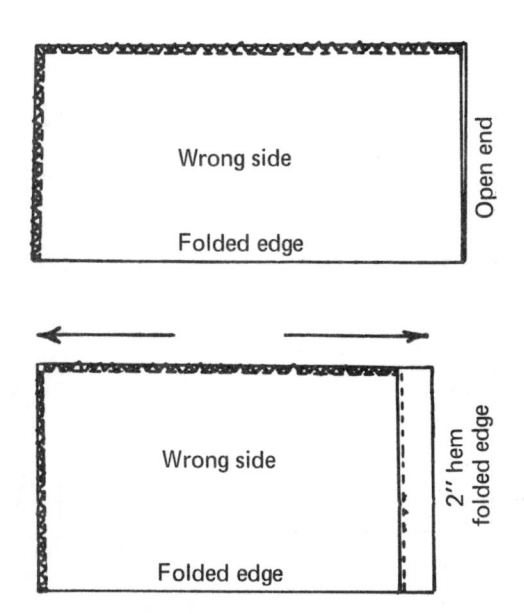

5. Lace can be applied with a zigzag upon the hem line. Be sure to zigzag both edges of the lace to the fabric. This looks much better than attaching one edge of the lace to the folded bottom edge of the hem.

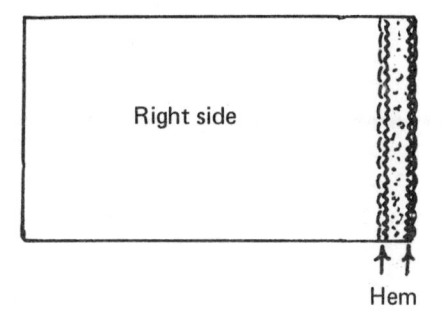

6. If a hem is not desired, and it really is not necessary, simply zigzag lace to the right side of the fabric barely covering the raw tricot edge. Then follow Step 2.

Zigzag lace onto tricot

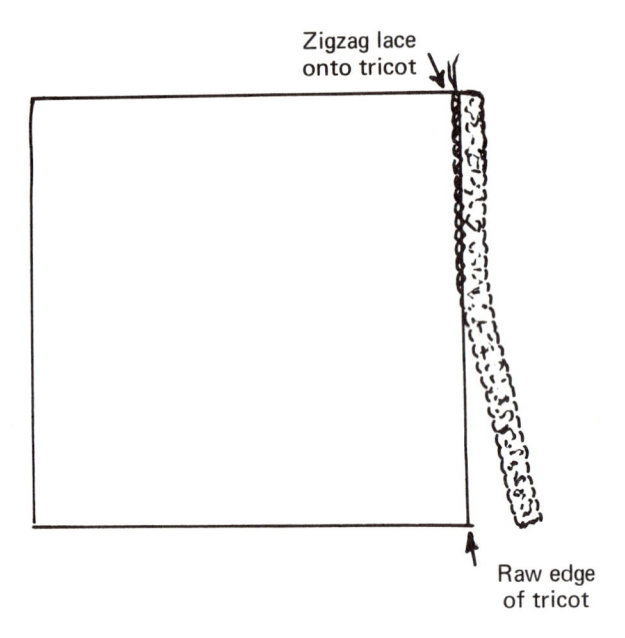

Raw edge of tricot

PILLOWCASES MADE FROM EXCESS SHEET FABRIC

Step-by-Step:

   1. Cut an 18-inch wide strip 2 yards long (wider and longer for king-size pillowcases).

   2. Fold the ends together lengthwise.

   3. Sew both sides with a straight stitch; then overcast the seam and the fabric edge with a wide zigzag and a short stitch length.

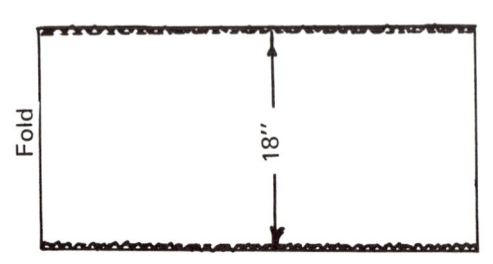

Fold

18"

   4. Finish the open edge as desired by following Steps 4, 5, and 6 of the previous pillowcase instructions.

   5. There will still be some leftover fabric from your sheets even after making a pair of pillowcases. Slips, gowns, panties,

scuff slippers, girdle crotches, bras, gloves, scarfs, etc., may be made from this. Never waste a single scrap of tricot. It makes wonderful bindings, facings, buttonhole loops, covered buttons, and tiny rosebud decorations. Just imagine having beautiful lacey sheets, pillowcases, gown, negligee, scuff slippers, slip, bra, and girdle all to match out of your favorite, most becoming color. Then your bedroom and your wardrobe will be truly "you."

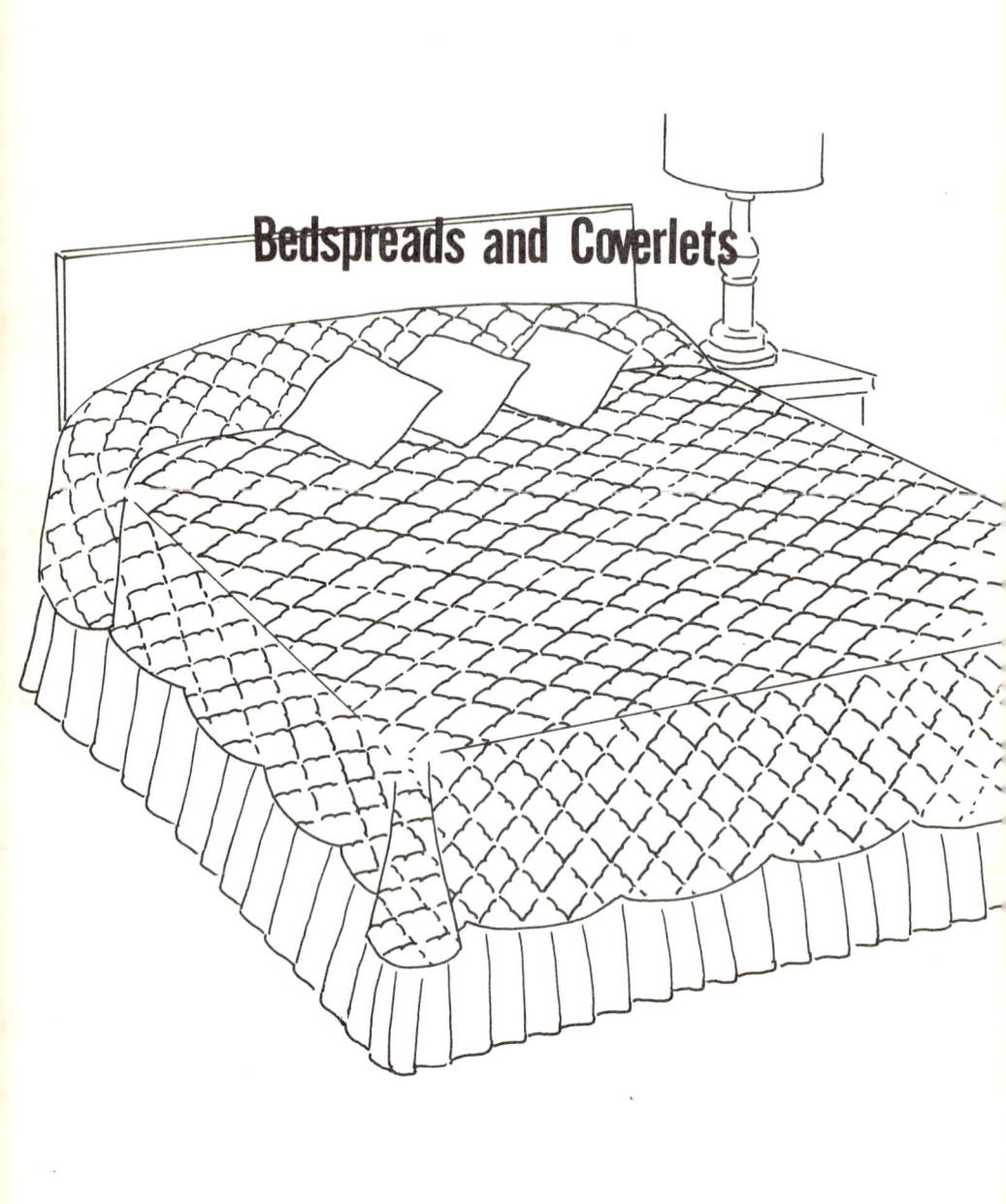

Bedspreads and Coverlets

CHAPTER II

BEDSPREADS AND COVERLETS

Bedspreads and coverlets are very easy to make, but they are bulky to work with. A washable fabric is usually less expensive, more durable, and much more practical because of drycleaning costs. If a washable fabric is chosen, it should not be one that requires ironing. The lining fabric, if one is used, should also not require drycleaning nor ironing. A quilted fabric is very beautiful and may be found in washable fabrics. It is also very easy to quilt any fabric by machine. Simply use a lining fabric with fiberfill or cotton as an interlining. Then baste the three fabrics together in the desired pattern, either in straight lines to make squares or around flowers, etc. After basting, machine stitch the fabrics together. The basting may be used for a guide. A lining or quilting adds weight to a bedspread and makes it look much more expensive. Nylon tricot makes a good lining, as does the quilted nylon tricot. Often the quilted tricot is used as a liner for the top of the bedspread, even if the outer fabric is not going to be quilted. This gives the bedspread a plushness and stability. The velvet-type brushed nylon fleece makes a very practical, durable bedspread that may be used in a very formal room as well as a tailored room. This versatile fabric seems to adapt to its surroundings and blend into any style.

No matter what fabric you use, you will be astonished at how easy it is to create a beautiful bedspread. In this day of odd-sized beds and windows, it is often extremely difficult to find draperies and bedspreads to match in just the right sizes. If you can custom-make your own, though, you will not be hampered by what is available in the size you need, and the result will more nearly express your taste and be an extension of your personality.

In this chapter you will find instructions for making several different types of simple bedspreads. These spreads are very attractive, yet very simple to make in a short period of time. By following these instructions or combining ideas from each of them, you will be able to create any type bedroom decor.

SCALLOPED COVERLET
Materials Needed:
> Fabric (must be bought according to bed size and fabric width)
> Lining fabric (tricot is excellent for a lining)—the same amount as the outside fabric
> Cord to outline the seams

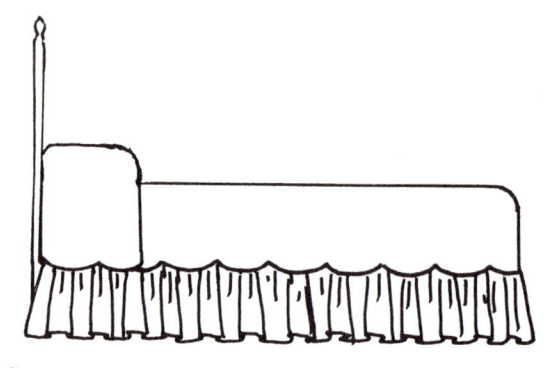

Step-by-Step:

1. Measure the mattress length. Then add 27 inches to the length for the pillows. Next, cut a piece of fabric in this length for the coverlet top. If the fabric is wider than the mattress top, trim the sides to the necessary width plus the seam allowances. If the fabric is not as wide as the mattress top, use this cut piece for the coverlet center and add pieces to the sides to make the top the correct width. Use a cord in the seams.

2. Cut two pieces of fabric the same length as the top in the desired width for the sides.

3. Cut a piece of fabric as long as the bed is wide for the bottom overhang. This piece should be the same width as the two side pieces.

4. Cut any lining the same size as the other pieces.

5. Place the right sides of the side and end overhang pieces together, and sew them into one long piece of fabric. Then sew the overhang lining in the same manner.

6. Pin together the overhang lining and outside fabric; then, using a pattern, cut large scallops on the bottom edges. Plan the size and position of the scallops before cutting the fabric so that

only whole scallops appear.

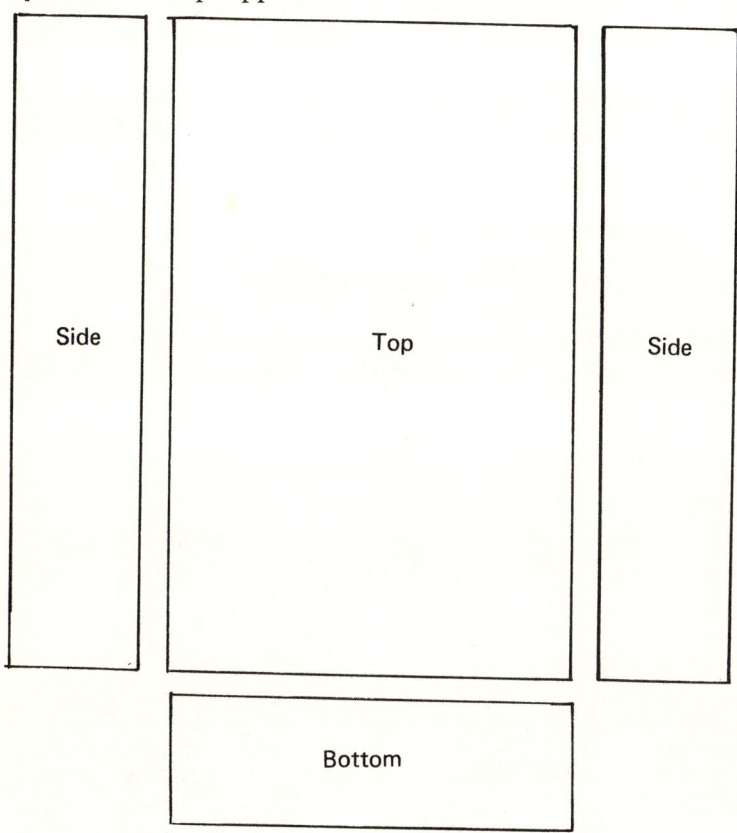

| Side | Top | Side |
| Bottom |

7. Place the right sides of the lining and the overhang outside fabric together with the scallops matched, and sew the scalloped edges together.

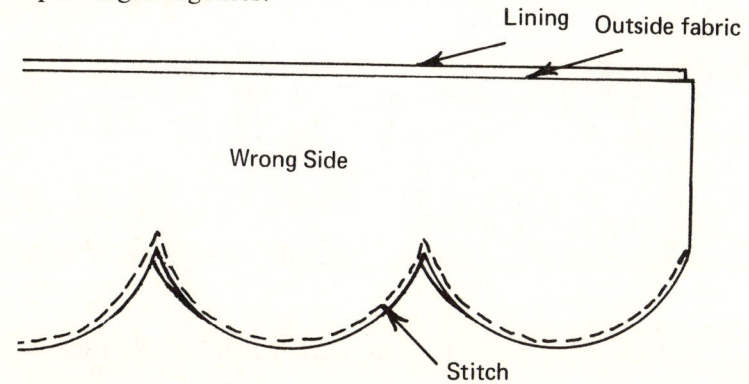

8. Turn the overhang pieces right side out.

9. Cover a cord the length of the sum of the two sides and the width of the bed.

10. Stay stitch the coverlet top and the top lining together.

11. With right sides together and the cord sandwiched between, stitch the top and overhang pieces together. A cording foot will make stitching this seam easier.

12. Hem the top by machine.

FORMAL AUSTRIAN SWAG COVERLET

Materials Needed:

Fabric (Measure the bed carefully; remember that only pieces as long as the bed are usable, except across the bottom end.)
Austrian gathering cord or beading lace
Ball trim or fringe, if desired
Two long zippers for the pillow cover openings
Fabric for the two pillow covers

Step-by-Step:

1. Cut four rectangular pieces of fabric the correct size to cover the pillows. Allow a little extra fabric for seam allowances.

2. Cut two of the pillow cover pieces in half, and insert a zipper in the center of each.

3. Place the right side of the pillow cover piece with the zipper against the right side of the pillow cover piece without the zipper, and stitch together on all four sides.

4. Turn right side out and stitch fringe on the edge of the pillow cover.

Bedspreads and Coverlets   237

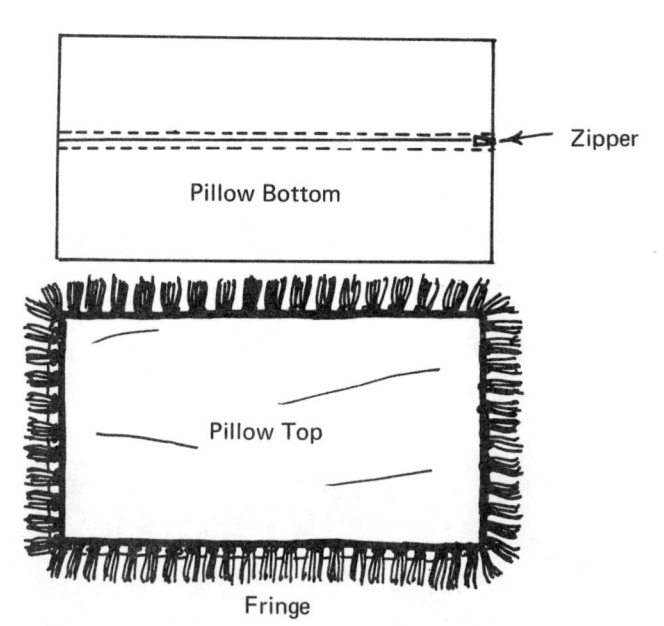

Pillow Bottom — Zipper

Pillow Top — Fringe

5. Repeat this process on the other pillow cover.

6. Cut a piece of fabric the length of the mattress plus six inches. If the fabric is wider than the mattress top, trim the sides to measure the width of the mattress with a seam allowance. If the fabric is not as wide as the mattress top, use this piece for the coverlet center, and add pieces to the sides to make the top the correct width. Use a cord in the seams.

7. Cut two pieces of fabric for the coverlet overhang the same length as the top and one piece for the coverlet bottom overhang as long as the mattress is wide. A wider fabric will make a wider overhang. The fabric should be at least twice as wide as you want the finished coverlet overhang to be. A wider fabric can be gathered tighter.

8. Place the right sides of the side overhang and the end overhang pieces together, and sew them into one long piece of fabric.

9. Sew the Austrian gathering cord or the beading lace, whichever is being used, across the width of the overhang piece at the two ends, the two seams, and at equal intervals on both sides and the foot of the bed. One gathering cord at the center of the side piece will make two swags; two gathering cords on the side piece will make three. Either design is very beautiful.

238   *Sewing The Unusual*

Austrian gathering cord

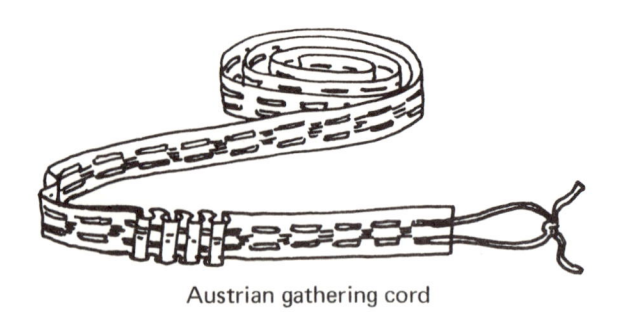

Beading lace

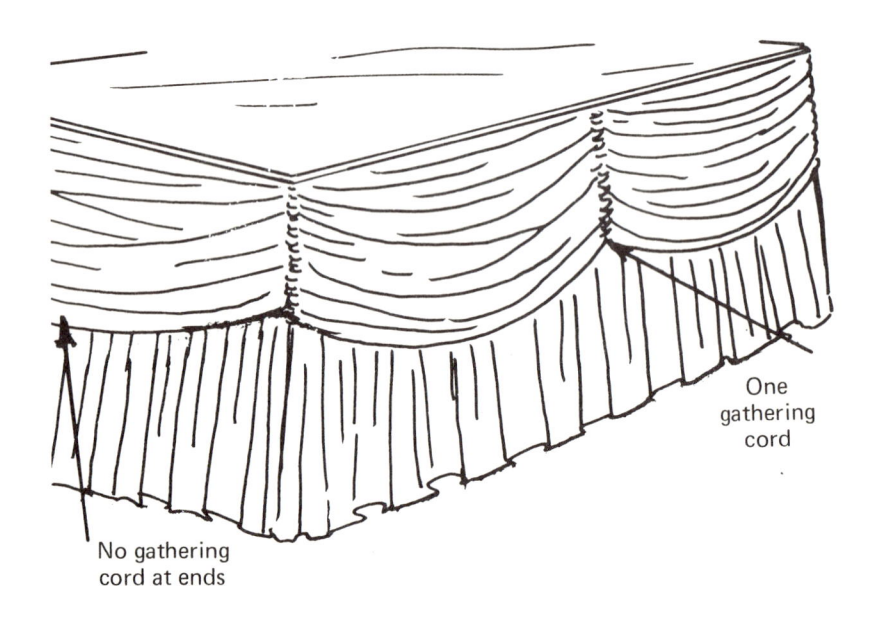

No gathering cord at ends

One gathering cord

One gathering cord at end

Two gathering cords

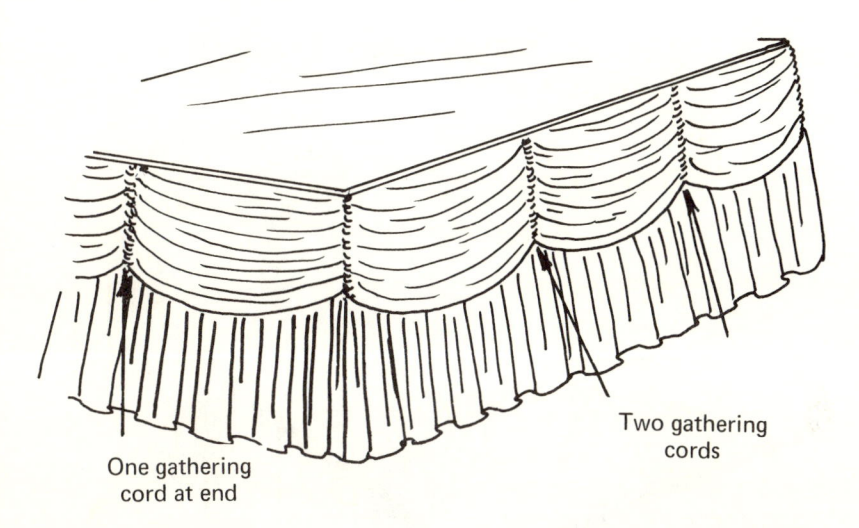

10. If beading lace is used for a gathering cord, run a heavy string or cord through the lace, and secure it at the bottom end.

11. Gather the overhang pieces to the proper length by pulling the cords tightly. Be sure that each side of the coverlet overhang is gathered an equal amount and that the overhang pieces are the same width all the way around. Stitch the cords in this position at the top edge so that the gathers will remain stationary.

12. Either hem the bottom edge of the overhang piece, or sew fringe to the edge.

13. Cover a cord the length of the sum of the two sides and the width of the bed.

14. With right sides together and the cord sandwiched between, stitch the top and overhang pieces together. A cording foot will make stitching the seam much easier.

REVERSIBLE BEDSPREAD

Many materials are reversible, and it always seems unfortunate to be unable to hide raw seam edges on one side of the fabric so that both sides may be used. This method is a simple way to make a bedspread with reversible fabric. You will also find that it is much easier to do than the standard method of making bedspreads with cord in the seams.

Step-by-Step:

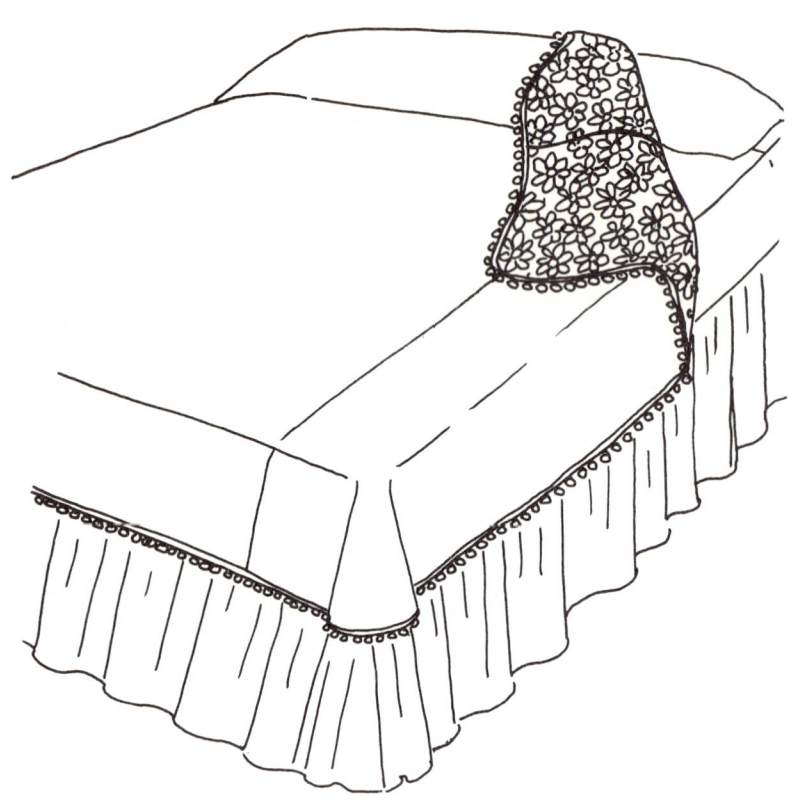

1. Measure the bed carefully, and purchase enough fabric for the bedspread. Remember that only pieces as long as the bedspread are usable.
2. Cut the fabric as usual for any other type bedspread.
3. To make the seams, overlap the two pieces an inch to an inch and a quarter. The wrong side of one piece of fabric will be against the right side of the other.
4. Stitch the two pieces together by sewing about one-half of an inch from the raw edge. This will leave a ½-inch raw edge on the underside of the spread, also.
5. Turn the raw edge down to make a folded edge. Then turn the folded edge down against the seam. Next, with the folded edge in this position and the wrong sides of the bedspread together so that they will not get involved in this seam, stitch along the folded edge very close to the seam.

½" on either side of seam

Raw edges

Right side

Right Side

Stitching line

Bedspread pieces being joined

Folded edges

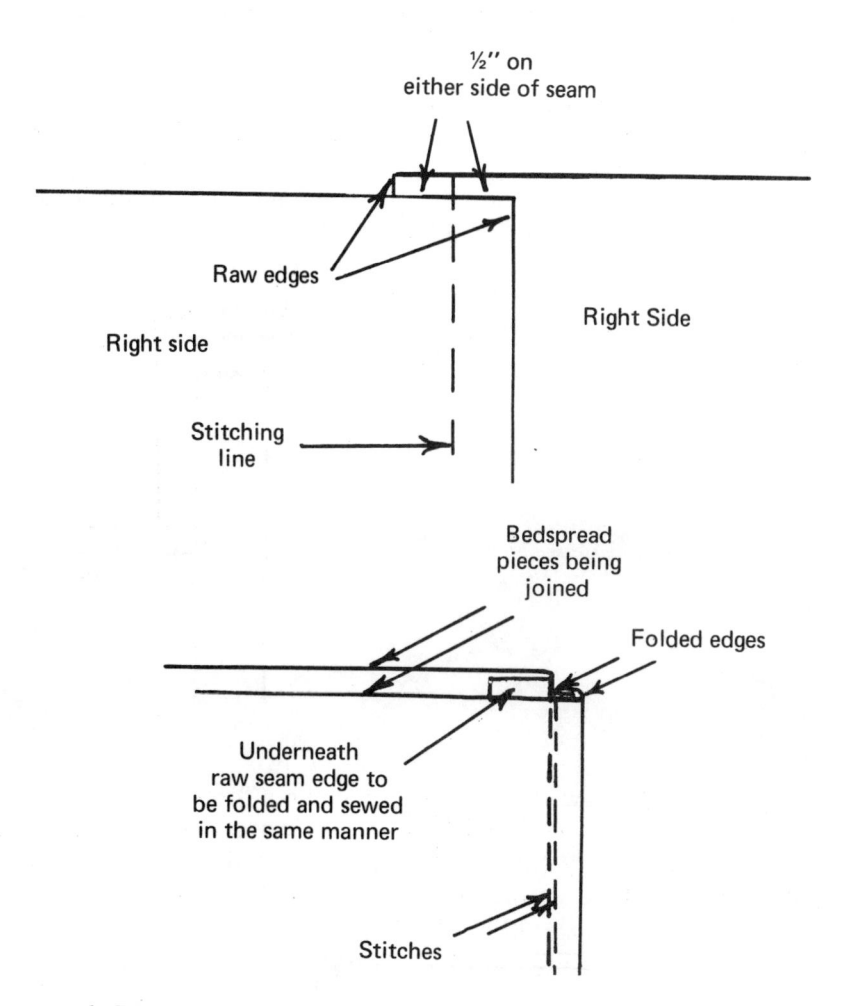

Underneath raw seam edge to be folded and sewed in the same manner

Stitches

6. Stitch all the right side seams in this manner; then turn the bedspread over and stitch the wrong side seams in the same way. Thus, both sides of the bedspread are neatly finished.

7. Hem all edges of the bedspread, or sew fringe on the edge.

NO-CORD, NO RAW-SEAM-EDGE BEDSPREAD

Often a bedspread fabric will ravel easily. This makes an unsightly, messy appearance when the spread is pulled back for sleeping. To get rid of these raw seams and also get away from the tricky job of inserting cording in the seams, try this method.

Step-by-Step:

1. Measure the bed carefully, and purchase enough fabric to make the bedspread. Then, cut the fabric as usual for any other bedspread.

2. To make the seams, place the wrong sides of the bedspread together and stitch 5/8-inch seams.

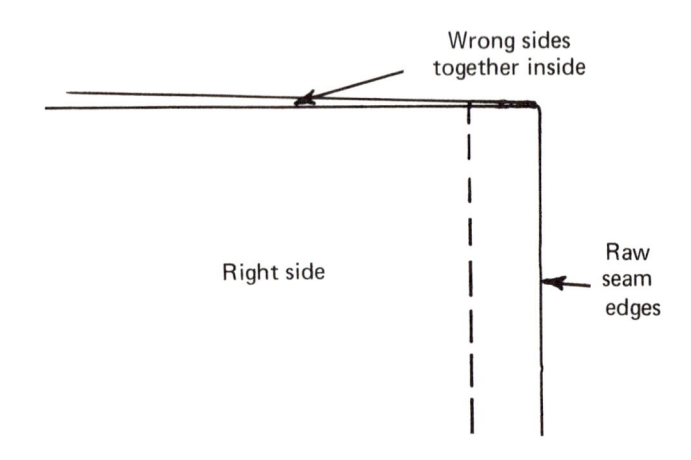

3. Turn the raw edges down to make a folded edge. Then turn the folded edge down against the seam, and stitch along the folded edge very close to the seam. This will look very much like you have used cord in the seams, but there will be no raw fabric edges showing on the wrong side of the bedspread.

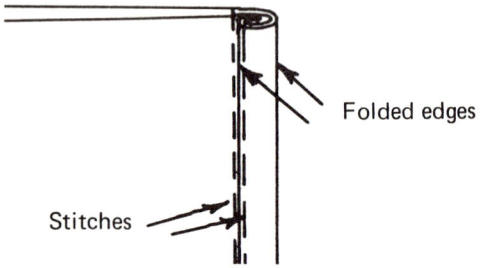

4. Stitch all the seams in this manner.

5. Hem the bedspread by machine, or sew fringe on the edge of the bedspread.

CHAPTER III

QUILTING

Every home seamstress has bags, closets, and drawers full of leftover fabric scraps that are too small to be used in another garment. These fabric scraps could make beautiful quilts. The quilts in this chapter are all machine made for speed and durability. However, the same patterns may be adapted to handmade quilts, if desired. Quilt making may provide the seamstress with a new hobby and furnish the family with cozy warmth for winter nights. Quilts are beautiful used as coverlets with a dust ruffle. The quilting techniques may also be worked into afghans, place mats, skirts, jackets, wall hangings, pillows, and potholders. It is truly wasteful not to use sewing scraps in a quilting project when they are too small for other uses. Let the imagination soar, and design unique and attractive creations that are beautiful as well as useful.

Most quilting projects are based on geometric shapes; therefore, graph paper and crayons or colored magic markers are indispensable for all but the most simple projects. Figure each square of the graph paper as ½ inch. Decide the outside dimensions of the quilt based upon the size and depth of the mattress. Outline the quilt on the graph paper, and then decide on the overall design. Decide if the quilt will be made up of geometric shapes sewn together to form squares, or if it will be geometric shapes sewn to make a large design over the entire quilt.

The easiest quilts are based upon squares. Quilt designs may be made by folding a square piece of paper various ways and copying the design made by the folds. The design may be used for small squares or one large square making up the entire quilt.

Draw the design to scale on the graph paper and color it in the desired color scheme. Then make each pattern piece out of paper by increasing the graph paper scale to the proper size. The pattern pieces should fit together snugly in the proper design. If the patterns fit, they may be used to make permanent patterns from cardboard, posterboard, or shirt board. Check to be sure that the cardboard patterns fit together properly.

After making the pattern, count the number of quilt pieces that should be cut from each pattern piece. As each piece is cut, allow for a 3/8-inch seam by cutting 3/8 of an inch beyond the pattern on all sides. Pencil around the pattern piece if it makes cutting easier.

Fabrics of similar weight and handling requirements should be used in each quilt. The completely washable quilt is especially practical. Fragile fabrics should not be used. Used fabrics are very acceptable, but they must not be worn out. Each piece must have approximately the same wear capability.

QUICK-SQUARE QUILT

Materials Needed:
Quilt scraps large enough to cut 5-inch squares—a large variety of colors and design is desirable
Polyester thread for machine stitching
Lining fabric sufficient to extend 2 inches beyond the quilt on all sides
Fiberfill or other type of quilt batting—polyester or dacron is best
5 packages of embroidery thread

Step-by-Step:
1. Make a 5-inch square pattern of cardboard and cut the prescribed number of squares (smaller squares may be used if they better utilize the available scraps). The squares will measure approximately 4 inches when sewn, so the precise number may be calculated.

2. On a bed or on the floor, place the squares side by side to form the quilt top. Do not have identical squares close to one another—variety is the object.

3. When the desired arrangement is obtained, stack the squares in each row in the correct order bottom to top. A basting thread may be run through the middle of the stack of

squares to stabilize them until they are sewn. Leave the thread knotted on the bottom, but not on the top.

4. Using a straight stitch and a ½-inch seam allowance, stitch each stack of squares into a long row. Stack the rows in proper order as they are sewn.

5. Sew the long rows together in proper order; then press all the seams.

6. Cut the lining fabric so that it will extend two inches beyond the quilt top on all sides; then sew.

7. Place the lining and the quilt top with wrong sides together and the batting sandwiched between the two. Pin the three together about every foot or so throughout the quilt.

8. Tack the pieces together with the embroidery floss. Push a threaded needle into the center of each square and pull it back through about an 1/8 inch from where it entered the quilt. Pull the thread through until about 1¼ inches of thread is still extending on top of the quilt. Cut the thread extending from the needle so that 1¼ inches of thread is extending on top of the quilt on that side, also. Tie the two thread ends together in a square knot. Continue to tack every square throughout the quilt in this way. Although the quilt will hold together with less tacking, it will not be as attractive.

9. Fold the lining edges over the top of the quilt and pin into place. Fold the corners into a neat mitre and pin. Then tuck under the raw edge of the lining as you zigzag along the lining edge that is folded to make a binding.

NINE-SQUARE QUILT

Materials Needed:
   Quilt scraps for 5-inch pieces
   About 2½ yards for strip spacers
   Quilt batting
   About 5 yards for lining
   Polyester thread

Basic design for squares.

Sewing The Unusual

Basic layout for quilt.

Step-by-Step:

1. Decide the overall dimension of the quilt by measuring the mattress top and sides and adding at least 20 inches for additional overhang.

2. Draw the basic design on a piece of graph paper. Use a scale of ½ inch for each graph paper square. Each 9-square section should be made up of five matching 4-inch squares and 4 matching 4-inch squares. The squares made up of the nine smaller squares do not have to be made of matching fabrics. Contrasting squares make an attractive quilt and help use leftover fabrics to a greater degree. The strips or spacers that go between the squares are usually of the same fabric. Strips the same length as the quilt and 4 inches wide should be used as vertical spacers, and 12-inch x 4-inch strips should be used for the horizontal ones.

3. Adding ½ inch to all sides for seam allowances, make a cardboard pattern for each piece.

4. Cut the prescribed number of pieces. Then sew the 9-square blocks. One of the 12-inch x 4-inch (13-inch x 5-inch with seam allowance) strips may be sewn to one side of the blocks at this time.

5. Place the blocks on the floor with the long vertical spacers between them. Make any changes necessary in block ar-

rangement to ensure a more attractive quilt.

6. Sew the blocks and spacers together in vertical strips; then sew the vertical spacers to them. Press all seams open.

7. Sew the lining fabric together to make it extend 2 inches beyond the quilt top on all sides.

8. Place the lining and top with wrong sides together and the batting sandwiched between.

9. Pin the quilt top, batting, and lining together in this position. The pins should be about 5 inches apart throughout the quilt.

10. Check the back of the quilt for puckering, which should be eliminated.

11. Roll the sides of the quilt into the middle in tight rolls, and secure the rolls in this position with large paper clips, hair clips, or clothes pins.

12. Straight stitch from the top of the quilt to the bottom along the seam line of the outside edge of the 9-square blocks. Work from the middle seam to the edge on one side by unrolling that side when necessary. Then sew the other side.

13. Tightly roll the top and bottom edges of the quilt to the center and clip into place.

14. Stitch lines straight across the quilt from one side edge to the other following the outside edges of the 9-square blocks.

15. Fold and pin the lining edges over the top of the quilt to form a self-binding. Pin the corners into neat mitres.

16. Folding under the raw edge, zigzag the binding into place. Press the quilt.

EASY TRADITIONAL PATCHWORK PATTERNS

Shoofly   *Triangles*

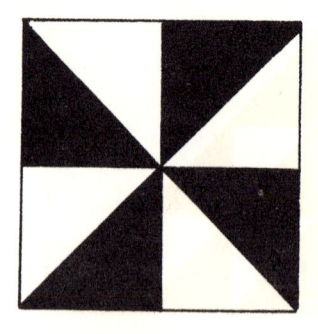

Broken Dishes

Granny's Star

Zigzag

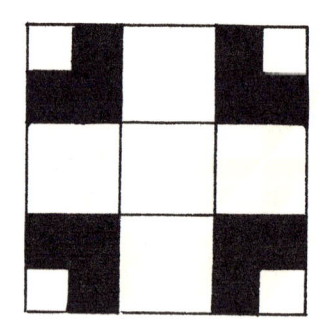

Cross And Crown

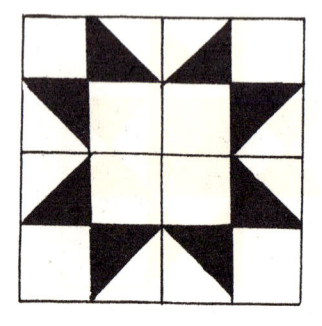

Triangles And Squares

Star

Quilts 249

Square In Square

Birds In Air

Basket

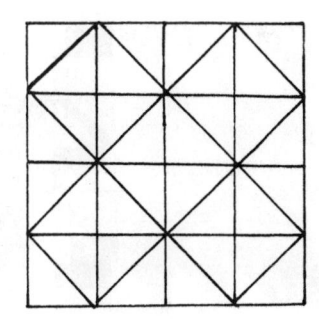

Broken Dishes

Flock Of Geese

Ohio Star

Log Cabin

Pineapple

Aunt Vi's Choice

CRAZY QUILT

The quilt that most efficiently uses fabric scraps is the crazy quilt. The scraps should be no more than 6 inches in length or width. A variety of sizes and shapes makes a more interesting quilt. The scraps should be similar in fabric content, weight, and handling care. The greater the variety of colors and patterns the better.

Materials Needed:
Bright heavy thread
Lining fabric

Fiberfill or cotton batting
10-inch cardboard square pattern

Step-by-Step:
    1. Iron the quilt pieces flat with the raw edges pressed to the wrong side to make a 3/8-inch seam allowance. If a non-raveling fabric is used, the raw edges do not have to be tucked under.
    2. To sew the pieces together, overlap the edge of one piece 3/8 inch over the edge of another of contrasting shape, color, and size, and sew into place by machine with a briarstitch, zig-zag, or other decorative stitch. The raw edge of the bottom piece may be pulled flat before sewing to better utilize fabric.

Crazy Quilt Square

    3. Continue stitching contrasting pieces of fabric together until a 10-inch square may be cut. Any excess left after cutting the square may be incorporated into the next square.
    4. Press the square.
    5. After constructing enough squares to complete the quilt top, place the right sides of the squares together and stitch a 3/8-inch seam. Sew the squares into long rows; then sew the rows together.
    6. Press open the seams.
    7. Sew the lining fabric to the desired size. The lining should extend beyond the edge of the quilt top about 3 inches on all sides.
    8. Position the lining and quilt top with wrong sides togeth-

er and the batting sandwiched between.

9. Secure the quilt together with pins at the corners and in the middle of each square. Check the underside to avoid puckering, and adjust accordingly.

10. Roll the side edges of the quilt into the middle.

11. Using the same decorative stitch that was used before, sew through all layers along the seam lines from top to bottom. Work from the middle to the edge. Keeping the quilt rolled makes it much more manageable.

12. Roll the top and bottom edges to the middle and stitch along the seam lines from side to side. The rolls may be secured with clips.

13. Remove pins.

14. Fold the lining onto the top of the quilt to make a binding. Turn the raw edge under and stitch into place. The corners should be mitered.

LARGE PATTERNED QUILTS

Any geometric quilt pattern may be used as a design for the entire quilt top. These quilts take very little time, but are strikingly beautiful. The entire quilt top is one giant quilt square rather than a series of small quilt squares. Careful planning and matching of fabrics will insure an attractive result.

Materials Needed:
Graph paper
Fabric for the top
Lining fabric
Batting
Thread

Step-by-Step:

1. Plan the quilt on graph paper, and decide the amount of fabric of each color that will be needed.

2. Cut the fabric into the correct shapes with a 3/8-inch seam allowance provided.

3. With right sides together, stitch the pieces together with a 3/8-inch seam allowance. Usually it is easier to sew the pieces

into strips and then stitch the strips together. If this is not feasible, begin at the center and sew the pieces toward the edge.

4. Sew the lining in the correct size to extend 3 inches beyond the quilt top on all sides.

5. Sandwich the batting between the wrong sides of the top and lining, and pin into place. The pins should be about 12 inches apart over the entire quilt.

6. Check the lining side for puckering, which should be eliminated.

7. Machine stitch along the seams of the pattern. Rolling the quilt from side to middle and securing with clips may reduce bulk and facilitate the stitching.

8. Turn the edges of the lining into position over the top to act as a binding. Tuck under the raw edge, and miter the corners.

9. Stitch into place with a zigzag or straight stitch.

COZY COMFORTER

Materials Needed:

Fabric sufficient for comforter size (about 5 yards for each side)
Fiberfill
Thread

A variety of fabrics may be used for a comforter. Contrasting fabrics may also be used for top and bottom. Some suggested fabrics are: sheets, plain or patterned; velveteen; brushed nylon; bandannas, red and blue sewn in pattern; satin; woven nylon.

Step-by-Step:

1. Sew the fabric together to make the top; then the bottom.

2. Spread the top on the floor and determine how the top is to be quilted. If bandannas are being used, they should be stitched down the seam lines. Fabric or sheets with fairly large pattern or flowers may be stitched in such a way as to outline some or all of the pattern or flowers. If the fabric is a solid color or a small pattern, plan an interesting geometric design for the quilting. The stitches do not have to be closer than six or

eight inches if dacron batting is used. Squares, diamonds, or a combination of the two are easy to do. Mark the quilting design on the comforter with tailor's chalk or pencil.

3. Place the comforter bottom and top right sides together and stitch a 3/8-inch seam on three sides.

4. Tuck under the raw edges on the unsewn end and press.

5. Turn the comforter right side out, and stuff the batting into place.

6. Seal the unsewn side with a straight stitch or zigzag.

7. Pin the comforter together about every 10 or 12 inches to hold it in place while quilting.

8. Roll the two opposite edges into the center, and clip into place to facilitate sewing the bulky comforter along the marked pattern lines or into the quilting pattern.

9. Straight stitch in the desired pattern to quilt.

APPLIQUÉD QUILTS

Appliqué is one of the oldest art forms in existence, as old as fabric making. The uses of appliqué are as numerous and varied as the shapes and fabrics that may be used. Appliqué is at home on clothing for men, women, and children; wall hangings; pictures; pillows; bedspreads; purses; scarves; quilts; potholders; tablecloths; place mats; hats; swimsuits; aprons; and many other items. Although quilted items will be the only ones covered in this book, appliqué techniques are the same no matter what the project.

Appliqué is the art of applying a piece or pieces of fabric to the top of another, larger piece of fabric in such a way as to make a decorative design or picture. Appliqué patterns may be drawn by the artistic seamstress or may be adapted from simple pictures or drawings, such as the ones found in children's coloring books. Cookie cutters, large designs on fabrics or wallpaper, and the comic strips are also good sources. Graph paper may be used to calculate size increases in the pattern. The simple picture may be drawn or traced onto graph paper; then the final dimensions computed by figuring how large each square must be to make the design the desired size. The pattern may then be made by drawing the squares the required size on cardboard or paper and then copying the design on the squares the same as on the graph paper. For example, if the figure drawn on the graph paper were ten squares tall and the height of the desired appliqué were 10 inches, then the squares on the cardboard should be drawn one inch square.

Embroidery is often combined with appliqué for a more detailed design. Embroidery may be especially useful for small detailing that is too minute to be cut from fabric.

Designs may be raised or padded by partially stitching the appliqué in place, then gently pushing batting under the appliqué. The unsewn portion is then completed. Another unusual treatment of appliqué is accomplished by leaving part of the appliqué detached. Flowers, animals, fruit, butterflies, and dolls are especially attractive in this application. A basket with embroidered checks for ribbing may be appliquéd with detached flowers or fruits extending from the top of it for an attractive design. Detached kittens, dolls, or puppies would also be interesting in the basket appliqué.

To make a detached appliqué, cut a front as well as back appliqué piece with a ¼-inch seam allowance. With right sides together, stitch almost all the way around the appliqué. Turn right side out and stuff batting into opening, if desired. Then blindstitch the opening closed. The appliqué may be attached by hand or machine. Embroidery may also be useful in attractively joining the detached appliqué. Sometimes only part of the appliqué is detached. This is done by cutting and sewing a backing piece onto the part of the appliqué that is to be detached. The appliqué is then stuffed, if desired, and attached the usual way, except the part to be detached is left free.

To prepare the appliqué for hand application, turn the outside edges under ¼-inch and press. Pin into position and either blindstitch or buttonhole stitch with embroidery thread into place. Any other embroidery work is then applied.

Machine appliqués are pinned into place, then straight stitched all the way around ¼ inch from the raw edges. The raw edge is then covered with a close zigzag stitch that also covers the straight stitching. Appliqués may also be made more sturdy by sticking into place with a fusible web before zigzagging the edge. This eliminates the need to straight stitch; however, the appliqué will not be quite as soft and pliable.

Many heirloom quilt designs are based on appliqué techinques. Dutch Doll, Dutch Boy, Dutch Girl, Sunbonnet Girl, Calico Cat, Gingham Dog, Umbrella Girl, Small Fry, Bunny, Butterfly, Lazy Daisy, and Old-fashioned Rose are probably the most popular of these.

Two newcomers, the Farewell Quilt and the Remembrance Quilt, are also appliqué-embroidery creations. In the Remembrance Quilt each square is designed and dated to relate an important event in the person's life. Strips of white or solid color fabric are used as dividers between the blocks. The Farewell Quilt is similar in appearance, but each quilt square is designed and sewn by a different friend. Each square contains the designer's name and the date and some special remembrance or memorabilia worked into a design. This quilt makes a special gift for a departing minister's wife, club member, or neighbor. In today's mobile society this quilt is becoming a favorite. These quilts may be quilted or tacked.

Appliqués may be placed on small squares or be extremely large so that they almost cover the entire quilt top. Strips or dividers of fabric are useful to set appliquéd squares apart. Finished appliquéd tops may be hand or machine quilted in a design or squares or hand tacked with embroidery thread. Any method will bring pride and pleasure.

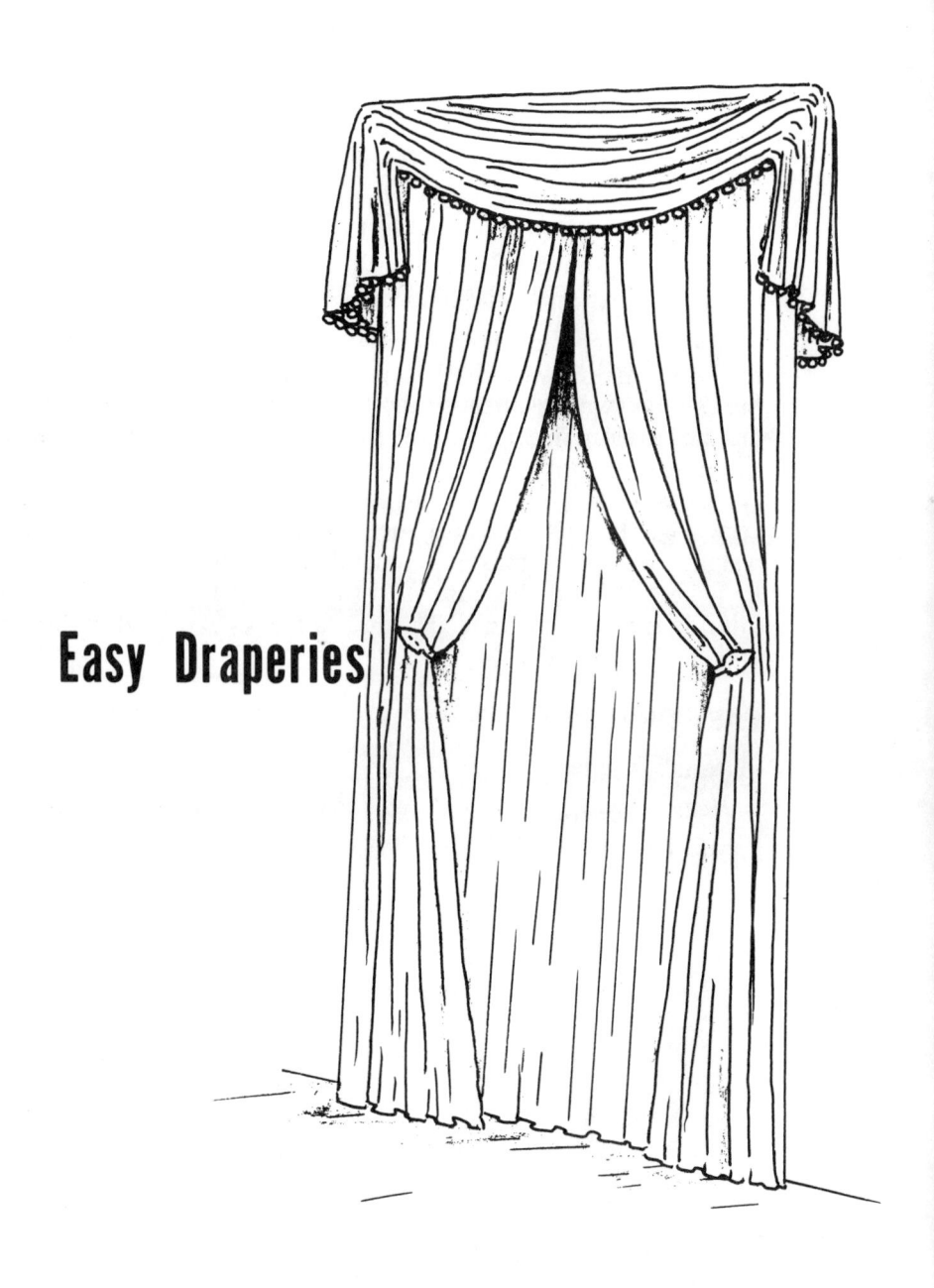

Easy Draperies

CHAPTER IV

EASY DRAPERIES

Since the cost of drapery drycleaning is so great, it is a real thrill to make washable draperies and bedspreads that are durable as well as beautiful. The heavy weight, velvet-type, brushed nylon fleece is excellent for draperies in any room in the house. It looks like velvet in the living room and yet has a casual look in less formal surroundings. The sheer tricot makes very durable and beautiful sheer draperies. The satiny, heavyweight tricot also makes beautiful draperies and curtains and may be self-lined, because no other lining fabric would be as durable or as inexpensive. Tricot also makes excellent bathroom and shower curtains.

EASY DRAPERIES

Materials Needed:

Heavy, brushed nylon fleece sufficient to prepare two panels the width of the window
Fringe for edging

Step-by-Step:

1. Cut the fabric into panels the desired length plus three inches for the top hem.
2. Prepare two panels that each measure the width of the window.
3. Hem the top and outside edge of each panel with a 1½-inch hem. If fringe or balls are desired on the outside edge, hem only the top edge.
4. Straight stitch the trim, either fringe or balls, onto the inside edge and the bottom of the panel. If fringe is desired on the outside edge also, stitch it into place.
5. Run a regular curtain rod through the top hem and hang. The drapery may be tied with a decorative rope or a tie-back made of the drapery fabric. The tie or rope may be released at

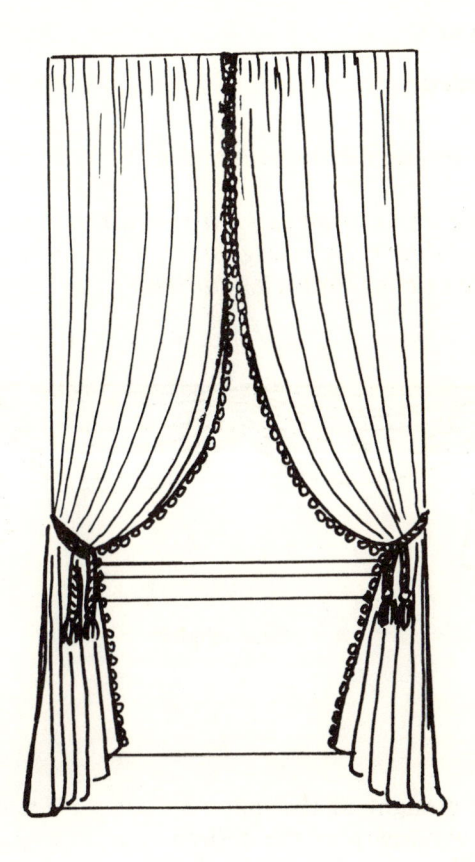

night for privacy.

SHEER DRAPERIES

Materials Needed:
Sheer nylon tricot enough to measure twice the width of the window in the desired length

Step-by-Step:
1. Since the sheer tricot is 108 inches wide, one large piece the desired length may be sufficient for a panel twice the width of the window. If the window is extremely wide, prepare two panels, each the width of the window.
2. Hem the outside edges of the panels with a straight stitch. Nylon thread and a small needle should be used.
3. Hang on a curtain rod.

EASY VALANCE

Materials Needed:
> Fabric sufficient in length to go across the window and hang down several feet on either side
> Fringe
> Beading lace or Austrian gathering cord three times the width of the fabric if two swags are desired; or one more width of lace or cord for each additional swag

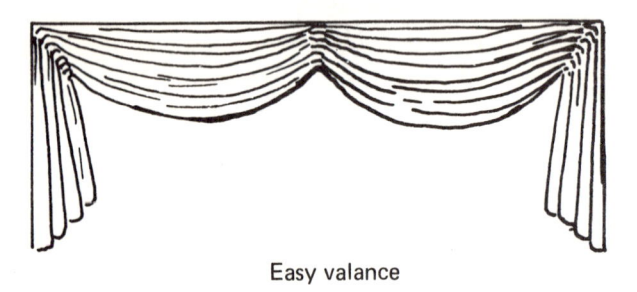

Easy valance

Step-by-Step:

1. On the straight of the material, cut a piece of fabric the width of the window plus the desired amount to hang down on either side. The straight of the fabric should go across the window, unless a design is being used that would not be suitable cut this way. If the design is not suitable to go across the window, cut the valance with the straight of the fabric going up and down at the top of the window and across at the sides. The width of the fabric, usually 48 inches - 54 inches, is the proper length at the top for the valance.

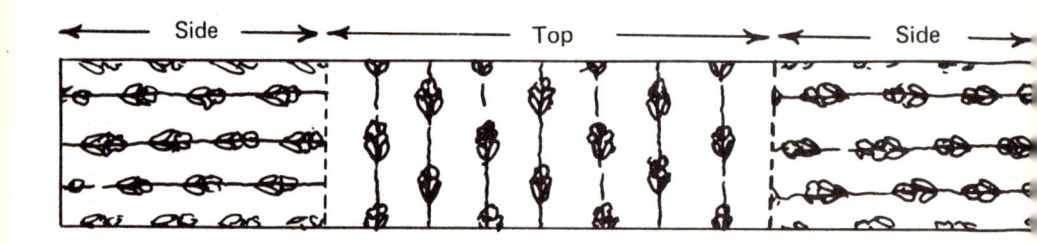

Easy Draperies

2. Cut each end from the top corner diagonally across the width of the material to a point two feet from the opposite corner on that same end. This will make the valance ends longer on the outside edges, instead of the inside edges.

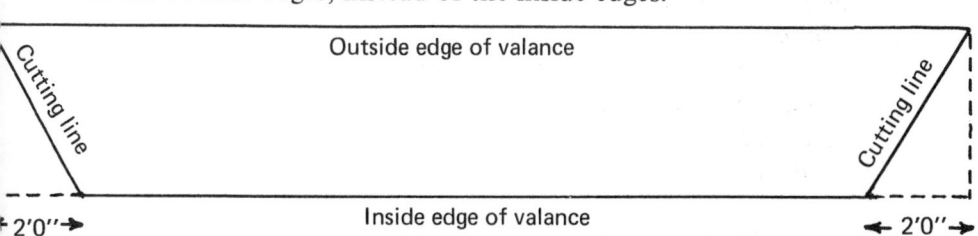

Outside edge of valance
Cutting line — *Cutting line*
← 2'0" → ← 2'0" →
Inside edge of valance

3. If fringe or ball decoration is desired, straight stitch it to the bottom edge and ends of the valance.

4. Hem the top edge of the valance by machine, either with a blind stitch or a straight stitch.

5. On the wrong side of the valance, straight stitch the beading lace or Austrian gathering cord across the width of the fabric at the point where the cornice board ends on either side and in the exact center of the valance if two swags are desired. If a different number of swags are desired, be sure that the gathering devices are an equal distance apart, as well as positioned at the end of the cornice board.

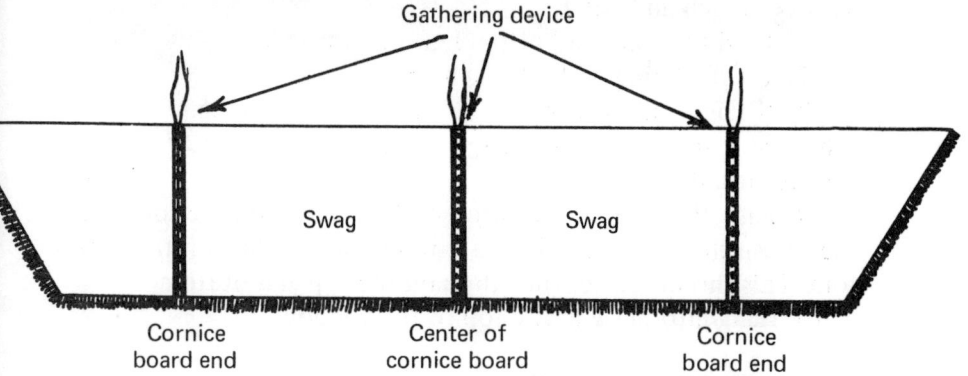

Gathering device → Swag | Swag
Cornice board end — Center of cornice board — Cornice board end

6. If a drawstring is not built inside the gathering device, attach a drawstring to the bottom edge of the valance at the gathering device. Then, run the drawstring through the device to the top of the valance.

7. Draw the string as tightly as possible; then secure it in this position.

8. Attach the valance to the top of the cornice board close to the wall with staples or tacks.

SHIRRED VALANCE

Materials Needed:
   Drapery fabric desired valance length plus 5 inches and width of twice the window width plus 5 inches
   Drapery lining for above fabric
   2 curtain rods
   Thread

Step-by-Step:
   1. Cut and sew the drapery fabric to make a valance the desired length plus 5 inches for hems and twice the desired width of the finished valance.
   2. Press a 1½-inch hem on each side of the valance and press a 2½-inch hem on the top and bottom.
   3. Cut the lining so that it will fit snugly within the hems of the drapery fabric. Allow a 5/8-inch seam allowance.
   4. With right sides together, sew the lining to the side hems.
   5. Turn under the raw edges on the top and bottom of the valance ¼ inch and stitch.
   6. Fold the top and bottom hems as pressed.
   7. Fit the lining under these hems.
   8. Straight stitch across these hems from one side to the other. This should secure lining and fabric and make a heading for the curtain rod.
   9. Push the curtain rod through the heading on the top, and then push the other curtain rod through the heading on the bottom. This should gather the fabric on the top and bottom.
   10. Hang into place at the top of the window.

LIGHTWEIGHT CORNICE

Materials Needed:
   Drapery or upholstery fabric
   Drapery lining
   Heavy cornice buckram (usually comes in 10-inch widths)
   Fringe, braid, or other trim, if desired
   Curtain rod

Step-by-Step:

1. Experiment with paper and pencil with various designs of cornice. Some suggestions are as follows:

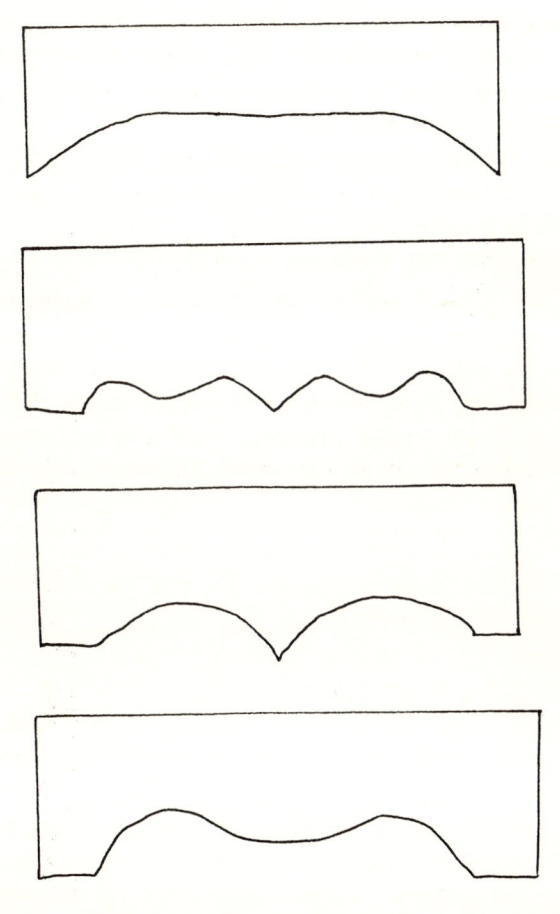

2. When the desired shape is determined, it should be drawn on newspaper taped together or butcher paper. Folding the paper in half to cut the shape assures a uniform design.

3. Tape the newspaper pattern onto the curtain rod or onto the wall or ceiling so that it will be approximately in place over the window. Adjust the pattern until it is visually balanced.

4. Use the newspaper as a pattern to cut the fabric, the lining, and the buckram. Some or all of these may have to be pieced together before cutting. The buckram is pieced together

by overlapping and sewing into place. Allow for a 5/8-inch seam allowance at the sides and bottom, and a 3½-inch seam allowance at the top on the lining and the fabric. Do not allow for seams on the buckram.

5. Place the right sides of the lining and fabric together, and sew a 5/8-inch seam on the sides and across the bottom. Press. Turn right side out and press again.

6. Slip the buckram between the lining and fabric.

7. Tuck the raw edges of the top of the lining and fabric inside and stitch into place.

8. Straight stitch any trims onto the cornice.

9. Fold the top hem down 3 inches and stick across the bottom edge.

10. Run a curtain rod through the top heading, and hang in place over the window. Crease the sides of the cornice so that it will curve gracefully toward the window. Tacks may have to be inserted at the bottom corners to secure them into the window.

CHAPTER V

ACCESSORIES

Very, inexpensive tablecloths may be made from nylon tricot. Since tricot may be purchased in widths up to 108 inches, and sometimes even wider, the length of the table cloth may be obtained from a width of fabric. Then all you need to purchase is the width of the table cloth. Allow 6 to 12 inches for an overhang in the cloth. Lace may be zigzagged around the edge of the table cloth for decoration; therefore, there should be almost no sewing involved. Over-all lace makes a beautiful table cloth. It may be purchased in widths up to 108 inches, also; therefore all you would need to purchase would be the width of the table cloth. The over-all lace fabric is often bonded with a sheer tricot, which makes it more practical. The over-all lace cloth could be edged with 2-inch wide lace, to give it a finished look. Sheer tricot also makes a beautiful table covering to be used over white cloths at parties. It comes in a multitude of colors, and helps to carry out a color scheme. The sheer should also be edged in lace.

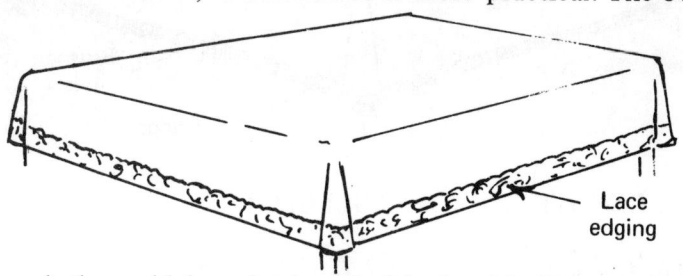

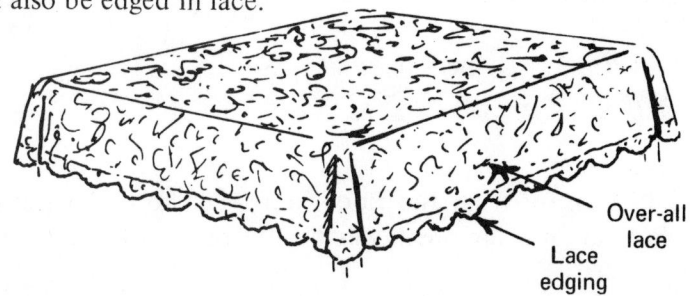

Sheer overlay
over regular tablecloth

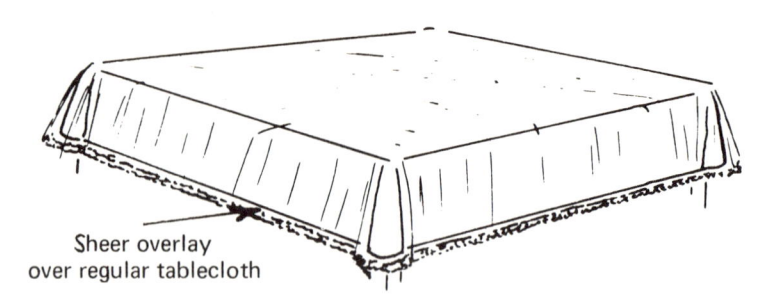

The brushed nylon makes a nice table cloth for families with small children. When milk or other liquids are overturned, the cloth absorbs it so that the spill need not be wiped up until after the meal. This may keep meals from being interrupted so many times. The nylon launders so easily that the homemaker will enjoy using it. This cloth should also be edged in either lace or fringe.

Brushed
nylon
Fringe

FLOOR-LENGTH ROUND TABLECLOTH

Materials Needed:

Fabric equal in length to twice the diameter of the tablecloth plus an allowance for a hem on either side
Any edging or ruffle
Thread
Pencil
String

Step-by-Step:

1. Measure from the floor straight up to the center of the table. This measurement will be the radius of the tablecloth,

and twice this number will be the diameter.

2. If the tablecloth is to have a ruffle, lace, or hamburg edging, subtract the width of the edging from the radius and add a ½-inch seam allowance.

3. Cut the fabric into two equal lengths. Each piece should be equal to the diameter plus two hem allowances or two seam allowances.

4. Cut one of the pieces of fabric in half lengthwise.

5. Sew one of the split lengths to each side of the uncut length. If the fabric has a nap, be sure to have the nap going in the same direction on all pieces. Cutting and sewing the tablecloth in this way ensures that there will not be a seam on the tabletop.

6. Fold the fabric in half lengthwise and then in half crosswise.

7. Tie the end of a long string around a pencil. Cut the string to equal the radius of the tablecloth plus one hem allowance.

8. Place the end of the string at the folded corner of the tablecloth. Mark the tablecloth from one side to the other by swinging the pencil at the end of the string.

9. Cut the tablecloth along the pencil markings.

10. Hem the tablecloth or sew on the hemmed ruffle or edging.

TABLECLOTHS WITH SEAMS

Often the fabric to be used for a tablecloth is not of sufficient width to avoid seams. These seams may be used to a decorative advantage. A seam should never be sewn down the middle of a tablecloth. Instead, after cutting the fabric in two lengths that equal the length of the table plus overhang and hem, cut one of the pieces to a 36-inch width. Then cut the other piece into two lengths that are the necessary width to complete the sides of the cloth plus a hem. Sew the side pieces to the sides of the 36-inch piece.

If the cloth is to be used for formal dining, sew lace of the desired width over the seams. If an open effect is desired, sew the lace on top of each of the two pieces so that only the lace touches each piece of fabric. In this way there will be fabric under the side edges of the lace only. To complete a more decorative tablecloth, sew lace across each end about 18 inches from the hem for a crisscross effect. Lace appliqués may be added to the squares formed at the four corners by the crisscrossed lace strips. The fabric may be snipped from behind the lace appliqués if an open or cutwork effect is desired. If more lace is desired, edge the hem with lace. This gives a very attractive hem that is easy to apply. Be careful not to stretch the lace as it is sewn on the hem. A little fullness may be eased into the lace as it is sewn to avoid a drawn look. Miter the corners.

More tailored tablecloths may be made by applying rickrack, braid, or decorative stitching onto the seams. A scalloped decorative stitch makes a very attractive hem.

PLACE MATS

QUILTED PLACE MATS

The purpose of the place mat is to protect the table or the tablecloth and to add beauty to the table setting. The quilted place mats certainly fulfill these requirements; and for an added bonus, they are also washable. Plan the place mat to be at least 15 inches x 20 inches. Any patchwork or appliqué design may be used. Detached or padded appliqués are not suitable, however, because they could cause spillage. Tacking may also cause spillage and is not recommended.

Graph paper is certainly an aid in designing the place mat, as in all other quilting projects. The place mat should be carefully planned before the patterns are cut and the fabric touched.

The stitching around the appliqués on the place mat may suffice for the quilting. The appliqués should be attached after the top, bottom, and lining are in position and the edges are sewn or bound. The appliqués should be outlined with a straight stitch ¼ inch from the edge of the appliqué and then outlined again with a zigzag that covers the edge and the stitching. The zigzag stitching will make an attractive design on the back of the placemat so that it is reversible.

Place mat edges may be finished by binding with a bias tape

or other binding; edging with lace, ruffles, hamburg, or fringe; or simply sewing with right sides together and turning right side out. The bottom of the place mat may be cut 1 inch larger than the top and folded over the raw edge for a binding.

GEOMETRIC DESIGN PLACE MATS

Materials Needed:
Graph paper
Pencil
Ruler
Shirtboard or cardboard
½ yard of 45-inch fabric for bottom for 2 place mats, or patchwork bottom may be used.
Quilt scraps
Polyester thread
Quilt batting (dacron)

Step-by-Step:
1. Design on graph paper a 15-inch x 20-inch place mat top based on a favorite quilt pattern. Some suggested geometric quilt patterns may be found in the previous chapter on quilting. Since geometric quilts are usually based on squares, add borders to increase the size of the design. Let each square on the graph paper represent ½ inch or some other convenient size.
2. Draw the quilt pieces the correct size on shirt board, cardboard, or posterboard. Fit the pieces together to assure accurate fit.
3. Cut out the quilt scraps by using the cardboard patterns as a guide and allowing an extra ½ inch beyond the cardboard edge for a seam allowance.
4. Machine stitch the geometric pieces together with a ½-inch seam allowance. Press the seams open.
5. Cut the lining fabric 1 inch wider and 1 inch longer than the completed place mat top. The lining or bottom of the place mat may be made in the same manner as the top if a geometric design is desired rather than a solid bottom.
6. Cut the batting the same size as the place mat top.
7. Place the top and bottom wrong sides together and sand-

wich the batting between them. Pin the three layers into this position and check the bottom to eliminate puckering.

    8. Straight stitch along the seam lines of the top. This should make the bottom attractive enough to also be used. Press the place mat.

    9. Pull the excess bottom fabric over the edge of the top, and pin into place as a binding. Miter the corners. The raw edges should be turned under and pressed.

    10. Straight stitch or zigzag the binding into place.

FRUIT PLACE MATS WITH NAPKINS

Materials Needed: (Makes two place mats and two napkins)
    1 yard of fabric for bottom pieces plus napkins (wrong side should not be noticeably different)
    ½ yard of contrasting top fabric
    3 inches of green fabric for leaves
    Dacron batting
    Thread-1 black or brown, 1 green, 1 to match fruit
    2 packages extra wide double fold bias tape
    6 inches of fabric for fruit appliqué

Step-by-Step:
    1. Cut two 18-inch squares for napkins.
    2. Press the raw edge under 1/8 inch, and then fold the edge again another 1/8 inch and press in place.
    3. Straight stitch the hem.
    4. Sew the other napkin hem.
    5. Cut an appliqué pattern for the fruit—cherries, apple, pear, grapes, or other fruit. Cut a pattern for leaves, as desired.
    6. Cut the fruit appliqués and leaves for the napkins and place mats.
    7. Cut two rectangles 16 inches x 21 inches from each of the two kinds of fabric.
    8. Sandwich the batting between the wrong sides of the contrasting fabrics and pin into place.
    9. With pencil and ruler, mark guidelines for quilting every 1½ inches vertically and horizontally.
    10. Straight stitch along the quilting guidelines with a thread

Accessories

that will blend well with all fabrics.

11. Pin the appliqués into place. These may be basted for easier handling, or stuck into place with fusible webbing.

12. If appliqué is not fused, straight stitch ¼ inch from edge all the way around each piece.

13. Zigzag around the edge of the leaves with green thread.

14. Straight stitch veins of the leaves with black or brown thread. Then zigzag to make stems.

15. Zigzag around the fruit with a matching thread that will contrast with the bottom fabric.

16. Press the appliqués and place mat.

17. Apply appliqués on the bottom right-hand corner of each place mat.

18. Straight stitch the bias tape onto the edge of the place mat.

19. Construct the second place mat in the same manner.

FLOWER PLACE MATS

Materials Needed:

30 inches of 48-inch fabric will make three place mats
4 inches of fabric for flower centers will make 6 place mats
Quilt batting

Step-by-Step:

1. Fold a 15-inch square piece of paper in half lengthwise, then in half crosswise, then in half diagonally, then in half diagonally once more.

2. Holding the center point like an ice cream cone, turn the paper so that the shorter horizontal pieces that are opposite the end being held are on top. Cut to remove the bottom layers that extend beyond the short horizontal pieces. The paper should more closely resemble an ice cream cone now.

3. From a point ½ inch below the top of the cone on the side that is open, cut a curved line to the top of the cone on the folded side. When opened, the paper should resemble a flower with eight petals.

4. With the place mat fabric folded so that the left selvage is 15 inches into the fabric, cut the place mat pieces with the paper flower pattern.

5. Cut two 4-inch circles from the center fabric. Pin the centers into place on the flowers and straight stitch ¼ inch from the edge to secure circles.

6. Place the right sides of the two flowers together and straight stitch a 3/8-inch seam around the outside perimeter. Leave one petal unsewn to insert the batting. Turn right side out and press.

7. Insert batting evenly within the place mat, and blind-stitch to close the petal.

8. Zigzag around the center circle so that the thread covers the straight stitching and the outside raw edge with a close satin stitch.

9. Either straight stitch or zigzag from the indentation delineating each petal straight down to the center stitching.

10. Press the place mat.

PILLOWS

FLOWERBASKET PILLOWS

Materials Needed:

18 inches fabric for back and background (green is a good color)
9 inches fabric for basket (yellow, beige, or light brown)
3 inches of several colors for 5 flowers
Pillow batting

Step-by-Step:

1. Fold in the left selvage of the basket fabric 6 inches. Cut straight across the bottom from the fold to a point 4 inches from the fold. This may be only a straightening operation.

2. Measure from the point 9 inches up the fold from where the fabric was cut. Then cut parallel to the first incision to a point 6 inches from the fold. This also may only involve

straightening the fabric edge.

3. Cut a diagonal line connecting the 4-inch cutting mark to the 6-inch one. Open up the cut piece, and it should be a trapezoid.

4. To make the basket handle, fold the right selvage of the basket fabric to a point 4¼ inches from the folded edge. Cut a half rainbow from the bottom of the selvage edge to the top of the folded edge. Then cut again 1 inch inside the first incision.

5. Fold 12 inches of the backing fabric in half lengthwise. Pin the folded basket handle so that the folded handle edge is on the folded background edge. The raw edge of the handle base should be at the bottom raw edge of the background fabric.

6. Cut the background fabric 1 inch above the basket handle from folded edge to raw edge. This background piece should now be a quarter circle that is 8 inches high on the folded edge and 6 inches wide on the bottom.

7. Pin, baste, or use fusible webbing to secure the opened basket handle centered to the opened background half moon. The raw edges at the bottom should be together. The basket handle should be 1 inch from all the edges except the bottom.

8. Sew the basket handle into place by straight stitching 1/8 inch from both the outside and inside edges. Then overcast these stitches and the raw edges with a very close zigzag. A brown or black thread should be used.

9. Place a yardstick diagonally across the basket base so that the edge connects the top right and bottom left corners. Mark the basket fabric with pencil or tailor's chalk along both edges of the yardstick; continue until the fabric is covered with parallel diagonal lines. Then place the yardstick so that the top left and bottom right corners are connected, and mark the base with parallel lines in this direction.

10. Zigzag or straight stitch with black or brown thread along these lines. Press.

11. Place the top background piece over the basket base so that the center raw edges are together and the right sides are together. Sew the center seam with a ½-inch straight stitch. Press.

12. Cut 8 petals 2½ inches long and 2¼ inches wide for each

of three different flowers. The petal patterns may vary in shape from flower to flower. These three large flowers will be used near the basket edge.

13. Cut 8 petals 2 inches long and 1½ inches wide for each of two different flowers. These flowers may vary in design, also.

14. Place right sides together of two like petals, and stitch around the outside edge with a ¼-inch seam, but leave the base of each petal open for stuffing. Continue until all petals are completed. Press.

15. Cut two 1-inch circles for centers for the two small flowers. Then cut three 1½-inch circles for centers for the large flowers.

16. Turn the petals right side out. Pad them with batting. Do not allow the batting too near the open edge. Then straight stitch across the open edges to close them. The petals on some or all of the flowers may be gathered across the base to make them fluffier and stand out more.

17. Position the petals on the background fabric inside the basket handle. The petals may extend over the basket edge and the basket handle, if desired. Straight stitch across the base of each petal to secure it. If the petals seem floppy, they may be stitched ½ inch up the center of the petal perpendicular to the base.

18. Position the flower centers on the petal edges. Straight stitch 1/8 inch from the raw edge of the petal center; then overcast the raw edge with a close zigzag. The petal edges should be covered as well as the center raw edges.

19. Place the pillow front over the backing fabric and cut the pillow back to match the front.

20. With right sides together, straight stitch the pillow front to the pillow back with a ½-inch seam. Leave 5 inches open at the basket base for stuffing.

21. Stuff the pillow with pillow batting. Then stitch the opening closed by hand.

PATCHWORK PILLOWS

Any quilt design may be used for an attractive pillow. The pillow size must be determined, and then the size of the patch-

Accessories 275

work pieces must be calculated so that the design is visually balanced. Borders of contrasting fabrics may also be used to extend a design to make a larger pillow. Experiment with ideas on graph paper or with newspaper patterns to determine the design. It is not necessary to quilt the pillow, although quilted pillows are very attractive. Appliqued pillows are very beautiful, also, and may even be works of art. The pillow maker is limited only by her imagination.

Some favorite patchwork pillow designs are as follows:

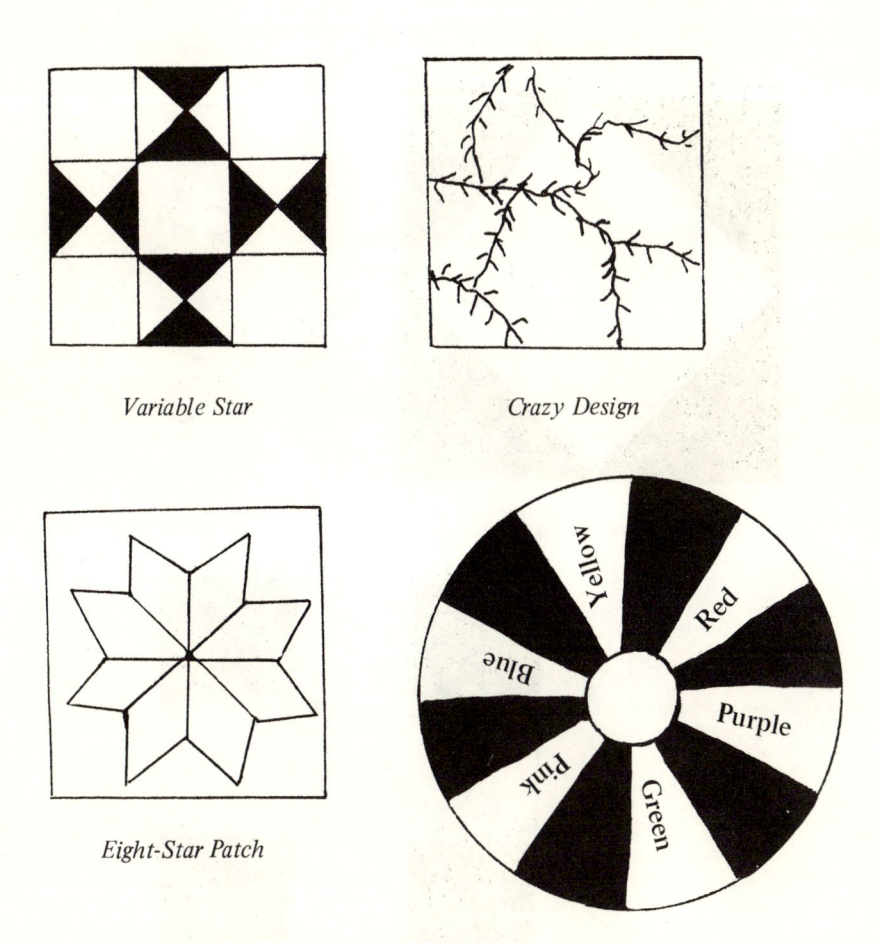

Variable Star

Crazy Design

Eight-Star Patch

Spinning Wheel

276   Sewing The Unusual

Shoofly

Calico Cat

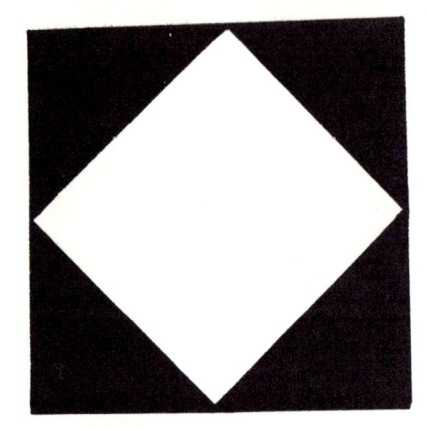

Square On Square

Calico Dog

Nine-Square Patch

After determining the design of the pillow, cut a paper pattern for each of the pieces. Then fit them together to assure that they fit perfectly into a total design. These paper pieces may then be used to cut permanent cardboard patterns. Cut around each piece of cardboard on the desired fabric about ½ inch beyond the pattern for a seam allowance. Then stitch all pieces together and press.

The back of the pillow may be patchwork or a solid piece of fabric. When both sides are completed, place right sides together and stitch around the outside edges. A 5-inch opening should be left on one edge for stuffing. Then stuff the pillow and close the opening by hand.

FLOWER PILLOW

Materials Needed:
13 inches of pillow fabric
4 inches of center fabric
Pillow batting
Embroidery thread

Step-by-Step:
1. Fold a 13-inch square piece of paper in half lengthwise, then in half crosswise, then in half diagonally, then in half diagonally once more.
2. Holding the center point like an ice cream cone, turn the paper so that the shorter horizontal pieces that are opposite the end being held are on top. Cut to remove the bottom layers that extend beyond the short horizontal pieces. The paper should more closely resemble an ice cream cone now.
3. From a point ½ inch below the top of the cone on the side that is open, cut a curved line to the top of the cone on the folded side. When opened, the paper should resemble a flower with eight petals.
4. With the pillow fabric folded in half lengthwise, cut the two pillow pieces using the paper flower pattern.
5. Outline the petals by zigzagging from each outside indentation straight across the center to the opposite indentation. These lines may be marked by folding the fabric in half at each

indentation and pressing the folded edge.

6. Cut two 4-inch circles from the center fabric. Pin the centers into place on the flowers and straight stitch ¼ inch from the edge to secure the circle. Then cover the circle edge and the stitching with a close zigzag. The circles may be secured into place with a fusible webbing before stitching, if desired.

7. With right sides of the flowers together, straight stitch the edges with a ½-inch seam. Leave one petal open. Press.

8. Turn the pillow right side out. Press again, if needed, and stuff with pillow batting.

9. Blindstitch the open petal edge to seal.

10. Optional—With needle and embroidery thread outline the center circle by allowing the needle to go through the circle on the backside and back to the top circle. Pull the thread tightly enough to cause the flower centers to be indented. Experiment with different embroidery stitches to arrive at the most attractive one.

BUTTERFLY PILLOW

Materials Needed:
13 inches of fabric for butterfly wings
6 inches of black fabric for butterfly body
Fusible webbing
Pillow batting

Step-by-Step:

1. Cut a 13-inch square from newspaper and fold in half.

2. Cut a ½-inch triangle from the four corners of the rectangle.

3. Fold the rectangle in half again to make a square. Then nip a ½-inch triangle from the corner that has the fold on only one side.

4. Open the newspaper and round the sharp outer edges into curves.

5. Using the newspaper as a pattern, cut the butterfly pillow pieces (front and back) from the fabric.

6. Cut a rectangle from newspaper that is 12 inches long and 1½ inches wide. Fold the rectangle in half crosswise and length-

wise.

7. On the unfolded narrow end begin cutting a curved line about 2 inches down from the corner and angle it in to the opposite top folded corner. This should make narrow points out of the two ends.

8. Place the narrow newspaper pattern on the black fabric and cut out two body pieces for the butterfly. Then cut out sixteen 1-inch black circles.

9. For an antenna pattern from newspaper, cut out a rectangle 3½ inches x 1¾ inches. Fold the rectangle in half lengthwise and crosswise. On the unfolded narrow end cut a curved line from a point 1 inch from the corner to the opposite top folded corner.

10. Place the antenna pattern on the black fabric and cut out 4 antennae.

11. Place the black butterfly body centered on the wing pieces and straight stitch into place. The stitching should be ¼ inch inside the raw edge. Then cover the raw edge and the stitching with a close zigzag.

12. To delineate the wings, begin close zigzag stitching ½ inch from the side wing indentations and angle it in toward the center wing, ending the line at the body. Then begin another line of stitching on the same side ½ inch on the other side of the wing indentation and angle it in to join the first line of stitching. Repeat on the other side.

13. Fuse the circles onto the butterfly wings with a fusible webbing. Place four circles on each side. Then zigzag around the outside edges of the circles.

14. Fit the antennae into the center indentation. With right sides together, straight stitch to the body and wings with a ¼-inch seam. Overcast the seam with a zigzag.

15. Construct the back of the pillow in the same manner as the front. Press both pieces.

16. With right sides together, sew the back and front of the butterfly together with a ½-inch seam. Leave an opening at the bottom for the batting.

17. Stuff the pillow with batting, and seal the opening with a blindstitch.

CHAPTER VI

STUFFED TOYS

Children love stuffed animals and all sorts of woolly creatures, and most teen-age girls also have their assortment of loveable creatures left over from childhood or newly acquired if found to be irresistible enough. The facial features are usually the most important aspect of the toy, and they are usually very bright and happy. Some animals have a sad, tearful face, however, and are especially welcome when the world has caved in. The nose and mouth are sometimes omitted, but never the eyes. The warm, woolly fabrics in fake furs are very natural looking, but the child's imagination can encompass a purple and pink polka-dotted bear as easily as a black furry one.

Gruesome creatures, such as lizards, snakes, spiders, and octopuses, are favorites of children. A snake smiling from his bed may make the child feel brave and take some of the fearsomeness from the unknown and hostile world beyond.

All decorations, such as eyes, buttons, and other indigestibles, should be sewn or attached very securely. The government has passed very strict safety regulations concerning children's toys, and the home seamstress should follow these regulations, too. Metal bells, although very cute, should be left off of toys for very small children. Buttons and eyes should be glued as well as sewn. A pellon or canvas backing should be used where buttons or other such decorations are sewn. All toys should be checked periodically for signs of wear and loosening.

Any creature may be designed into a stuffed toy very easily. Simply capitalize on the varmint's main identifying features, and stress those in making the pattern.

The toys in this chapter are very simple to make without a

purchased pattern, and they use a variety of techniques that should help the seamstress design and make many other original and fascinating varieties.

PILLOW DOLL

Materials Needed:
12 inches of fabric (chintz, gingham, calico, or a solid color cotton/polyester)
1 skein of yarn for hair
1 package of black embroidery thread
1 package of red embroidery thread
1 button for nose
1-inch square of pellon
Pillow batting

Step-by-Step:
1. Cut two 12-inch circles from the fabric.
2. On one of the circles sketch two eyes, nose circle, and a mouth. Then embroider the outline of the eyes, eyelashes, and iris with black embroidery thread. Glue and sew the button nose in place with a piece of pellon to reinforce the underside of the fabric. Embroider the mouth with red thread.
3. Place the right sides of the circles together and stitch the outer edge with a ½-inch seam. Leave a 3-inch opening for stuffing.
4. Stuff the pillow with pillow stuffing and close the opening with a whipstitch.
5. Thread a large needle with yarn. Beginning at a point on the side seam, insert the needle in and out of the seam and pull the yarn through until only three inches of yarn remains to be pulled through. Snip the yarn on the needle side the same length as the other side. Then tie the two pieces together with a square knot close to the fabric. Continue sewing the yarn hair in this way to a point directly across from the starting point. The yarn hair may be clipped to an inch across the top of the pillow to keep it clear of the eyes. Three or four rows of yarn hair sewn on or near the seam should be sufficient.

BEANBAG FROG

Materials Needed:

14 inches of one or two kinds of fabric
Two ½-inch or ¾-inch shank-type buttons
2 small pieces of pellon
6 inches of braid, rickrack,
 or felt for eyebrows
Beans, rice, popcorn, or other stuffing
Sheet of paper or newspaper

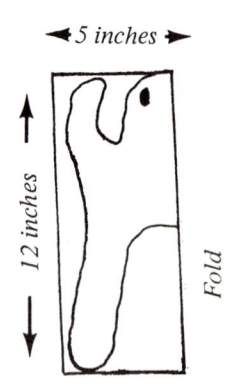

Step-by-Step:

1. Fold a 12-inch x 10-inch piece of paper in half lengthwise. Sketch a frog pattern as in the illustration, and cut it out.

2. Using the pattern, cut two pieces of fabric, either the same or contrasting. Cut ½ inch beyond the pattern to make a seam allowance.

3. Machine stitch the eyebrow braid from a point 1½ inches toward the body on the side of the head to the center point of the head 1 inch toward the body. Then continue the braid in the same manner to the other side seam allowance. The braid should be curved like eyebrows.

4. Sew the shank buttons on either side of the head with pellon reinforcement underneath the fabric.

5. Place right sides of the frog together and machine stitch with a ½-inch seam. Leave a 2-inch opening for the filler.

6. Fill the body with popcorn, beans, rice, or other dry, round substance. Then seal the opening with a whipstitch.

FRIENDLY OCTOPUS

Materials Needed:

10 inches of fabric
2 skeins of yarn
Black felt scraps
Another color felt scraps
96 inches of narrow ribbon
8 small rubber bands
Pillow stuffing

Step-By-Step:

1. Cut a circle with a 6-inch diameter from the fabric. Then cut 4 pie-shaped wedges that are 8 inches deep and 5 inches from side to side across a curved bottom.

2. Stitch the side seams of the wedges together.

3. Cut two 1-inch-long elongated circles from the black felt and position them with the length of eye going up and down on one of the pie-shaped pieces. Stitch into place. Then cut two small circles from the other piece of felt and stitch into place on the eyes at the bottom of the elongated pieces. A round nose and smiling mouth may be added or omitted.

4. With right sides together, pin the 6-inch circle onto the base of the wedges. Some seam adjustments may be made to ensure a good fit. Then stitch into place with a ½-inch seam allowance. Leave a 2-inch opening for turning and stuffing.

5. Turn the head right side out and stuff the inside with the batting. Seal with a whipstitch.

6. Cut 72 pieces of yarn that are 2 yards long. Thread a large needle with a piece of the yarn and insert it at the seam at the base of the head where a side seam intersects the base seam. Remove the needle from the yarn, and pull the two ends of the yarn to equal lengths (about 36 inches). Continue until nine pieces of yarn have been inserted into the head at this intersection.

7. Divide the yarn into three sections of six strands. Then braid the yarn. Secure the end with a rubber band and tie a 12-inch piece of ribbon into a bow to cover the rubber band.

8. Make seven more braids in the same manner. Place one at each seam intersection along the base and one midway between the seams.

WOOLLY MOUSE

Materials Needed:
6 inches of fake fur fabric with short to medium nap
Scrap of pink felt
2 eyes or buttons
1 nose button, small fuzzy ball, or piece of felt
36 inches of yarn

Step-By-Step:

1. Fold the fur fabric in half and cut a half-moon that is 5 inches long at the base and 4 inches tall at the apex.

2. Cut two 1-inch x ¾-inch petal-shaped ears from the pink felt. Insert them in two slits cut 1½ inches from the base corner of the half-moon and ¾ inch from the top cut edge. Sew the ears in place.

3. Fold the half-moon as cut. With right sides together stitch the top seam. Avoid catching the ears in the seam and leave a 1-inch opening for stuffing.

4. Position the eyes and the nose and secure them in place.

5. Stuff the mouse and close the opening with a whipstitch.

6. Pull the fur from the seam with a needle.

7. Thread a needle with the yarn and insert it at the seam on the back of the mouse. Pull the yarn through until there are two equal lengths. Twist the two lengths together, and then tie by pulling the two through a loop.

HUNGRY CRAB

Materials Needed:
4 inches of solid fabric
6 inches of patterned fabric
2 eye buttons
Pellon scraps
Batting

Step-by-Step:

1. Cut two 6-inch circles from the patterned fabric.

2. Cut a 4-inch circle from the solid fabric.

3. Cut an arm pattern that is 1 inch wide, 6 inches long, and semicircular with a two-pronged claw on the end. The claw should be larger on one side than the other. Then cut 2 pieces of fabric with this pattern for the right side and two for the left side.

4. Place the right side of two arm pieces together and stitch the seam all the way around the arm except at the bottom end where it joins the body. Then stitch the other arm in the same manner. Be sure that you have a right and a left arm.

5. Stuff the claw of the arm. Then machine stitch across the base of the stuffing. Complete the stuffing of the arm, and stitch across the base of the stuffing so that at least ½ inch is left unstuffed for a seam. Then make the other arm in the same manner.

6. Place the solid circle on top of the figured circle with the raw edges together on one side. Machine stitch the raw edges where they meet.

7. Position the other figured circle in this same manner onto the solid circle and stitch into place.

8. Place the eyes about 2 inches from the mouth opening and glue and sew into place.

9. Place the two figured circles so that the right sides are together and the solid circle areas are together.

10. Position the claws on each side midway back from the mouth. The claws should extend to the interior of the circles as the circles are wrong side out.

11. Stitch from the seam attaching the solid circle to a point 1 inch short of being opposite the solid circle opening. Then stitch the other side in the same manner. Be sure the seams are very secure at the beginning and ending by backstitching.

12. Turn the crab right side out and stuff the interior. Put plenty of stuffing above and below the mouth as well as everywhere else. The mouth should be agape. Then close the stuffing opening with a whipstitch.

LOVEABLE IMP

Materials Needed:
- 14 inches of fabric
- 4 rubber bands
- 1 skein of yarn
- 24 inches of narrow ribbon
- 1 curtain ball
- 18 inches of ½-inch wide ribbon
- 2 buttons for eyes
- Felt for mouth

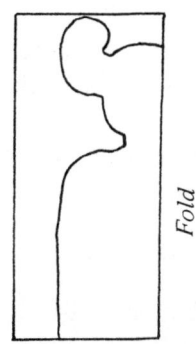

Step-by-Step:

1. Sketch a pattern for the body and head of the imp as shown.

2. Place the pattern on the fabric and cut two pieces.

3. On the head of one of the pieces, glue and sew eyes with a small piece of pellon behind for reinforcement. Glue and sew the nose ball and glue and sew the mouth. Cut six pieces of yarn that are 1½ inches long, and glue three of them on each side of the face to extend from the nose to the cheeks.

4. Place the two pieces of fabric with right sides together and stitch almost all the way around the body, leaving a 2-inch opening at the base of the body for stuffing.

5. Turn the body right side out and machine stitch across the base of the ears where they join the head so the ears will not be stuffed.

6. Stuff the body and head and close the opening with a whipstitch.

7. Tie the ½-inch wide ribbon in a bow around the imp's neck.

8. Cut 37 pieces of yarn 36 inches long.

9. Thread a needle with the yarn and insert it on the seam where the arm should be. Pull the thread through until the ends are of equal length. Continue until nine of the 36-inch pieces have been inserted.

10. Divide the yarn into three equal portions of six strands each and braid the yarn. Secure the braid with a rubber band and a 6-inch piece of the narrow ribbon tied into a knot.

11. Complete the other arm and the two legs in the same manner.

12. Thread the needle with the last piece of yarn, and insert it in the center back about two inches above the bottom. Pull the yarn through until there are two equal pieces. Then twist the two tightly and knot them by looping the ends over themselves and through the loop.

SWEETIE BEARS

Materials Needed:
Fake fur sufficient for the bear's height
2 eyes or eye buttons

Felt for mouth and eyebrows
Buttons for boy and lace for girl
12 inches of ribbon for each bear
Stuffing

Step-by-Step:
1. Make a paper pattern for each bear as follows:

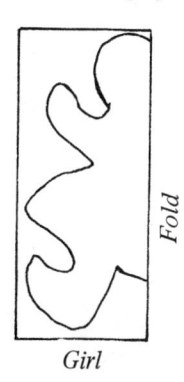

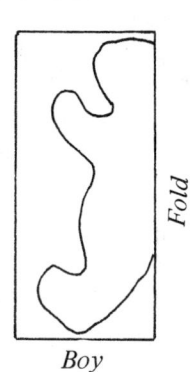

Girl — Fold

Boy — Fold

The bears may be made any size from small to large. Either allow for seams in the patterns or cut the fabric larger than the pattern to allow for seams. The boy and girl may be cut from the same pattern to assure uniformity of size and simply extend the skirt to make the girl differ.

2. Cut the folded fabric by the patterns.
3. On the front side of each bear sew and glue the buttons, eyes, and mouth. The black felt may be cut in zigzag pattern and placed behind the eyes for a pleasing effect. The boy should have buttons sewn down his front, and the girl should have lace sewn from the shoulders to the waist and then outlining the skirt.
4. Place the right sides together of one bear and stitch around the perimeter. Leave a 2-inch opening at the top of the head for stuffing.
5. Turn right side out and stuff. Then close the opening with a whipstitch.
6. Pull the fake fur from the seams with a needle so that the seams will not show.
7. Complete the other bear.

SCOTTIE DOG

Materials Needed:
15 inches of fake fur for a dog 14 inches tall
2 eye buttons
Batting

Step-by-Step:
1. Construct a paper pattern as shown:

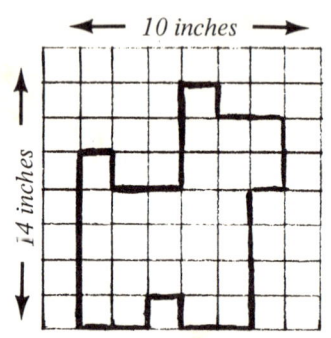

2. Fold the fabric so that the left selvage extends sufficiently far onto the fabric to cut the dog. (This will cut the two sides.)

3. Cut the dog by using the pattern (cut ½ inch beyond the pattern edge to allow for seams).

4. Measure the outside perimeter of the dog. Then cut a piece of fabric 4 inches wide and as long as the perimeter plus 1 inch for a seam allowance. This piece may be cut a little longer than needed to ensure sufficient length.

5. Glue and sew the button eyes in place. Pellon reinforcements may be sewn to back the fabric.

6. With a ½-inch seam allowance, sew the two narrow ends of the long piece together. Then pin this piece around the outside perimeter of the dog. Some adjustment may have to be made to the length of the long piece. With right sides together, stitch this piece as pinned.

7. Pin the other long edge of the long piece to the perimeter of the other side of the dog right side to right side. Sew these two pieces together except for a 2-inch opening on the underside for stuffing.

8. Press the seams and turn right side out. Take a needle and pull out the fur caught in the seams.

9. Stuff the dog, then close the opening with a whipstitch.

CREEPY SNAKE

Materials Needed:
1 yard of 48-inch fabric
2 large eyes
4 inches of red felt for tongue and mouth

Step-by-Step:
1. Cut a pattern from newspaper as shown:
2. Fold the fabric in half crosswise and cut out the snake by using the newspaper pattern.
3. With right sides together, machine stitch the outer perimeter of the snake. Leave a 3-inch opening behind the head for stuffing.
4. Turn the snake right side out and stuff with batting. Close the opening with a whipstitch.
5. Cut a smiling mouth from the red felt. Cut a 4-inch-long slender forked tongue from the red felt, also. Sew the tongue into place on the snake, and then slit the mouth in order to insert the tongue through it. Secure the mouth into place with glue and stitching.
6. Position the eyes, and secure in place with glue and stitching.

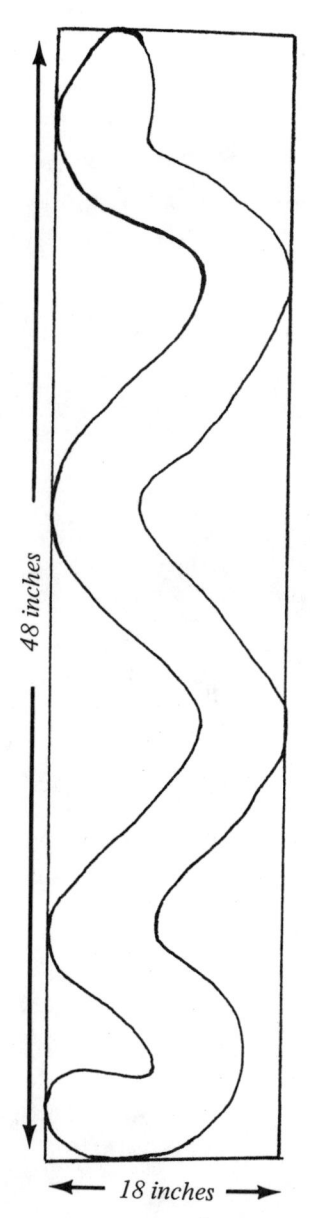

48 inches

← *18 inches* →